EMILY & VIRGINIA

For Susan,
As precious as
these two,

Robert

May 2021

EMILY & VIRGINIA

A novel

Robert McDowell

Homestead Lighthouse Press
Grants Pass, Oregon

ISBN 978-1-950475-10-0
Library of Congress Control Number: 2020948240

Homestead Lighthouse Press
1668 NE Foothill Boulevard
Unit A
Grants Pass, OR 97526

www.homesteadlighthousepress.com

Distributed by Homestead Lighthouse Press, Amazon.com, Barnes & Noble, Daedalus Distribution

Homestead Lighthouse Press gratefully acknowledges the generous support of its readers and patrons.

Book design by Ray Rhamey
Photographs by Alissa Lukara
Art by Jane Mary Katherine McDowell (Fox)

Is there not a sweet wolf within us that demands its food?

Emily Dickinson

୧ରୁ୬

Now then is my chance to find out what is of great importance and I must be careful and tell no lies.

Virginia Woolf

Contents

For Jane Mary Katherine (Fox), who knows where the portals are and travels back and forth unafraid

Part One

The Portal

One

Lily Ramsay looked at the clock, its news a reproof as she slapped her colored pencil down on the table, abandoning once again the drawing of Inari the fox messenger of the Japanese fertility goddess; she could not finish and grabbed her jacket, the sage-colored one her mother wore when she hiked the Pacific Coast Wilderness Trail. If she waited any longer, she'd be late.

Lily and Shaya, best friends since they'd met as little girls at a horse-jumping lesson, walked up a wooded path from town into Ashland, Oregon's Lithia Park at 6:00 a.m. Lily Ramsay, 25, not famous, yet developing what she hoped would become a successful career as a respected writer, artist and commercial illustrator, visited a special place in the park every year on this date, the anniversary of her parents' death. Shaya, blonde, blue-eyed and also 25, would leave in a month for a year in England to work on a relative's farm in Sussex. As they'd always done when they walked anywhere together, the young women held hands.

At the playground, they paused to read a newly posted sign warning about a cougar sighting, then veered to the right, crossing a small bridge spanning Ashland Creek. The creek burbled, pooled, swirled and raced on, big with snow melt and rain water. The girls turned left and continued on, passing the band shell where they had graduated from high school one sticky summer night in June (an especially lonely summer night for Lily who couldn't help feeling that great grief and graduating were synonymous) then crossed a road and walked up a green embankment to the Japanese garden.

The garden featured a series of descending ponds connected by a walking path and tiny bridges, like the bridges one sees at a miniature golf course, though these were more stylish and ornate. Here and there the girls also admired small, spontaneous rock sculptures (one could see them throughout the park) created by...who knew? Lily and Shaya stopped at one of the middle ponds where lush lotuses feathered the surface.

The pond had an oval shape surrounded by Japanese maples and polished granite boulders. One of these was a flat rock, and it was here that Lily shed her backpack, opened it and took out a book by Courtney Weber about Brigid—Pagan Goddess and Catholic saint— two white candles and two red candles, a clump of sage, a writing tablet, a Blackwing pencil and a small brass bowl. She also laid out two more books, a slender volume of poems by Emily Dickinson, *Selected Poems,* and a well-read copy of *Moments of Being,* excerpts from Virginia Woolf's diaries.

Shaya took from her backpack a woven mat the size of a large napkin and spread it out on the flat surface. Gold flecks in the turquoise-green of the mat sparkled in the early sun. Lily knelt by the pool and said a silent prayer to center herself and reach out to the Goddess, then dipped the brass bowl into the water and brought it up half-filled.

Wiping off the bottom of the bowl on her left palm, she placed it at the center of the mat. The friends silently divvied up the candles, two each, lit them and placed them on the four corners of the mat. A windless morning, Shaya thought; thank you for cooperating! Shaya produced from her bag a role of twine and a bundle of reeds the girls had collected the day before, and the two sat down on the stones. Together they unwrapped sixteen reeds, four small rubber bands, two scissors and began to make Brigid crosses.

Both were experts, and though they did not hurry, they made short work of the project. With two Brigid crosses completed and laid above and below the water bowl, Shaya and Lily stood on opposite sides of the mat.

"Adjuva Brigitta! Adjuva Brigitta!" Lily cried, inviting the Goddess in. "365 days the sun traveled far away from that awful day when my mother and father were killed. The sun traveled far away and has come back again to that day—Adjuva Brigitta!."

Shaya opened the book of verse, and in a clear sweet voice read the Dickinson poem:

> Because I could not stop for Death -
> He kindly stopped for me -
> The Carriage held but just Ourselves -
> And Immortality.
>
> We slowly drove - He knew no haste
> And I had put away
> My labor and my leisure too,
> For His Civility -
>
> We passed the School, where Children strove
> At Recess - in the Ring -
> We passed the Fields of Gazing Grain -
> We passed the Setting Sun -

Shaya stopped there in mid-poem and lit the two red candles. Lily opened *Moments of Being* to one of Virginia Woolf's most famous passages about marriage. Finding the passage, she gathered herself and read aloud. She recited the prose in a clear, quiet voice.

"Arnold Bennett," Woolf wrote, "says that the horror of marriage lies in its 'dailiness'. All acuteness of a relationship is rubbed away by this. The truth is more like this: life—say 4 days out of 7—becomes automatic; but on the 5th day a bead of sensation (between husband

and wife) forms which is all the fuller and more sensitive because of the automatic customary unconscious days on either side. That is to say the year is marked by moments of great intensity. Hardy's 'moments of vision'. How can a relationship endure for any length of time except under these conditions?"

Lily closed the book and lit the two white candles. Candles flickered above all four corners of the mat. Taking up the bundle of sage, Lily held it out so that Shaya could light the burnt end. The sweet, pungent scent of the smoldering sage wreathed around them and drifted away towards the stand of giant sequoias fifty yards away. Slowly, Lily circled the altar, speaking these words:

> *Queen of Ice, Queen of Stone,*
> *Hear me from your Frozen Throne,*
> *Be here, be here, be here now!*

After two circles of the altar, Lily handed the sage to Shaya, who took it and walked her own slow circles saying:

> *Brigid has come! Brigid is welcome!*
> *Brigid has come! Brigid is welcome!*

Completing her second circle, Shaya ground out the sage on the side of the altar, placed it next to the brass bowl of water and crossing her legs, settled down on a stone bench. Across the small pond, across from Shaya, so did Lily. The two dropped into meditation as the candles flickered and the water bowl sparkled.

"Lily? Lily! Come on, Lily, open your eyes. It's me, Shaya! Come on, you're scaring me."

Lily's eyes fluttered open and squinted, as if the daylight were too much, too much. Getting used to the light as she sat up, Lily's eyes opened wider and came into focus on Shaya. "What. What?"

"Here. Drink some water," said Shaya, raising a water bottle to Lily's lips. Lily sipped a little and turned her head to one side. "Have more," said Shaya, but Lily shook her head no.

"I...went somewhere" said Lily. "What's wrong?"

"Nothing's wrong," Shaya answered. "It's just that you seemed to disappear in your meditation. I mean, I stopped after ten minutes, like we said we would, but you kept going. I waited five minutes, ten, then I spoke to you, but you didn't hear me. I spoke louder. Still, nothing. I thought you were kidding, but then realized you weren't. So I got up and touched you. Still, nothing. That's when I got rattled, I guess. What happened?"

"I'm not sure," said Lily. "I was climbing a green hill. I was crying for my parents, for my work. I was crying for purpose, I guess, and love. Yes, that's it!" Lily's eyes fired as she remembered. "A face, yes, a woman with fiery red hair and milk-white skin came out of the earth and flew down the hill at me. I thought she was going to hit me, but she seemed to pass through me. I felt her everywhere inside me. The non-impact was so great I fell to the ground as if I'd been tackled or run over, but I was alone."

"It was Brigid, Lily! You met her!"

Her head clearing rapidly, Lily's eyes brightened with greater focus.

"Did she say anything? She must have or why would she appear to you like that?"

Lily fixed on the candles, which had burned down half way since the two had lit them. A memory jolted her and passed on. She trembled. "Someone's coming," she said.

"Who?" said Shaya. "Did you say someone's coming, or did Brigid? Come on, Lily, don't go catatonic on me again."

"What?" said Lily. "Oh, I guess I said it. No, it *must* have been Brigid who said it. Why would *I* say that?" Lily took a long drink of water on her own and cupping her hand, splashed a little on her face.

"There was something else, too. A disturbance at the base of a dying oak, like that one up the trail we noticed last week."

"Well, go on!" said Shaya. "*What?*"

"For a moment," Lily continued, "the tree was, like, on fire and the ground shook. Then I saw two people—I think they were people—scramble out of the smoke. They seemed distressed. They looked wild and scared, like lost dogs or cats. Suddenly they made a grab for me, then they vanished and...and I heard your voice."

"Well, there," said Shaya. "Are they the ones that are coming?"

"No!" said Lily, surprising herself with her swift and emphatic response. "I'm sure of that! Someone else is coming. I don't know whether to be frightened out of my mind or eager and excited," she said.

"Well," Shaya said, "since you aren't sure which, why not settle for eager and excited?"

Shaya could make her laugh, Lily thought, and as usual, she made a lot of sense. "Yes," said Lily, "I'll try that." Again, they stood on either side of the altar, their hands pressed together at their chests. Shaya recited:

> Oak! Open the door!
> Brigid the Warrior, light the way!
> Shine your fire into the shadow,
> Truth shall prevail!

Shaya extinguished the red candles and packed them away. Lily spoke:

> May her song be pure as water
> May her light guide me
> Wherever I go in this world
> Or the next world.

Lily extinguished the white candles and wrapped them up. Shaya lifted the brass bowl to her lips, kissed it and sipped the water. Passing the bowl on, Lily did the same. She walked the bowl to the base of the maple tree nearest them and kneeling, poured out the water on the tree's mossy base. Returning to the flat stone, Lily saw that Shaya had already rolled up the mat and packed it with the candles in Lily's backpack. The sage, wrapped in linen, and the brass bowl followed. They had been in the garden for an hour. A doe and two spotted fawns emerged from the brush to munch on the green grass; the deer paid the women little mind as they passed by. It was a threshold morning, Lily thought, rife with memory yet promising discovery and adventure. Perhaps contentment, success and love would come, too.

On the Plaza, they stopped at Mix for coffee. Because the morning was bright and dry (so far, though it would certainly change), they took their cups to one of the wobbly iron tables out front and sat down to watch the other businesses waking up. "I love it that we do this Brigid ritual every year," said Shaya.

"Me, too, and thank you," said Lily. "My mother kept an altar to her. I grew up with Brigid's love and guidance." She leaned over and kissed her friend on the cheek. "You're my sister forever," she said. "It means everything to me to do the ceremony with you. You were with me in the beginning and, I don't know, it brings my mom and papa closer to me. Does that make sense?" Shaya nodded. Resting her arm across Lily's shoulders, they people-watched and enjoyed the silence they made together.

I need somebody, Lily thought. I need someone now. She sat up in bed and switched on the nightstand lamp. She had already done so twice before, and now that it was just after 3 a.m., she gave up any hope of going back to sleep. She sat there, making effort at meditation, imploring intervention. I am hungry, Lily thought. I am ravenous, like an animal. She ran her tongue over her teeth. Were they longer? Sharper? Lily wondered, was there any meat in the refrigerator?

Lily got out of bed to check. Half-way down the hall, she remembered her new resolve to eat vegetarian; she had given away the frozen pot roast, the lamb cutlets, the lean luncheon meat to her neighbors in the building. What's the point of going on? She thought, exaggerating as everyone does in the dark hours of early, early morning. Three steps onto the kitchen's tile floor she drew back in pain, a shard of a broken flower vase having punctured the sole of her right foot. Once, weeks ago after an awful date, there had been lots of pieces on the floor. She thought she had swept them all up, but here was a lethal, stray fragment just waiting for her errant step. It found me, Lily thought and hopped to the bathroom where she sat on the edge of the tub to wash and bandage the wound.

"*There*," she said, exaggerating her limp as she staggered back to the kitchen; "I have done something useful." The kitchen, she thought, is a sacred place of usefulness and rejuvenation. Did she write that once? Did someone else? Where had she heard it? Not from one of those awful cooking shows, though secretly she liked some of them more than she'd ever admit. She stood alone in her kitchen, the room where days launch, where mid-days pause, where evenings arrive with their gauzy gold light, their changing bars of purple and blue and say, 'rest; replenish your exhausted body and spirit with food, drink and talk'.

Yet, there was no one to talk to but herself, and that wild, undisciplined chatter wore on her. Like a physical body bumping into her in the street, knocking her off stride, the chatter upset not her equilibrium, which was already off, but the likelihood that she would be able to regain it any time soon. Besides, it was too familiar, this chatter, and she loathed it. She knew the voices, her parents pleading for their lives and the lives of other passengers, random, terrified voices consoling each other, the pirates terrorizing the ship's crew, bullying and yelling orders, the mass confusion, the pistol and rifle shots, the bodies falling overboard, smacking the water.

"Who loses their parents to pirates in this century?" Lily blurted out. She was kneeling when she said it; she was kneeling as if half-way to a prayer that was hung up somewhere, just beyond her. "I need somebody. I need somebody now. Could Shaya be up at this hour? Could I call her? No, I won't wake her for this again. I'll go back to bed. I'll read Emily; I'll read Virginia."

But before she read, she punched up Brandi Carlile on her phone singing *What Can I Say*, her song of heartbreak and loss. Lily quietly sang along—*Look to the clock on the wall/ Hands hardly moving at all/ I can't stand the state that I'm in/ Sometimes it feels like the walls closing in/ Oh, Lord, what can I say/ I'm so sad since you went away/ Time, time ticking on me/ Alone is the last place I wanted to be*...As she sang, Lily's mind raced through past relationships. There are healthier things to do through a sleepless night than play over a failed love life, Lily thought, yet reminiscing so at a terrible time is also oddly satisfying. It tells me I've lived a little, Lily thought. Now that she had started, she followed the thread leading to a night that summed up, for her, the Nothing she had so far achieved in her love life.

She thought of a dinner that began late because Reuben, the man she was seeing, had been delayed and did not call. Men were often delayed and did not call, Lily thought. So, the dinner began badly and got worse. When he finally arrived, they tried to talk their way out of their agitation; hoped that words would smooth out their scratchiness, and though this should work every time, how often it fails! But something clawed to get out of them, Lily remembered, something between them, something between them and so many others wanted out into the space between them. They tried. They talked, unsuccessfully, probably going on too long for Rueben's poor male brain to keep up. "The soup's cold," he'd scolded. "The country-green salad is brown-tipped and wilted and you're shaking your head and rolling your eyes at me!" By the time the river trout arrived, neither could eat another bite. Even worse, both forgot the To-Go boxes on the table and did not think of them until they arrived at Lily's door. This despite the utter silence in which they drove. "All that food gone to waste," Lily had grumbled.

Back in Lily's apartment, they'd found agreement on one thing: sex, and neither wanted any of it. Even so, though she thought she did not want him to, Lily also thought of how she had half-waited for this man to put his arms around her and kiss her, to exercise that male magic that irritates and excites women. She had wanted him to turn the entire unsatisfactory evening on its ear, but probably he was wondering how he could extricate himself from the encounter without making matters even worse. She knew that his male brain, shut down and numb as it was, could not think of intimacy with Lily or anyone. So he plopped on her sofa in his miserable man's truth, defeated, murmuring platitudes like 'I really like you' and 'why can't we just have some fun?' Inadequate to maneuver in or out of what was happening to them and trying not to show it, he managed to call down a spotlight on his foibles, his insecurity and imbalance. He even sat scrunched up to one side as if he could not wait to get out of his body.

She knew, of course. Like all women, she knew. Lily thought of how she was at least one or two thoughts ahead of that man, any man, but she, in her own way, was also paralyzed. She could turn him around like that! Lily thought of how she'd imagined snapping her fingers and a transforming puff of smoke would rise out of the man's head. Instantly, he would be changed. He'd stand up, become animated, walk around the room with a bounce to his step, asking his puppet master questions about her day, what she thought, how she felt about the plight of the tiger, the missing airliner, the new puppy she hoped to find soon. Oh, yes! *Now* she yearned to feel his

arms around her. But the smoke and his enlightened transformation had only occurred in her head. Instead of standing up changed
for the better, the man put on his jacket with the threadbare elbow
patches and headed to the door. "I'm sorry," he stammered, pulling
the door back and hesitating in the opening, in the space they shared
before the door closed and isolated each of them, one from the other,
even more. "I'm sorry," he'd repeated, though it was clear to both
that he wasn't sure what he was sorry for. His *sorry* had been a Gen-
eral Sorry—a ranking officer in the familiar army of Sorry, Confused,
Disappointing and Inadequate Men.

In that evening's closing gloom, Lily had stood alone in her
kitchen; her anger bubbling and sizzling. She had wanted to throw
something, had wanted to hear the sound of anything breaking. She
had wanted nothing so much as to shatter the empty flower vase on
the counter. The vase was in and out of her hands in a heartbeat,
and there were hundreds of shards and pieces all over the floor that
would take weeks to clean up. She had felt her anger flatten and go
out of her. Exhausted, she'd shuffled into the bedroom, kicked off
her shoes and fallen like a knocked-over lamp onto the bed. She
would begin to clean up the mess in the morning.

"So, that's my love life," Lily, back in the present, said aloud, as
if hearing herself say it might make a joke of it that even she could
laugh at, as if saying it would make it almost bearable. Propped up
in bed, feeling fragile in the small light of a reading lamp, Lily put
aside her ramble through dating and no sex and brought herself back
to Emily, to Virginia. She read aloud Emily Dickinson's poem that
begins, *After great pain, a formal feeling comes.* She read it aloud, her voice
sounding otherworldly to her—and as always happened when she
read the poem silently or aloud, she wept. She remembered sitting
on her mother's lap listening to this poem and looking up, she saw
her father leaning in a doorway, also listening, with tears in his eyes.
Sliding down a little in bed, she laid aside Emily's poems and opened

her mother's well-used paperback of Virginia Woolf's *The Waves*. It had been her mother's favorite novel and Lily remembered having the first section read to her over and over when she was a child. Now she opened the book and pressed the pages to her face, imagining she could still catch her mother's delicious Jo Malone tobacco and Mandarin scent. As Lily got older, she enjoyed reading passages to Shaya on sleepovers. Now she read aloud to herself, loving the voices of the six children that are introduced as the novel begins and somewhere in the middle of a monologue by one of the children—Jinny (the vivacious one, the child who stirred the emotional pots)—she drifted and began to half-dream of someone peering through a hedge. There was water nearby and there were other eyes, too, watching her through the bushes. Lily thought of the Brigid ceremony. She thought of the scent of sage and the words, the abyss and surprise of her meditation and Shaya's concern, the sweet taste of the water, and as she drifted off again, Mother Brigid's message: someone *is* coming.

Two

"You see how it is," said Virginia to the woman ladling water from her well into a bronze bowl. The water-gatherer looked as one would expect Brigid, the Mother of Ireland, Goddess of the forge and the well, of music and poetry to look. Yet, she seemed perplexed by her supplicant's impatience. Brigid's flame-colored hair (the color of Maureen O'Hara's in *The Quiet Man*), wrapped up in a coil shape, looked damp, but not from perspiration. Indeed, those of the next realm do not perspire. A warm mist rose from the well. "What am I supposed to see?" she asked.

"That I must go to her, of course!" said Virginia. "The poor girl needs my protection; she requires my assistance! I am needed. I feel called to some extraordinary adventure. I am shot from a bow. I am blind with urgency and speed!"

If you lived in Lily's world (Earth 2021), you would guess that the woman making demands on Brigid was in her mid-thirties to early forties. Tall and thin (some might say 'gaunt') with deep-set, large dark green eyes, you'd say that her beauty would be conceded by anyone in either realm. Her nose and chin were long but perfect, her ears exquisite, her neck as elegant as a swan's, her thick, brown hair, with flecks of gray, pulled back in a careless bun from which wispy strands escaped to flick at her cheeks. Everything about her appearance looked disheveled, just a little, but that only added to her elegance and charm. Even her impatience made Brigid smile in spite of herself.

"You know," said the Goddess, "the one thing we discourage is our kind flying off to the Before Time on any old whim or pretext.

The poor dears would be scared to death with spirits whizzing all over the sky! Remember! Earth isn't a playground—even for us!"

"Why not!" said Virginia, stamping her foot like the excitable, frustrated six-year-old cricketer she had once been. "The most serious play is truth-play; that's what I'm after. My young woman—*our* young woman—is threatened by the De la Nuit, our derelicts here. They want to force her to lead their sordid, evil rituals, or worse. She calls to me in meditation and prayer...through you, of course, dear Mother. I want to fly to her aid! She has dreams and ability, yet she is unsure of herself. She lacks divine feminine confidence. And she grieves for and feels guilty about her lost parents. I can help her. Please, mother, send me back!"

Virginia's infectious, flirtatious plea was impossible to resist unless one was a Goddess, yet though she was, Brigid smiled wider and wavered. But she was not ready to give in. "What does Leonard think? she said. "And Vanessa?"

Now Virginia looked annoyed and answered in a sullen voice. "Leo's against it, and Nessa is bored by it all, but no matter. I've gotten around both of them before."

Brigid knew there was no dissuading her, yet she put Virginia off. "I'll consider it. After all, the poor girl appealed directly to me," said Brigid. "I heard her. You'll know my decision when you do."

"What does that mean?"

"If you find yourself on your way," said Brigid, "there will be your answer; and if you find yourself rooted here, there is yet another."

Virginia watched the Goddess cover the light of her well with a star-shawl and walk vibrantly up the hill to her chapel surrounded by laurel trees and wispy clouds. "How like my mother Julia she is!" Virginia thought. "So beautiful and so *right* about everything."

꩜

Because Brigid had inspired Virginia's great Feminist book, *A Room of One's Own* (an Otherworld legend says that Brigid suggested, in Virginia's dreams, the word *Well* in place of the word *Room*, but the author resisted) *and* because she had read it at least a thousand times, Brigid had no doubt about Virginia's conviction. Brigid had never met a more passionate being, save one other, in either realm. She knew that Virginia despised the oppression of women and was endlessly fascinated by the mysteries of the human condition. She also knew that Virginia had more than a passing reason for wanting to save the young woman threatened by "our derelicts", as she called them. Brigid knew that Virginia herself had barely escaped them when she transitioned and that it was only she, Brigid, who had saved her.

The mortal Lily's slim biography was familiar to the Goddess. It included the tragic loss of the girl's parents while she was still in her teens—a double tragedy the young woman shared with Virginia, her would-be protector. Brigid also knew all about Lily's lack of confidence and deep desire for love. The woman yearned for affection, yet, so far, was unhappy in love. Doubtless, Virginia could be a tonic for that, too, for few mortals, few women had ever, in an effort to understand, so passionately and meticulously penetrated the human heart like Virginia had in her life and work.

These details, and the interest of the De la Nuit (the frightening Unmentionables in her realm) in the girl were more than enough to pique the Goddess's sympathy. Yes, she would let her headstrong Virginia go. Yet, as she contemplated Virginia's mission, she remembered how the earth realm had been both fascinating and terrifying for Virginia, the girl and woman. Suddenly, the Goddess smiled at the acorn-bursting thought that came to her. She would send Virginia back, yes, but not alone.

꿍

As she waited for Brigid's decision, Virginia spoke to a lark singing with all her heart from a nearby branch. "I float in this magic bubble of your song," said Virginia, "and contemplate the thin membrane between worlds. I've always been able to come up with a name for anything, for anyone, though once I declared, rather provocatively, that the names of characters in a novel were irrelevant. Can you imagine a world with no need for naming? Dreadful! I must be wary of mediocrity. I must avoid delusions, like the king spewing obscenities from the bushes, or birds talking to me in Greek, or the walls of my room roistering like a storm at sea. I am the person I wrote about. I could make more of this, but what would be the point of that?" The lark trilled a conspiratorial melody.

Brigid carried out her plan with minimal fuss. Having enlisted Emily's enthusiastic aid, the Goddess would send her through a portal just ahead of Virginia. The poet required no coaxing. In fact, she shared with Brigid that she herself had received imploring spirit messages from this same young woman of the earth realm. She also understood, with no need for the Goddess to explain it, that the De la Nuit was on the prowl and would no doubt show up to oppose her. Lily *was* in danger. Possibly Emily was in danger, too. She understood that, yet she felt excitement at the prospect of returning to earth for the first time in over 130 years. At the last minute, Brigid decided to keep to herself that Emily would have company and help. She had done the same with Virginia. Why, she thought, deprive either of such a sweet surprise?

Rain had come. After promising relief in Oregon's Rogue Valley for weeks, finally, rain had come. It fell, not all at once, but slowly. A big drop splashed on the sidewalk, another skipped off the crown of an unprotected head. Beginning slowly, drops accelerated, pinging the leaves of the maple trees, drumming on awnings and waking sleeping babies in their strollers. Thunder echoed up and down the valley from Gold Hill to Mount Ashland. The vast, penned, heavy-headed sky opened up as if someone holding back grief broke down and wept, unable to contain any longer an overwhelming emotional front.

Rain fell like a riot of golf balls the drops were so big and round and loud. Rain gnatted pedestrians ill equipped to meet it. Only one in ten produced umbrellas and opened them with a flourish that said 'I am prepared; I am *always* prepared'. Others chose a drenching, walking with quickening pace or breaking into trots to wherever they were going; the rest camped under awnings, clogging entrances to little shops, cafés and bars—the candy store, the hat store, the Theater Guild—as they waited out the deluge. A couple of men who still smoked and a woman, too, lit their cigarettes and ignored the annoyed stares of nonsmokers stranded near them. They blew clouds of smoke upward into the wet, charged air as if their exhalations completed a ritual connection that the storm wrought. Almost insolent, they blew their smoke-clouds and waited out the rain.

Peal after peal of raucous thunder reverberated on high, beyond sight, and boomed down, echoing through squat tunnels made of buildings on both sides of Siskiyou Boulevard. Rain pelted the woody Lithia Park path beside Bear Creek, drenching surprised walkers and roistering the creek water, which rushed and chuckled and ran wildly like a child freshly risen from a nap and finally let outdoors. Lightning slashed across the dark sky, chasing thunder with its zigzag fire.

In the next realm, celestial Brigid bowed her head. Her wild, long hair floated in circles and stirred up the surface of one of her better-known ancient wells. Mystics everywhere knew that this well high up on the green flat top of Ben Bulben in County Sligo, Ireland was surrounded by an ancient grove of sacred portals between worlds. Other portals emanated from other Celtic sites and crisscrossed the globe, though many earth dwellers never saw or were aware of them; others saw them but did not fathom what they were; some who were ready came upon them with recognition. These last awake beings knew adventures and existence-changing dreams.

On this wild day, as Brigid stirred the well water, magical channels opened, creating passageways allowing travel back and forth between the worlds of the living and the dead. On this day, the channel through Brigid's sacred well aligned with portals near the footpath in a faraway park in southern Oregon. There were many unassuming portals off that walking path in Lithia Park, mostly at the mossy bases of trees; at two of these, within moments of each other, two women came through, returning to this dimension of flesh and blood and bone.

They came through for the first time since each had left—one more than a century ago, the other on a late March day in 1941. Objectively, they looked well, much as they had in their prime—spirited, beautiful, daring and passionate. One had grown famous in her lifetime, even more so beyond; the spotlight did not find the other until after her death. Now none of that mattered. Their return was borne of a shared desire felt and followed separately, much as they had lived. Equals with few peers, there they were, drawn back by the same young woman whose devotion and need called to them. Why her, though? Why them? Why not?

"I am not unhappy in the spirit world," said Emily, who had just left her sister, Lavinia, after telling her about Brigid's plan, "yet I am Compelled—to go! Perhaps it's that I *can* go—I who stayed so close to Home—living Circumference mostly in my mind when I was Alive. The thought of that young woman, Lily, began to Buzz—in my Hive—& someone else. A boy I knew? A Woman, too!

"Yet, who or what has driven such Force through me? What Gardener planted bulbs—just so—whose stalks pushed up through worms & loam to bud & flower in the Radiance of Father Son—the cool heat of Mother Moon? Mother Brigid—Decrees that I must go—and that is All."

Kneeling before Brigid at her sacred well, Emily had looked up at the Goddess and smiled. "I am the Bee—prepared To Exit—the hive—though she Loves the hive," Emily said. She bowed her head to receive Brigid's blessing and protection.

"Go to the old world, child, with your new powers," Brigid murmured. "Be discovery and delight and do not be afraid."

"Hope is the thing with Feathers—I wrote that," she reminded the Goddess, "desperately wanting—to Fly! I Exulted in Being—the Fly, the Bird, the Bee—the angel Unseen—rather, Seen by me. So I hid behind corners—Retreated to the edges of Diadem Light—Refracted and redolent, ribbon after ribbon, I saw the sun wake up and the Currents Defined—Inviting me to Try my wings. And so I did—I always rose to try. Once wings were mine I could not keep them Folded!"

Brigid walked with Emily, who carried a basket of goodies she had baked with her sister, to an opening at the base of an ash tree. They prayed and Brigid concluded, "I am never far from you, dear One." Then Emily shrank or the opening expanded, she couldn't tell which. She was in a whirl of light and shadow, free and moving with remarkable speed. She was on her way.

"I am Content! Invention Increases," she thought, "whenever I think of it—the Mind so much more elemental—so Magical. I will be gone for an instant only, as we perceive comings and goings. Yet, I will do some good, I think, for that young Woman, Lily. Yes, I am Compelled to go! I am Off—like the Bee!

☙

The portal Brigid chose for Virginia's journey was her favorite, high up on a green hill. She could feel the teeming energy of the writer's brain at work and so did not delay releasing her. The opening, at the base of an ancient oak, expanded, or Virginia shrank. She knew she was flying, or swimming, dissembling and coming back together and doing both over and over. She was moving, she was traveling fast. She knew that. She traveled light, with nothing more than the clothes she wore. They would be somewhat dated, she knew, but she'd prevailed on Vanessa's superior taste to dress her, and her sister never failed her. She looked right enough to pass in the 21st American century. As she shot through the light show, rather like the aurora borealis she had seen once on a holiday in Wales, she met vivid scenes of her earth life. There she was as a child, holding forth in the nursery, telling a story about the next door neighbors before bedtime, and there on a warm summer day were all of the children cricketing. She shot past her wedding day and one family death after another; she slowed down as she observed her own death.

Was she the person she'd written about even then when she walked under the river? I must have been, she thought, else why go through with it? She remembered how she had come to a turning point, a crisis. It was like so many before, and she was tired; she was older and the war frightened her. Going through it all became unmanageable. No doubt she could have recovered, just as Leonard said, but she was tired. She was tired and she was tempted and the war terrified her. Yet, if she walked into the river, what came next? She remembered thinking that, over and over, yet she wanted to know! On that late March day, at that noon hour as she rushed out of Monk's House and got away, transitioning became her only project. She had to know! How else could she have stayed under water long enough to die? Anyone can tell you that drowning is at first a hard death, and almost impossible to do when one tries. The rough, icy-cold current helped—so did her appalling thinness and the rocks in her heavy coat—but she had stayed under because she wanted to. She wanted to know. She remembered expecting a door to open, a watery door to slide open revealing passage to the next world, and so it happened just that way, as if she'd written it. As her lungs filled with water she felt as if she had sprouted gills to ease her transition and thanks to the sudden appearance of Brigid, she had eluded the blind, grasping hands of agents of the De la Nuit. They had almost hijacked her, their hands like claws catching in her clothes and undone, wild hair. Yet she broke away and passed through the watery, aquamarine-colored French doors opening onto Brigid's realm where her journey continued and new-old stories began. I have been making them up ever since, she thought.

Slowly, steadily, Virginia moved through the drama of her earth death and continued on. She was growing younger again, she could feel that, and there was something else. Yes, the De la Nuit had wanted her. In the river, under the water, they had clutched and pulled at her. She remembered fearing them more than the cold water and death itself. She had struggled against them, holding them off with her formidable will even as she was dying. She fought them until they suddenly vanished, driven off not by her opposition, but by the intervention of Brigid. Now, approaching the Earth realm, Virginia felt the Goddess's love and protection and thus fortified, focused on the new/old world she would once again be part of.

Scanning, close up, earth's progress in many areas as she neared her destination, Virginia was delighted to see that brain research was finally describing the transition of consciousness from this world to worlds beyond. At the intersection of astrophysics, quantum mechanics and physics appears Biocentrism—a field that comes closest to describing what occurs when the soul migrates, when it leaves the body. Virginia's friend Wells (H.G.) was the first to approach this unreal reality in his story, *The Door in the Wall*, which he wrote in 1894-95; hadn't she lived in an age of talented wonders! she thought, but her thoughts wandered. She thought about naming things. She thought of consciousness and the soul residing in the microtubules of the brain cells. When one 'dies,' this energy or information—this consciousness—is intact and released from one's body. Identity remains inviolable.

She thought of how all of them, the living and the dead, are like Russian dolls that have other, almost identical dolls inside them. That was the metaphor she believed in. Consciousness is non-local, she thought. It is not made by my body, she thought, so when the body dies, consciousness goes on; but to where?

It goes on to the same body, Virginia thought, in another dimension. She knew this. She had seen it. In the tunnel of light, under the river, she had seen it. Her consciousness could have turned left or right and gone through beautifully open doors to her body there, or there. She could have gone into the abyss with the De la Nuit, yet Brigid and her own desire had guided her to the best exit where she entered the astral body at once and righted herself, laughing. There was mother and father, and Thoby and Stella; Julian, Lytton, Carrington and all the dogs and cats she'd known. Rupert and Roger were there—and Leo's marmoset! Of course, Leonard, Nessa, Vita, Adrian, Clive and Duncan would come later; Tom Eliot, Quentin and Angelica would follow. Only Katherine was missing, an absence that troubled her in the spirit realm just as her early loss on earth had troubled her through most of her life.

Virginia felt a heaviness attach itself to her as her passage neared its end. What was it? It wasn't too awful to bear. It wasn't fatal, but it was palpable, a sensation she'd rather not have if she had any say in the matter. But what was its name? As she slowed down approaching the earth portal, she felt a rush of excitement. She knew! The heaviness she felt was 'God'! She was coming back to a place where people spent an inordinate amount of time thinking and talking about God!

Every time I said the word 'God' in this realm, Virginia remembered, I felt derisive, dismissive, impertinent, but not in the world next door. Derision and impertinence are not feelings or conditions there, and 'God' as most Earthers think of him or her, does not exist. Other feelings and conditions are also missing. Fear is missing. Avarice and jealousy are missing. Guilt is missing. Regret is missing.

Virginia remembered how easy it was to disengage from reunited loved ones and walk with Shakespeare and question Jane Austin and playfully spar with Sappho and Sam Clemens. Since there is no time, she thought, we are never pressed by appointments or deadlines; we're never in a hurry. When I return, Virginia thought, after this Earth mission, the next name on my dance card is Emily of Amherst! Virginia knew all the poems and letters. She had absorbed them, really. She imagined the Belle of Amherst becoming a third sister to her. Virginia had already observed that her young woman, Lily, appeared to like the poet's writing as much as she liked Virginia's own, if that's possible. Virginia thought about the strange tale she would have for Emily once she returned home and they met.

Virginia's Portal in Lithia Park

Three

Ignoring the rain that suddenly softened and slacked off, the first woman through a portal sat down on a wooden bench above the creek.

She sat down and began to speak as if in a dream that gradually gave way to wide awake consciousness. She had tied up her russet-colored hair in a bun for the journey and she wore an antique summer dress, off-white, that had a pocket, large enough to hold a notebook, sewn onto the area that covered her right hip. The woman spoke out loud though no one was near, but if others had heard her, they would have sworn that she was speaking to everyone. It was like that, her voice, like water rushing, wild and almost breathless; babbling a thousand stories it could sweep to the sea. The voice bursting out of the diminutive woman said: *"Little Cousins, Called Back. Emily.* These words—my last—feel like summer sunlight through heavy willow branches. They pass through me—again—like the sound the wings of Poetry Birds make as they swoop low out of the barn and whirl around me in the garden. They Dazzle me. I was lying a-bed, breathing with difficulty, feeling for all the world as if I were leaving the world. *Called Back*—as if I had somewhere to go—as if someone urgently required my Presence."

A beautiful heron, blue, silver and grey, dropped down through the tree canopy, alighting in a calm pool among rocks directly in front of Emily. She gasped.

"Gibraltar! Oh, Planet Bird—You set me—ablaze! I was telling how—I shall tell you! I dropped—deeper—as if descending—surrounded

Emily Dickinson's Bench in Lithia Park

by the cool round walls of a sacred well—and I saw—Everything. There! At the edge of a far field—spattered with morning glory—father and mother—walking; it had to be spring. The sun was nowhere in the sky; or it was in the sky but not where it should be—yet it shone so bright, a panache of Gold! Bees everywhere. They hummed—they delighted me.

I buzzed with them on the Highway of Scent. I alighted on the stamen—covering myself with sticky pollen. My mother wrapped up her arms with a shawl fearing that I—would sting her; father reassured her. He knew—there was no danger from the honeybee his Daughter. Leaving my Parents—as I left the buttercups in their earthy beds—I soared into limitless blue and headed straight to the Hive to deposit my bounty!"

That's how it was, Emily thought, crossing over—like a bee returning to the hive. She studied the heron who walked with infinitely slow precision and grace, scanning the water. She thought again of that transcendent day—the crossing—and spoke aloud, delighting in the sound of words and her own Voice—restored!

"My love for you is Great, Little Cousins, so remember me—I did not go so far away. I am sweet and hot, like carnival taffy pulled in two directions—more than Two! My words then—and now—are almost Delirious. They are White Words; all of them like little people wearing white dresses, like my white dress. I remember that I lay in state in the parlor—with a face so beautiful and young—said Higginson—that he remarked on it in his account of my death and funeral service. That was the last face I showed this World, and the first face I shared—with Eternity!" She stared down the bank hoping to see her reflection in the water, but the heron, slowly exploring, took all her focus. "Thank you, Great Bird—for Welcoming me! Already I feel—so much more—at my ease Here." Heron lowered its long neck, as if bowing to her, then folded its wings and moved deliberately upstream, pool by pool.

"My tongue requires a Resurrection!" Emily cried. "The words that take shape are White Words mixed with Blue Words—Blue like the high summer sky, Blue like the robin's egg, Blue like you—my dear Heron. As always, the Words that come from me build a Nest for me—a Nest from which I declaim in a voice like a waterfall; one must listen very carefully—and feel deeply—to make meaning of a waterfall. I am tumbling, racing, roiling with inspiration and intent. I see Truth. I know it; I tell it *Slant*. Am I speaking to my later reputation—or did I always talk like This?" The heron, slowly making its way from pool to pool, stepped up on a tall boulder and balanced on one leg.

"I think of my Transition. I see myself breathing hard in my bed. I left my body in the same way that I always left my Room—but I knew a new thing. I was certain of this: that I was required somewhere. There was work—and Play—waiting for me. Travel, adventures and resolution awaited me. It was not so very different—But—what did I Mean? Words—came to me—White Words, higher up than Blue, and always changing. I caught them like doves in mid-flight. They fluttered—they resisted, then calmed down quickly in my hands and my hands took flight.

"I will come and go again, startling visitors in hallways with my Shadow, stopping them on the stair—with my voice. I am dressed in white for my Odyssey. I speak Yellow Words—Aegean Words—I've never known. The Greek is in me! Seaweed, foam and spray call to me. They wrap me up and carry me away to this—Land, and This!

"Oh, my Judge appears, greeting me with open arms; mother, father; my little nephew, darling Gib! Part of us went with him when he died. So many I knew, so many! We made—a seamless Insect Union. Such Promise—waylaid—Deferred. I came to each of you and in a White word, flashing moment—We divulged. We shared and said again—all the stored up and oft-told stories and in the telling and listening I hear and feel that I am—Back. Not a reverse trip; not a Punishment; not in error. I return on a Tangential Odyssey—to what Purpose, well, I shall soon know. I shall reveal More. *Internal difference/Where the Meanings, Are.* The whirling all around, the excitement—oh, I am giddy! *Called Back*—yes, *yes*! My Galleon in the harbor heaves at high tide, the wind Favorable, the deck hands casting off lines, my Captain at the wheel—raring to go!

"But wait! Who stands behind me—in the Shadow of the Black Oak?"

"Hello, I am Virginia. I just came out of a tree, there, up the trail. May I sit down? Is there room for another? I wonder if we might close our eyes and pretend we are aboard ship. May we tack close to the lighthouse? I love lighthouses! I love light in its myriad forms. I loved writing the quality of light on the sea, the depth of light in every human being. I said once that my life would pass like a shadow on the waves. I was half right.

"I know you! I was thinking of you before when I was coming through the portal. How I have wanted to meet you! Do you think you could have fallen in love with me? Would we have been friends? I was four years old when you went on ahead of me, though I didn't know it then. There was an ocean between us and a dark fin slicing through waves as they pitched on the shore and pulled back. I saw it first, the dark fin slicing through waves, as I looked from my writing window over the Downs. I looked over the heads of children playing on a great green lawn and saw the fin rise and slice the ocean's tapestry before diving and disappearing in the black water."

"Virginia!" said Emily, who stood up to receive and give a long hug. After the hug, they sat down together on the bench. "Would you like a cookie?" Emily opened her basket and Virginia selected a cookie fat with currants and pecans. "Yes," said Emily, "you would have been one of my Beloveds—my Specter of Eternity! I have read you, too; I read it all. How did you do it? How? How could you string so many Words together like pearls—the pearls flawless—each one gleaming in sunlight, in moonlight–Pristine? How? If I could have done that–I would have written novels and stories, too! I found my voice, my method, in Nature and in my own heightened–what would You call it?–*reality*. Yes, reality! A busy Insect Reality–that was Emily! That's me! Tell me something about your Words!"

"If you ask me the meaning of the dark fin slicing through waves," said Virginia, "I will tell you I do not know. I do not respond in this way to be difficult, but because I do not know. I never knew. I was never good with symbols. The lighthouse meant the lighthouse; the light meant light."

"Then tell me," said Emily, "were you a contrary child?"

"I was precocious, irreverent, a pistol and painfully shy. I became the cricketing demon bowler, the storyteller of the nursery. I was skittish, sly and I led revolts. I became ubiquitous. I undermined. My fingernails skittered over walls and chalkboards."

"Forgive Me!" Emily interrupted. "Oh–I was about to Say–my Impatience will be–the Death of me!" They both laughed. "Speak of the Deaths," said Emily. "We both Endured–so Many!"

"My mother died," Virginia answered, "my older half-sister, too, when I was young; then my father and my older brother. Too young! A half-sister, born an idiot, spent most of her life in an institution. When our much older half-brothers attempted to introduce us into Society, Nessa (my sister) and I aggressively proved ourselves ridiculous: eccentric dressers, indiscrete conversationalists, bad dancers. We inclined towards alcoves where we sat alone; sometimes I read a book.

"I can see you," said Emily, "soaring, unpredictable, like an exotic Bird. Alas, I also See–you–jumping out a window the first time– You tried–to kill Yourself." The heron had slowly circled back and was directly below them again. The bird watched.

"What a gorgeous creature!" Virginia exclaimed as tears came to her eyes.

"Tell me," said Emily, "when did you fall in love—with Words?"

"When I was growing up. Was it not the same with you? My father's proudest possession, in addition to his breathtakingly beautiful wife, my mother, was a vast library; he gave me the run of it. I devoured books like a lion tearing into a zebra. I read and I wrote, falling in love with the alchemy of words. I always felt I was nothing without books, without words. I fell in love with ink and pen points and the page. I loved finding and bringing home papers of different colors and textures; my delight was visceral, filling pages with smudges and doodles and words, words, words. I wrote and read and wrote. I walked miles and miles every day, making up rhythm, sentences and situations and saying them aloud, trying them out as I ambled everywhere, climbing over stone walls, crawling through hedges. Sometimes I sang, scaring children who thought I was a witch! They laughed at me just as the early critics laughed at me, but I went right on being myself. I lay in my bath saying out loud the phrases and sentences I'd written the day before so I could hear them and change them if I wanted to. I set type and bound books and made a world of words and stories, much as you did."

Emily stared at the mottled pattern the sun through leaves made on her forearm. She touched her arm there, feeling the patterns in the flesh, her flesh. She felt a gust of wind riffle the hairs at the back of her neck. Something—an ache—seized the big toe of her left foot. She smiled, dazzled, remembering earth sensations, earthiness.

"Some people," said Emily, "believed that I was born with more Awareness of my star-stuff than others. I don't know if it's true. But I was always—a body at risk—flinging my Heart against high heat and extreme cold, threatening always—to fly apart."

"I also loved dissembling!" Virginia said. "I rolled my own cigarettes and smoked them with a long, tapered holder. Later, I smoked cigars. I attended concerts, the opera, theatre and I went to the movie palace now and then. I saw friends, Bloomsbury friends and others, on holiday, at tea, at dinner, at parties, in London, in the country, abroad. And, yes...at times I was quite mad. I'll spare you more autobiography for now. Isn't it fun, having forever to know each other better and better?"

"Always, yes—and Eternity," said Emily. "To know—to know you—there—and in Me, I had my own room, upstairs—a lock on the door just as you prescribed. I anticipated you. A pity we never met or read each other then, separated as we were by an ocean—and fifty years or so. Oh, I would have loved to discover you playing—hunting butterflies down in my Garden. I would have lowered treats to you—in a basket like this one. I would have sent You—Poems in a Bundle—tied with Ribbon the color of—Lavender. I would have shown you the hiding places of the Daddy Long-Legs—the Amherst Lepidoptera & the footprints of mysterious cats."

"*Your* mysterious footprints and hiding places will suffice," said Virginia. "Belle of Amherst—a royal title! I had none so grand. What *would* they call me? Misfit of Monk's House! Yes, how's *that*? But this is our shared vision, our co-creative time. We return, together in form, in our lovely earth bodies." A squirrel chattered above their heads, leaping from wispy branch to branch in pursuit of its mate.

"I'm surprised," said Emily, "that our Bodies aren't surface-cracked and creaky—like furniture abandoned in an attic. I'm surprised that we do not bear—the mottled faces of long-abandoned ceramic Dolls." Virginia gazed into the opaque creek water and imagined the faces of dolls just under the surface.

"Emily, we will enjoy this keeping company! We shall be busy bees together; we shall be vivacious aunts coming into our Lily's life. She needs our help and protection. What she cannot grasp, what she does not know, will become clear to her in time, because after all, she must still measure the world that way, in the ridiculous, arbitrary, incremental chains of Time. There! I have capitalized the word just for you, in deference to you, because I am feeling your thought rhythms, your riffs of speech, your soul's expression. Let us joust and spar and conspire because we've returned to this realm of competition, of women and men contesting with themselves and each other, but to what purpose? Yet, isn't it fine to feel the wind on our good bodies again, a wind-whipped tear on our cheeks, and solid ground beneath our feet? Even the long-asleep sensation of my teeth aching almost brings me to tears." Suddenly, the heron spread its wings and launched itself skyward, rending the air with a whooshing sound. Virginia's eyes followed its departure and trajectory, turning her head from Emily in the direction of the upper path. Thanks to the bird, something else caught her eye.

"But wait!" Virginia cowered close to Emily. "Do you see them, the sinister pair lurking behind the Manzanita? *There!* They're watching us, they're measuring us for an assault, perhaps. They know we're the enemy. Now, run, Emily, run! Before they can act, come with me into the brush. There is a fox path they won't be able to follow. *Run! Keep low!* If they catch us they may win! They would destroy us and take Lily!"

Together, the women plunged into the brush. "The De la Nuit!" Emily spat out the words as if they burned her tongue. They watched the two rancid figures lurking in the bushes, clumsily trying to sneak up on them. "We must meet Lily—Before They do!" Off they ran, crouching, across a wooden bridge to the other side of the creek.

"There," said Virginia, catching her breath; "we are safe now. We can stop. We have eluded them. They wander away in the park hopelessly lost. We are too swift and clever for them. Now we can straighten up and step out into the sunlight again. Shall we walk together? We have work to do. It is so *good* to set off on this journey with you. Oh, what a pair we are! You may call me Goat, or Billy Goat, or Billy if you wish!"

"Thank you, Virginia—Goat—" said Emily as she came out of hiding brushing brambles from her dress. "You may call me Emily, or Em for short."

"Oh, bother!" said Virginia. "So formal, so stuffy! Are we *both* snobs? I used to think I was the only one! That's not true. All the Stephen children were snobs, but in different ways. I digress. How's this—(your dash again, *I* love the ampersand) I'll call you L-Bug, short for lightning bug; or firefly. Both embody your dash, your spark & effervescence. Dearest, you *must* have an animal nickname!"

"Oh, very well...Goat! Call me L-Bug if you must. It sounds almost— naughty. It Amuses me! You amuse me. I see in you—the Astonishment of Delight! Now— Do you have—Money?"

"Oh, lots!" said Virginia. "Mother Brigid is like the Bank of England!"

How shall we—Begin?"

"In this way, L-Bug, in this way. We are shepherds for Lily, our young woman unsteadily swaying towards the dawn of a difficult day. Earth lives teem with vulnerability. Everyone needs a little help surviving and moving on in light. Say it in a poem, and take us there!"

"I have a poem born whole in my resurrected mind," said Emily, "and here it is:"

> *Alone in alabaster sheets*
> *Our Lily rises blue*
> *To all the world of weighted Harm—*
> *She cannot find her flow—*
>
> *She wants for allies—See—how she*
> *Shakes her head—her hair a nest*
> *Of Dreams disheveled, Dashed*
> *Within her brambles, her leaning—Breast*

Four

"Someone is coming," Lily thought, heeding the voice that said *Wake up! Lily, wake up!* The voice was not Shaya's; the bed—but it was not a bed—pitched and lurched. She lay on a hard, wet surface. Water lapped all around her and over her. Wind howled and lashed her flying weightless through space, then plummeting down, down, impossibly heavy, rejected by currents of air.

A bird landed beside her. She was not falling. She pitched and rolled like a wave. Yes, she thought, that's it. I'm a wave! She pitched and rolled and recognized the bird. "You're an albatross," she said in her mind to the bird, and tried to remember everything she had ever read about an albatross at sea. Yes, *The Rime of the Ancient Mariner.* She remembered that. She remembered Warning; she remembered Foreboding; she remembered Disaster. She became a wave riding waves. No, she was on a boat. Yes, she could make out the bumps and cracks in the deck beneath her body; yes, there were doors, and steps descending into the hold. There was the mast, and unmistakably from it, like a knife through her heart, whipped the Jolly Roger, the pirate flag.

Lily moaned. It began as a low cow sound that rather than ending in contented chewing grew louder and darker and crackled in the air like a shower of broken crockery. At the terrible sound, anyone nearby would have ducked instinctively; the albatross lowered its head, pecking furiously in a little half-moon at the slick, rollicking deck under its breast. Energized by the sight of the flag and her primordial cry, Lily sprang to her feet and began to climb the rigging.

She climbed past the lofty passenger cabins; she climbed above the captain's deck; she climbed to the flag and the lookout roost.

"It's the wrong ship!" she said high up in the rigging. "Why am I on a sailing vessel? Why not a cruise ship? Frantically, Lily searched the ship above and below deck for her parents, but they were not there. Then why am I here?"

Pelted by rain and wind and ocean spray, Lily wrapped the rigging around her legs so she could sit down and rest. Then she saw the unexpected; she saw herself sprawled out sound asleep far below on the rolling deck. "See how I move with the ship," she told herself; "I look like a wave on a wave." Where had the bird got to, she wondered, for the albatross was nowhere to be seen. A ghostly cawing overhead solved that mystery. Looking up, she could just make out the off-white wings of the albatross circling the ship.

She reeled. Lightheadedness engulfed her and the stunning pang of separation from her parents stabbed her chest. Was she feeling the loss of the bird, or the distance from her body? Slowly, carefully, she began her descent. Ever so slowly, she climbed down hand over hand, foot-by-foot, inch-by-inch until she was close enough with a little jump to land beside her still sleeping body. "Mother and father are gone," she murmured; "mother and father are gone." The feeling of separation that struck her in the rigging throbbed and grew in her chest and skull until she felt as if everything she'd ever loved was flying away from her. She felt how easy it would be to give it all up and fly away, too. "You can stop this," said Lily to herself. "You know how." She lay down beside her sleeping body and began to breathe slowly, deeply, rhythmically, like cows at rest, like whales endlessly journeying. Lily breathed, and her body breathed. The moon peeked out of clouds and shone through her window. Her sense of separation vanished. Then there was one body—one Lily—lying there, sound asleep in her own bed.

Lily lingered in bed an hour past her usual waking, gazing drearily at rain-streaked daylight slanting through window blinds. The paneled light made steep, transparent stairways out of floating dust, and Lily fancied she could see small, foggy people going up and down and dropping into unlit air. Oh, it's here again, she thought, another day. She thought, how will I go from here to there and back without falling apart, as I did yesterday at my drawing table over the picture of the Crone in the woods?

An hour later she was showered but not dressed. She stood before the bathroom mirror, the steam clearing, looking like a jungle goddess materializing out of clouds of wavy white ferns. Sometimes this post-shower vision of herself energized and inspired her, sending her out the door on a goddess-powered morning, but she did not feel much like a goddess today. As the last steam shriveled and evaporated off the bottom of the mirror, Lily regarded her body under the hard bathroom light. It was a good body, she thought. If she were signing up on a dating site, she would choose the description 'athletic and toned'. At 5' 10", she was tall, but not tall enough to be gawky or to trigger the word 'hoopster' in peoples' minds. She turned to one side and looked over her shoulder at her damp hair that tumbled half way down her back. The color of chestnut (though it lightened almost to blonde in summer), her hair looked disheveled and unruly, and Lily squared herself up in the mirror again to avoid it.

It was then she looked at her face, a morning reckoning she often put off as long as possible. If you could watch her like an unusually intelligent and reflective fly on the wall—like the fly with a human head from the movies, perhaps, but without the terror—you would wonder why. She thought that her large, oval gray-green eyes were rather too far apart, but in fact no one else had ever said that, and they were one of her best features. They were her mother's eyes and her mother always told her how striking they were. Her chin, though, was her father's. Not angular but resolute, chiseled in a strong feminine way. Lily's eyes shifted from side to side, trying to evade the dangerous territory of her face in the mirror, but like dogs racing from one end of the yard to the other and suddenly flattening out on the grass, Lily's eyes stopped and took herself all in. Yes, she was pretty. She knew that. Some even called her beautiful, but people commenting on her looks unnerved her. Their compliments gave her pleasure, but they also embarrassed her. Looking at her face in a mirror gave her pleasure and embarrassed her and this morning there was a third thing; this morning, looking at herself in the mirror depressed her. In the steamy room she looked greyer and cracked somehow, like an old doll. Get out of the bathroom, she told herself and she stumbled backwards, as if pulling away from someone's unwelcome grasp.

Back in her bedroom, she stood before the small closet—should she wear this or this or that? "Oh, what's the point," she sighed, and decided to crawl back into her Betty Boop flannel pajamas (a last present from her mother) because why not? *I'll tell you why*, said the crew-cut, square-chinned Coach Clapper in her head, *because anyone who gets back into pajamas after taking them off in the morning is a lazy bum, a loser! Is that what you want? Is it?* He never visited her in a normal tone of voice; he was always screaming, then screaming louder. Some people had the coach in the head, and some did not. Lily had it from volleyball and swimming in high school.

"I don't know if I'm going to leave the house today," said Lily, mocking the hectoring coach-voice. Though she thought it would take more effort, her simple defiance worked; it was enough to neutralize that demonic voice of duty, that crabby, sadistic fiend of push-ups and jumping jacks, that tormentor of squats and laps who never invaded her except to criticize, to run her down, to spoil her day. Well, her day was already bad, but it was early, and so she still turned over and over the question: *how much worse can it get?* She knew full well that she was in for some surprises she would just as soon miss. The point was to survive the onslaught, minimize the damage, perhaps turn the emotional tsunamis around. Even in my pajamas, Lily thought, I'll give it a try. Determined to kick-start her day, to do *something* useful, Lily got up again and plodded down the hall to the kitchen. Her eye caught sight of a business card on the counter and she picked it up. She sighed.

"Dammit! It's today," she muttered. The card belonged to a young man, Aidan, with whom she'd enjoyed an interesting conversation while standing in line at the post office. She was mailing original artwork to her editor while he was mailing art announcements from the gallery where he worked and they laughed that anyone their age would be using a post office. "Almost like using a phone booth, if you could find one," Aidan said. Lily recognized the gallery by name but had never been there. As her turn at the window was about to come up, Aidan asked her to have coffee with him. Not having time to think of a reason to say no, Lily said yes, and today was the day they'd agreed to meet at Rogue Roasters. "I can get out of this," Lily grumbled. "I *should* get out of this." But then a more welcoming inner voice said *why should I?* As sour as the morning had been, Lily smiled. She would go. She would meet this guy because...because why not?

Alone in her swept kitchen, Lily resolved to start over and do it well. She thought, 'be healthy', so she blended a smoothie—an orange, an apple, three kale leaves, and a vitamin supplement for good measure; she ground rich, shiny beans from Peets and brewed a small cup of coffee. Thus fortified, she sat down at her table and stared at her drawings. Was there too much of her current personal turmoil in them, she wondered. Was her professional commitment strong enough to balance the two? Yes, she was sure it was. After all, she had been at it a long time. She had drawn for as long as she could remember. Up until the age of six or seven, she thought she was really a dinosaur and she drew complicated societies of them. She could look back now and see that her artistic vision had softened thanks to Disney films, a guilty pleasure she still loved and all of these influences led her to Manga, especially to the work of Arina Tanemura.

Before recently breaking with her longtime publisher, Tanemura had produced Manga art and stories that inspired a generation of artists and writers. She had won Lily over at an early age, who was fascinated by Tanemura's seemingly effortless ability to blend love, romance and the supernatural. Because of Tanemura's example, Lily wanted to produce her own series of books, some featuring her art and storylines, some featuring her art only. Until then she was kept busy with contract work for Manga publishers in the U.S. Lily loved her work, yet she was stalling.

In the drawing on her table, two young Manga characters, a boy and girl, one poor, one well off, stood side-by-side, their backs to the reader. If they weren't already in love, they soon would be. They held hands and gazed at an awesome, arched celestial display of undulating purple, blue, black, green and white. The free arms of the two characters were extended out and slightly bent at the elbows. It was as if they were exclaiming, *just look at this!*

It was beautiful, her drawing, but she was stuck as to what came next. She was stuck and already late, having uncharacteristically missed her publisher's deadline by three days. Lily was tired. She felt uninspired, and she felt as if she had been awake for years. She had hardly slept and she had dreamed the same horrible dream that always haunted her this time of year. There was the albatross, friend or foe, pecking furiously the ship's deck in her brain. She stared at the figures in the drawing and suddenly saw how they reminded her of her mother and father when they were young. The pencil stilled between her fingers and she wandered into memory.

A Drawing from Lily's Project

There she was at sixteen the day her parents booked their Caribbean cruise. They'd wanted her to go—as a belated sixteenth birthday present—but she had begged off. Too much school work, she told them. Polite. The truth, of course, was that she did not want to go. The last thing she wanted to do with a chunk of her summer was to be confined on a boat tour with a bunch of old people. She had parties to go to, camping and swimming and horseback riding and two boys, Zach and Eli, one a jock, the other a local heart throb actor who were interested in her. Summer was for finding out which one she liked best.

So, Lily got out of the trip. She loved having the house to herself and Shaya. They reveled in their emancipation. They got out of bed whenever they wanted to, left their clothes where they fell, stayed up late, hosted parties and sleepovers and ate whatever they felt like making. At the last party, several friends got into the liquor cabinet and it took hours to refill bottles (partially) with water (as if that would fool anybody). Lily and Shaya also began working on a good story to explain the four-inch burn in the dining room carpet where Eli dropped a joint and forgot about it. Yes, this was a pivotal moment in which his stock as a potential boyfriend plummeted. Still, Lily thought of it as the happiest summer of her life until the phone call that informed her that her parents had been killed during an incident aboard ship. Lily and Shaya were alone together in the house and of course the call came at 3 in the morning when the worst calls always come.

In the middle of the phone call, Lily felt herself free-falling through a bottomless tunnel; the tunnel filled with the sound of her screams, which felt disembodied, as if they were coming from a source other than herself. Then she felt groggy and bed-bound, hardly able to move and unwilling to speak. Later, Shaya, who never left her side and fended off the reporters, would tell her that she'd lived like that for two weeks. And then one morning she appeared in the kitchen in her pajamas and asked for coffee. Shaya French-pressed a mug, sat down with her and Lily started talking. "Did I make this happen?" After two weeks of total silence, that was all she could get out. Then Lily talked for three days and nights.

"I played a part in this, yes. If I'd been there, if I'd been awake, if I'd been thinking of them instead of myself...How can I live after this?"

Lily talked and Shaya listened. Lily faltered and Shaya took her hands. Lily cried; Shaya cried with her and held Lily in her arms. Shaya listened as Lily told many versions of the story of her guilt. Why hadn't she gone with them? Perhaps she could have saved them. If she'd been willing to go, too, she might have persuaded them to vacation somewhere else. She had acted selfishly and stupidly and now her mother and father were dead. Because of her, they were gone and she would never be able to say to them, or hear from them, all the things she'd assumed they'd share in the many years ahead. Her cell phone going off made her jump.

"It's me." It was Shaya's voice. "Are you beating yourself up?"

"Are you psychic? I almost called you at 3 a.m."

"You can call me any time. Where are you? Are you sitting at your drawing table feeling like crap? You know you have a coffee date today."

"Yeah," said Lily. "I just found his card and remembered."

"You're going, right?"

"What are you? My ......" Lily broke down, crying.

"C'mon, honey, I'm sorry." Shaya's voice was soothing, like a warm compress on the back of the neck. "Want me to come over?" Lily gulped back her tears and blew her nose.

"No, I'm ok. Don't worry. I'll pull myself together. I'm going."

"Ok! You sure you don't want me to come over? No? Call and tell me how it goes, then, ok? I love you, Lily."

Calm again, Lily smiled. Shaya loved her. "Screw this," she sighed, tossing down the pencil in a pique and choosing another before attacking a field of white within bold lines. I need to go horseback riding, she thought. I need to tramp in the woods. I need to shut off my smart phone. What good is a smart phone when one feels so stupid? She always felt better when she rode Ed, her favorite horse. Ed was 12, a palomino and looked just like the old TV star, Mr. Ed. His real name was Driver's Ed, but to Lily he was always *Mr.* Ed.

After Ed, I need to avoid all of my friends except Shaya, Lily thought. She is the only one who can be with me no matter what. The others, Tillie and Star and Rua, they mean well, but I feel inadequate, unsocial! I'm no good to anybody like this. Lily shaded the white space within character lines on a new drawing. The page was framed and dramatic, full of youthful characters and one direful crone brewing a foul concoction in her forest hut. This new series had begun with such promise. Where did *that* go? Lily wondered. Where was that enthusiasm, the way one feels waking up in a tent beside the Rogue River on a bracing, sunny spring morning? Where did it go? Compulsively, she thought of the cigarettes she had hidden when she quit four months earlier, but new thoughts saved her before she could fish them out and light one up.

Lily desperately wanted answers, but which were right? She knew that every year, around the anniversary of her parents' murders, she plunged into depths she did not want to revisit, but here she was again back at the same story. There must be a purpose, Lily thought, a reason for circling and circling back on herself like a snake swallowing its tail, like a salmon flailing upstream—some indomitable urge that wells up and drives one, relentless, to a place of significance where all life changes in an instant. That's what she supposed she wanted. Didn't everyone? For life to change, for whatever was lacking to be found, for the hole in one's middle to be filled like a piñata with treats and surprises. Yes, that must be it, Lily thought, the reason for it all, the purpose. So she would abide. She would sigh and wallow. She would replay the incidents as she understood them, and she would feel herself changed, transformed in that moment of notification, of discovery, and transformed every day and every year since by replaying what had happened and, incrementally, ever so slowly, what it was making of her.

The fire trucks down the block came to life screaming and burst out of the station heading south. They passed directly by Lily's windows and shook her from one layer of reverie.

Truth is, she felt like cutting herself. She hadn't done that for a long time, yet there they were, the faded scars on her forearm to remind her. Her father had worried himself sick over the habit. He feared that the act of cutting was a rehearsal for suicide; others thought so, too. Nobody but Shaya believed her when she told them it was a coping mechanism for high school. She didn't blame them for thinking what they did. Her father's sister took her own life when she was 37, leaving behind four small children. What could she tell him? She had tried, but she wasn't certain that he had ever heard her. She told him she cut herself to relieve the pain, the anxiety. '*Anxiety—about what?*' He'd wanted to know. "The pain and anxiety of being alive," she'd said. Well, what could he say to that? What could anyone? Her father had talked about *real* pain and *real* anxiety and *real* loss, and Lily had quickly tuned him out. The tantalizing sharp knives in the kitchen sometimes called to her, mocking her. Did she hear their voices now? Lily paused in her act of shading and listened. No, it's not their voices I hear, she thought. The urge she felt was interior, otherworldly, all her own. From what world was it speaking? Was it this, the one where she, Lily, sat at her drafting table unable to work, paralyzed but for the smallest, insignificant motions? She finished shading a circle that changed a character's mood. That must lead to alterations in the moods of other characters. Oh, the uncertainty built and built!

How insidiously plays the fragment of a popular song, Lily thought, circling and circling in the cerebellum until a stumble over a rock or crack nudges the needle out of its rut. Here at my drawing table I am blocked, Lily thought, prevented from descending deeper to the kingdom of the miserable and past it, to the liberation and joy of originality.

What *is* that? she wondered. Originality. The dove's ascent feels original, yet it's repeated over and over through more days and stories than a mind can hold. Originality is a feeling, then, a rush that elevates, a strange song that comes as one wonders from where it comes yet is grateful to have it, hear it and feel it in place of the familiar song, the song of the silly, of the well tested.

Lily addressed her drawing of the young boy and girl: "So I say to you, my little colored pencil figures of today, that you're original. The color of your necks and faces and arms rises, not without pleasure, as your posture improves, as your eyes sparkle. You will share that light with someone you don't know and he will never discover how you came by it, or even fully grasp what it is about you that is different than the you of some other time."

Lily wondered what else she might do with this bounty, but her fear and boredom saved her from thinking obsessively about it. Yes, she thought, I am free of thought, free of feeling burdened by my lack of originality, but the voices—the voices continue.

But if it was not this world from which the inner voices were rising, which world was it? *Where* was it? Could she choose a door or window or curtain or portal and pass through? Or was it on the other side of the galaxy, requiring that she locate and board a soul ship for transport? There were also two faces, a man's and a woman's, and they were not smiling. They leered at her. Their hands reached for her; the woman held a knife.

Lily shifted, focusing on the soul ship image. Wouldn't that be a pretty thing to do, Lily thought, to be able to book passage and travel to another world as one books a tour of Greece or Egypt. I have been to Greece as an exchange student in my sophomore year, Lily thought, but not Egypt. Not yet. She had always talked about taking that trip with her mother. She would still like to go, but it would be different. I would like to wander, Lily thought; I would like to feel freedom surging through me and guiding me to surprising places and situations. Yes, that is what I want shipwrecked at this table on this wet, gray morning, Lily thought.

Perhaps now she could focus. Maybe now she could make herself work. Her doorbell rang—once, twice, three times. It rang with the persistence and urgency of someone who is expected, but Lily expected no one. "Oh, who could it be?" she grumbled. She stamped her foot.

Five

At the fourth ring, Lily got up from her desk shouting *All right! Just a sec!* She stomped to the door, her temples and the back of her head throbbing. The sensation made her feel half-headed, and she wondered what effect she might have on her unwanted callers if she flung open the door with only half a head teetering on the stalk of her neck. She peered through the spyhole for a moment—her hand on the deadbolt—and saw two middle-aged women, one short, one tall, the taller one wearing a straw hat with a wide brim, the shorter one in a white dress. They held antique umbrellas and the shorter one also carried a picnic basket. "They don't look like Jehovah's Witnesses," Lily muttered. She threw back the bolt and opened wide the door.

Before her, smiling, stood two of the oddest, most attractive women that Lily had ever seen, and she felt inexplicably drawn to them. That was enough to fascinate her and invite them in. Suddenly she welcomed the distraction; she wanted to study them. She loved stories and characters, and she simply wanted to know more. Much more. She wanted to draw them.

Both women were eye-catching but not in the same way. The taller one was more angular, sophisticated and elegant. The smaller one's face was rounder, softer. I can see that the tall one lives on the edge of something, Lily thought, but the edge of what? Does it have to be something with a name? Aren't I feeling the same way?

The diminutive one—she was shorter than her companion by four or five inches—was not unsophisticated or inelegant. No, but it was this—her sophistication and elegance were of a different order.

She seemed to stand inside a faint bluish-white aura; one could see her pulse racing through her whole body. The soft yet urgent sound of wings surrounded her; She almost vibrated. Lily thought of a hummingbird, or a bee, especially when the sun shines on them at a certain time of day and they appear to be translucent. Yes, she wanted to draw them.

Lily realized that the style of both women was of a different order than what she was used to. It wasn't that their styles were 'off'. There was something, though, that ruffled the surface contours of Lily's brain. They had come from somewhere, but where? It was not a place that Lily recognized, yet there was something so...familiar about each one! A tickling sensation played up and down the back of her neck, like the feeling one gets from the tiny hairs that survive a haircut until one sponges them off, like that isolated spot on one's back that itches awfully yet can't be reached by one's fingers. She sat up straight as the word *urgently* blinked on and off like neon in her mind.

"Hello, yes?" Lily said. The women looked at each other; the tall one giggled. They looked at each other as if they were enjoying a private joke. This irritated Lily. Perhaps they sensed it, because the taller one suddenly looked serious, explaining that she and her companion were from Community Gardens, a local organization that Lily had vaguely heard of but never paid any attention to. "Oh," Lily said, thinking they had called on her for a donation, "you're like Meals on Wheels or Food Angels or something, right?"

"Oh, Food Angels!" The shorter one exclaimed. "*That* approaches the Circumference! But no—we are not much like Meals on Wheels. We're representing people who grow—Food," she said. "That is, the people who eat the food also learn to—plant and grow it." Lily concealed her embarrassment that she'd been unaware of this distinction.

"It's all right," the tall one said. "People mix us up all the time! Not to worry! Now, there's a chill outside, so grab your woolly, or what do you call it here—your *hoodie*—such a *word*—and let's be going."

"What? Go where?" Lily felt her heart racing.

"Why, to the gardens, of course!" The short one said. "We've much to do, much—and we're grateful to you for volunteering."

"There must be a mistake," Lily said. "I didn't volunteer."

The tall one produced a piece of paper from her leather handbag, which dangled from a shoulder strap down her right side. She unfolded the paper and handed it to Lily. "This is your name, is it not, and your address, and your offer to volunteer?"

Every phrase felt like a sting, a rebuke, and Lily could feel herself cringing under the tall woman's lash as she examined the writing. It appeared to be in her hand, all right. What was wrong with her? When had she volunteered and why did she have no recollection of it? Once more, the clairvoyant tall one interrupted her thought.

"Nothing at all to worry about, Lily! Doubtless you forgot because you are doing so much! You have a very full plate, I can tell, and you are to be commended for it. Salud! But let's hurry now. We don't want to waste more daylight. We'll talk on our way. Shall we?"

Lily sensed the futility of refusing and she privately acknowledged something else. She felt that it was important to go with these ladies, wherever they were taking her. She actually wanted to go. So, she grabbed her hoodie, tied it around her waist and the three of them set off.

Off to the gardens, they sat three across, Lily in the middle, on the very back row of the #10 bus, which drove through the heart of downtown Ashland. From the corner of her eye, she studied the clothes of her companions. Their dresses were summery, demure, pleasant enough, but they seemed to Lily from another time. That's it! she thought. They're *vintage*. She felt a pang of remorse that she hadn't spent more time studying fashion in school. Clearly, these two had made a conscious choice to dress Retro, but Retro what? Yes, she thought, if she drew them she would have to catch that antique quality. And how old were they? It was a wide range, she knew, but she guessed mid-thirties to early-fifties.

"Close enough," said the tall one, startling Lily again so that she hopped a little in her seat like a jumping bean. Lily noticed how the tall woman with exceptional posture had a way of looking out from under the brim of her broad hat with the dancing eyes of a devilish pixie. It was obvious that the woman liked hats whether they looked silly on her or not. She was having a good time.

"Oh, look!" said the shorter woman. "Look there, there, and *there*!" She saw everything, or so it seemed, every street vendor, outrageous costume, musician, the boy dressed as a yogurt cup and the shoppers as if for the first time. She was agitated, but not in a fretting way. She was...excited! Yes, that was it. Lily felt herself drawn to the woman's joyful habit of surveying; she peered out the window, hoping to see what the woman beside her saw. The tall one gazed out the window, too, with variations of a playful smile always on her lips. Even the beggars seemed to amuse her.

"They do!" she said, turning her gray-green eyes on Lily.

"How do you know what I'm thinking?" Lily asked.

"Oh, good guesses—I guess!" said the short one, and then to change the subject, "We never told you our names! I—am Emily—and this delightful if somewhat vexing creature—is Virginia."

"*Aunt* Emily & *Aunt* Virginia," said the tall one.

"Excuse me?"

"Think of us as your long lost, eccentric aunts. It's more fun!"

Lily sat back. It was absurd, of course. These women weren't her aunts! Had she traipsed off on a bus ride with a couple of lunatics? No, the six other bus riders were not looking at them with alarm. "Anything to get out of working," she grumbled. Yet there was something charming and endearing about these two, something eccentric, yes, that's the word, even irresistible. Once that word had filled her head, it surprised her. I am drawn to these women, she thought, baffled. They even have the same names as my beloved authors. They rather look like them, too, now that I think of it. Wow! They look a lot like them.

"Coincidence?" Virginia's eyes dazzled as she laughed.

"It's a little unnerving when you do that," said Lily, "but I'd better get used to it, right?" She saw from Virginia's reaction that for once she had anticipated *her*. "I don't know how you do it," said Lily. "It's like you're able to read my mind. Are you psychic? Can both of you do it?" Emily looked sheepish. "I don't have any aunts," said Lily, thinking of the suicide aunt she never knew, "but I've always wanted some. Once, I had a cat I named Aunt Betty."

"Splendid! It's settled then," said Virginia; "everyone gets what she wants."

"Aunt Emily—Aunt Virginia? Well, anyone who knows me knows I love your names. They are special to me."

"Eureka! Here's our Stop!" said *Aunt* Emily.

"I was never quite right for this country," Virginia said, thinking of the beseeching invitations to lecture in America that she had turned down. "Just look at all this corpulence & racing around! But I was always too critical of the eating habits of others, even my friends. They were too picky or too glutinous."

"Americans weren't obese in your time," said Emily, "and certainly not in mine."

"Really?" said Virginia. "Then how do you explain your porky presidents? What were their names—Taft, Cleveland, Arthur?"

Lily tried shielding her thoughts as she listened to the odd conversation between the women. They had taken Lily to tea after their garden work and the three sat around the table of the meeting room at Pony Espresso, one of Lily's favorite coffee shops. One wall of double-pane windows looked out on the street; they admired the purple, white, rose and yellow pansies, peonies and petunias overflowing two flower baskets that hung side by side from a lamppost across the street. The room's two large sliding glass doors, their panels mostly obscured by privacy tape that had been foolishly applied to them, stood open to the larger room beyond. They sat close together though the table was long with ten soft leather chairs around it. They had the room to themselves and only three other people took up chairs in other parts of the shop. One was the famous compiler of a popular *Bathroom Reader*; the other two were young girls dressed like Romy and Michelle from the movie; one's hair was dyed lime green, the other's pink. Lily watched a town regular, the Goat Man, tie his companion, a mature goat, to a bumper and run in for a latte to go.

Virginia rapped the table-top. "This is long enough for table tennis," she remarked. Lily looked at the table as if for the first time and laughed.

"Yes," she agreed, "it's like that!"

"Lily," said Virginia, "do you come here because you love horses?" Lily looked at her new 'aunt' with confusion. "Because you love horses," Virginia said again. "You ride them. The name of this place is Pony Espresso. Is that why you come here, because of the name?"

Lily regarded Virginia carefully and saw that she wasn't kidding.

"I love horses," Lily said, "and I like the name, but I don't come here because of it. I like this room, actually and I love a couple of the baristas who work here—like Abby who brought us our drinks. She studies acting when she isn't here. She's a friend. Another barista who isn't here today is a jeweler. He made my necklace." She held it out, a silver heart framing an amethyst, for her 'aunts' to admire. "Aunt Virginia," Lily asked, "did you ever ride?"

"I rode when I was younger. Nessa and I liked to ride—Nessa, my sister—though I never much cared for the tacking up and so on and so forth. It's said that horses 'sense' the emotional state of the rider.

That worried me. Did horses know that I was sometimes cracked? How would they process such information, and what would they do with it? But I loved the canter and the gallop! I loved the sensation of speed and flight! One day I was seriously thrown. I was not really damaged, but I never rode much after that. Mostly I stuck to tramping through London or all over the Sussex Downs; later, we had a motorcar. I took lessons and learned to drive. I enjoyed it, but I soon ran our Singer through a hedge and I vowed then and there to leave the driving to Leo. I willingly became a passenger and hander of tools to my husband when he sat on the road to fix flats, which occurred quite often."

A 'Singer'? thought Lily. What a cool name for a car! What kind was it, she wondered. She'd never heard of one. And though Virginia's accent should have raised no doubt about her country of origin, Lily only just now fully awoke to the fact that her tall 'aunt' was English. The names 'Nessa' and 'Leo' were also familiar to her. She felt anxious, the way one feels when something momentous is taking shape in one's mind, yet is not consciously clear. What was it? Well, these two, of course, Lily thought. Who were they really? If they could both hear her thoughts, they were letting her go off on her own now without interruption. Lily wished they would speak up and help her and she was glad they didn't.

"I rode a little when I was a girl," said Emily, distracting Lily from her thoughts. "Many friends and cousins did. A school friend galloped into a low-hanging branch—Killed Instantly. Some I knew died—a-horseback in the Great War, including a boy who used to bring me Books—a boy I loved—Before I knew much about Love. It was peculiar—all the Death around me when I was young—all my life, really. Yet, horses in my Mind lived Forever—galloping over the furze like Messengers so far afield the Myopic could not see them—But *I* saw them! I saw them and I rode them in Dreams, and we passed the Greek runner, the Roman with dripping sword, King Cyrus in his chariot—all those dying with the plague, those tortured and roasted at the stake. We rode all night—Forever—through it all, above them all and circled Eternity to my own sleigh bed on the second floor, with the window overlooking the graveyard."

The milk steamers hissed behind the distant counter and an un-awake customer dropped a plate too heavily into the dirty dishes bin. Emily fell silent, then erupted anew. "I saw the pony express in Sil-houette," said Emily, "dashing through Orion—helter-skelter beyond the Milky Way; below my Tribe conundrum might have been had not the Moon—Good Mother—parsed a Meaning we could Tailgate."

Virginia and Lily stared at her, waiting. As Emily spoke, she seemed to be climbing, like musical notes skittering up the scales on a piano. As she reached the summit, she became more breathless, as if she were about to pass out. They waited, relieved as seconds ticked by and she did *not* pass out; Virginia poured her a glass of water. Emily took it and stared at the glass for a moment as if she had never seen such a thing. Suddenly, she tossed it back, all of it, like a sailor in a shanty bar, and rapped the glass on the tabletop. "I lived before cars," said Emily, "yet I coined the word—*Tailgate*—because I saw a red fox once wanting to but unable to run, its swishing tail—so beautiful—caught in a swinging field gate. The fox got away, as if the spring in my heart streamed out of me and filled it with the Power—to escape!"

They were all quiet. A customer banged through the shop door haranguing his hangdog friend about who knew what. Lily thought again of the something Momentous that was not yet fully formed in her brain as she watched Abby cleaning tables outside. Intuition told her it would be wonderful, yet there was something terrifying about it, too. In her thought, the names of her 'aunts' throbbed, dim then bright then dim again; she couldn't fully get past the names.

Virginia could be silent no longer. She cocked an eyebrow, an expression she was good at. "Our names are common enough," she said.

"Yes," said Lily, "they're common enough, like mine. But your names just happen to be the names of my favorite authors, Emily Dickinson and Virginia Woolf."

"Oh?" said Virginia, sniffing slightly, "who are they?"

"Like I said, they're writers. Great writers. And why do I feel that you *do* know who they are?"

"Who's psychic—now?" said Emily. "How flattering! Imagine that, Virginia! We remind Lily—of *great* Writers. We must look them up!"

"In person that would be difficult," said Lily. "They're dead."

"That's no obstacle," said Virginia. "I talk to the dead all the time. We both do. We all do."

"Oh—all the time, Lily! Every day," said Emily. "Why would We think it strange?"

"I have a question," Lily said. "It's about something Aunt Emily just said. You said you 'lived before cars'. What did you mean by that?"

"I meant *exactly* what I said!" Emily chirped. Lily waited for more, but there *was* no more.

"Suppose I told you," said Virginia, "that we lived in a horse and buggy age (though I also lived long enough to own a car), died & have come back to earth." Lily looked at them and out the window at passersby as she turned over in her mind what had just been said. She wished her parents were coming into the shop now to hug her and tell her that they were all right and not to worry so. But they did not come.

"Then I guess I'd have to say you're ghosts," said Lily.

"Do you believe in ghosts, my dear?" Virginia asked.

"I've always said I do," said Lily, "but I've never had tea with one—excuse me, Aunt Emily—with two." Lily reached out and touched Emily's arm as if to convince herself that her companion was real. Touching her felt like—Home. "Can others see you, Aunt Ginny?"

"Thank you for using a diminutive form of my name!" said Virginia. "Already our intimacy grows! Yes," she went on, "everyone can see us if we want them to. Didn't I order the tea and coffee and didn't the barista engage with me?" It was true. The baristas saw them. People looking in the window as they passed by saw them. The bus driver had seen them. Yes, the two women were as visible as she was.

"All right, then," Lily demanded, having made up her mind to play along, "why *have* you come back?"

"You know the—Answer! Dear Girl!" said Emily.

"You called us," Virginia said, "last night and often. Think, Lily," said Virginia. "You've experienced overwhelming grief, guilt and presentiments of danger. You fear something, but you don't know what, so in dreams you have called us."

"Wait! Are you suggesting—are you trying to say that you *are* my favorite authors, the women I turn to for comfort and security and guidance? Do you expect me to buy that?" Lily felt lightheaded, as if she were emerging from a dream and lingering half in and half out of two worlds.

"Yes, it's exactly like that," said Virginia.

"Think of us," said Emily, "as your guide Animals—your guardian Angels, your spirit—Friends!"

"Or," said Lily, "I can think of you as a couple of loons I stupidly let into my apartment." Lily was sorry, seeing the hurt look flash across Virginia's face like a cloud obscuring the moon the moment she said it. "I'm sorry," she said. "I don't think you're crazy but... but...who would believe this?"

"All that matters—is what—You Believe—my Dear," said Emily. Lily stared out the window and finished her ginger tea. She sat up straight. She looked at Virginia; she looked at Emily. She could see it now. Yes, the women looked exactly like her beloved authors. Her mother had loved them and taught her to love them. How many times had she sat in this very room and listened to her mother read their prose and poetry with joy? These two (if they were real) had been responsible for some of the deepest pleasures in her mother's life. Looking, clear-eyed, she said "All right! This makes me the luckiest woman in the world!"

"Let's not be *too* rambunctious," said Virginia, patting Lily's hand. "We have serious work to do."

"Yes," said Lily, "I've prayed and prayed for help with my work, with my life. And...*am* I in danger?"

"As a Fawn—Is—threatened by rampant—Fire!" said Emily.

Before Lily could respond, Virginia cut in. "This broaches a subject we must take up with you," she said. "Have you ever heard of the De la Nuit?"

"No, never," said Lily. "Who or what are they, the De la Nuit?"

"Those of the night", said Virginia, sighing deeply. "Their cult is so ancient even their origin is unclear. Mother Brigid told me she believes that they are Celtic in origin, precursors even of the Banshee. They're the mysterious, shunned souls of the world next to this one. They are transition-challenged. Despised, anti-social in dirty white robes and hooded cowls, they slobber, stagger and stink as they wander forever in the next world and occasionally in this one; they return here on sinister missions that are never quite clear to anyone. This much is known. Their nightly processions must be led by someone new snatched from the earth realm."

"Gob-smacked—stolen from their beds," Emily added, "poor Mortals are made—to sleepwalk—carrying symbols of their new Office—a side-ways cross or cauldron or candlestick—a task they must perform until relieved by other unfortunate Mortals—Snatched! Relieved—there is no relief. The former—standard bearers—become part of the—Crowd—wicked—Lost."

"No one in the earth realm is safe from the treachery of the De la Nuit," said Virginia, "but they must make do with their own kind in the world next to this one. Yet, they possess rights of those that have traveled on. In the next realm judgment exists in a way, but it is not human judgment. There is more wisdom and no competition in it. One might know it as a judgment of enthusiasm or encouragement, nothing more or less. One is aware of degrees of feeling for another and towards oneself; the sensation is satisfactory or not, pleasing or not. When it involves the De la Nuit, the sensation is neither satisfactory nor pleasing, especially for vexed and terrified mortals."

"All of this is a lot to digest," said Lily. "So, you're telling me that there's a world next to this one and some bad beings from there come here to kidnap people, is that it?"

"Close enough," said Virginia, who thought 'how *local* I sound saying that!'

"So," Lily asked, "are you warning me that these inhabitants of the world next door have it in for us, for people like me, here?"

"No—No—No!" Emily exclaimed. "The happier Souls of the World next to this one—which is to say everyone who does not belong to the De la Nuit—enjoy a much different relationship with people—Here."

"They're neutral observers," said Virginia. "They're divine protectors and friends. Sometimes, they favor and even adopt certain people, encouraging and nudging them along; these guides look after and mentor people who live here. They are granted great leeway in their methods of intervention, allowing for uniqueness and exhilarating expressions of style."

"So, they're constantly spying on us?" Lily asked.

"Poor dear!" Virginia added. "It's rather a lot to take in all at once, isn't it?"

"Maybe more than a lot," said Lily. "Look," if you're having a good joke with me, hah-hah, I've needed cheering up, but when do we get to the punchline?"

"I'm Afraid—It won't be that—easy," said Emily. "We are Who we say we are—and the De la Nuit are as real as the cup in your hand"—at that, the yellow cup exploded, scaring the daylights out of Lily and startling Abby who was walking by–"and potentially dangerous."

Picking up the bigger pieces of her cup, handing them to Abby and collecting herself, Lily supposed that people and the dead were hopping back and forth from one world to another all the time. She wondered why she'd never had 'visitors' before?

"Haven't you?" Virginia asked.

"One needs permission–to return to earth through a Portal–that isn't so easy," said Emily, ploughing ahead. "It's a Myth–that the citizens of the realm next door can do–Anything–they want. Even in the Divine Realm there are *some* rules; there is Order."

"Brigid, the great Goddess, watches over all the portals but one," said Virginia. "Immortal though one may be, without a pass from her, nobody goes anywhere. In what amounts to the most recent week in your earth time, for example, Shakespeare, Emma Goldman, Bela Lugosi and Joe the Green Grocer were turned back (I include this last Unfortunate so that you understand it's not all about celebrity). Why they were refused passage is unimportant; they were. Sadly, there have been cases of immortals meddling in the lives of earth people for their own entertainment and Brigid does her best to put a stop to it. She is not always successful–in the next realm, everyone is clever–but unfortunate earthly incidents of needless meddling have sharply de-clined thanks to her scrupulous management style."

"It's always helpful to have a well-organized CEO," said Lily, feeling that her rational response was somehow wholly inadequate to the moment.

"Mother Brigid is rigorous, even severe in her office, yet one mission in particular softens her divine heart," said Virginia. "Even Brigid's dear friend and colleague, ballistic Kali, sheds a tear now and then when someone applies for portal passage with the intention of protecting or rescuing a mortal from the clutches of the De la Nuit. In fact, she hugged me and wept before I departed to come here."

"Wait," said Lily. "If Brigid, a good Goddess, controls the portals, how do the creepy folk get through?"

"Ah," said Emily, "we said Brigid controls—all but One! The ruling council of the De la Nuit controls one—Portal—only one. It is also they who select acolytes to send through their rundown Portal—on what they euphemistically Call—a *Harvest Mission*—snatching an Earth Person—out of earth life—and bringing them back to the council."

"Fortunately," said Virginia, "most De la Nuit members are so demented they do not look forward to a trip back to a world full of mortals, so there are seldom volunteers."

"Still," said Emily, "it is only—Fair—to Warn You—that two of their Agents—are here & Looking—for You." The women studied the alarm and confusion on Lily's face, and Virginia spoke up.

"Just keep in mind that most of the De la Nuit are classic grumblers and carpers," she said. "Not really so much to worry about!"

"Well, to be fair," said Emily, "they *are*—Something—to worry about."

Lily's head was reeling as she wondered, what am I to believe out of all of this? Are these two women alive or dead? Or both? Are they escaped lunatics? Am I in real danger? Am *I* nuts? Are they my...

"Oh, dear Lily!" said Virginia, interrupting the young woman's thoughts. "Same names, power of suggestion, time of day, perhaps something you ate. Who knows why we hear what we do, and how we interpret evidence and information? Pinwheels and fractions! Pass me the veronal. We bend reality—gluten free—because there is no reality, yet we must be about the business of frowning clowns bending, or we would simply fly *whoosh* off the earth..."

"Virginia!" Emily interrupted her. "You're getting—carried away, dear. Shhh! Free association—voices! You'll frighten Lily!"

"Aunt Ginny," said Lily, "you're shuddering. Have you caught a chill?"

"Thank you, dear Lily, no. I'm fine, fine, fine. I'm fine. I am. Fine. Truly! Emily, quite right; thank you. Lily, I'm fine." Virginia's elegant, tapered fingers shredded her paper napkin.

"It's late; I must go," said Lily. She had much processing to do! "I have to meet a friend." Yes, she had to go. She truly had to go. She was meeting Aidan. She stood up thanking her 'aunts' who assured her they would meet again soon, very soon. And as she headed toward the door and out into the rain, Virginia was still reassuring her. 'I am fine, dear Lily. Truly, I am fine."

The two women left the coffee shop and were silent until they reached the bus stop. "That was a pretty thing to do," said Virginia, who had fully regained her composure after the short walk.

I should have kicked you," said Emily, laughing.

"I couldn't resist," said Virginia. "It was spontaneous. I opened my mouth and the words poured out. I always had that unsettling habit. I'm sorry. I think, though, that we managed a deft retreat and gave her an 'out', as they say here. Lily needs a good meditation-stop!"

"Let us hope so," said Emily. "I want her to embrace—Truth. Oh, I wish the Bus would arrive! I forgot—how tiring it all is in this Realm, all the Waiting, the standing around, the dull chatter, the irregular heartbeats, smells, competing sounds—so many it drives one batty just filtering, filtering. What *is* that smell? It's everywhere! I—don't Remember it! It's—a Machine smell—permeating—Everything. And now there is Lily's—relationship Life—we must add to the Mix."

"We must pace ourselves in this land of the too swift, the unknowing & the wicked. There is much to do, but first you need a good lie-down, L-Bug. Come, the bus is here."

Six

Ashland provided a welcoming home for The Homeless, who came in two versions—the authentic and the counterfeit. The authentic Homeless were just that, unlucky, drug-addled, emotionally scrambled and life-battered; the counterfeits collected street money all day and retired every night to apartments or shared homes in the hills above town. Most of the town winked at them—the counterfeiters—because it would be too complicated to sort out the phonies from the real deals; besides, the act itself would call into question the fiction most Ashlanders preferred to live by—that they were far more tolerant than the citizens of other towns.

The two agents of the De la Nuit that had arrived on earth shortly before Emily and Virginia found this unexpected Ashland characteristic, based as it was on self-deception, immensely appealing. Within hours of their arrival, they began to ingratiate themselves with the local Homeless population because they looked so much like them.

On their first bright morning, Ula (the name the woman chose, pronounced *Ewe-lah*) claimed a well-trafficked spot on the Plaza and busked for hours in an otherworldly, strangely hypnotic voice, while her companion, Dick (the man insisted on Dick, not Richard), walked all over town, keeping his eye out for Lily, their prey, and Emily and Virginia, their nemeses. Among the Homeless, their odd robes worked to their advantage rather than against them. More than one of the street people enthusiastically commented on how 'cool' and 'chill' they looked.

Ula and Dick enjoyed being 'cool' and 'chill', though neither of them remembered how many centuries it had been, exactly, since someone had thought of them like that. Had they ever been that way, 'cool'? 'Chill?' Honestly, they weren't sure what it meant, to be 'cool' or 'chill' and they tried not to dwell on it, reminding each other of their reason for being there.

Their legion in the other world required a new, entranced mortal to walk ahead of their processions and the current leaders had chosen the young woman, Lily, because—who could say? The leaders had their reasons and they were not in the habit of sharing them with underlings. That was all that Ula and Dick needed to know, that and the fact that they should be honored by the assignment. "Bring her back!" the De la Nuit leaders said and Dick and Ula went, traveling through the one sordid portal reserved for De la Nuit use. It was the ancient hole of what had been an outhouse and their sensitive noses couldn't help but detect a lingering ripeness, a faint, foul fragrance as they groped their way through to earth. The journey made them grumpier than usual, which was bad. Ula wanted to grab that girl, Lily, the mortal and go, and if they could torment and perhaps even exterminate two of the next realm's beautiful people in the process, all the better!

By early afternoon, Dick had twice walked all over town without spotting their prey. At the Plaza, he joined a small crowd around Ula and listened to her sing. She wailed more than she sang, Dick thought, yet people stood around her with dreamy looks. One emaciated young man sat down at Ula's feet and stared up at her with adoration. Two others looked funny. The descriptive word that eluded Dick was 'stoned'. Worried about not blending in, Dick affected the same look on his own face and after several minutes, he actually felt like they looked, dumb and dreamy. This transformation lasted until Ula ended her song and the little crowd slowly dispersed. Bending to pick up the blood-red shawl she'd spread out on the sidewalk for tips, she told Dick to help her.

"Look at this!" said Ula. "I overheard someone calling this their 'money'. We can get stuff with it."

"Stuff? Like what?" said Dick.

"There's a shop across the street," said Ula. "Smell it?" Dick sniffed the air. "It's pizza," said Ula, "you know, like a pie with meat or vegetables and sauce on it—and cheese!"

"What are we waiting for?" said Dick. "I haven't tasted cheese in almost 200 years!"

Seven

While Dick and Ula gorged themselves on pizza, Lily and Aidan settled down with lattes at Dave's coffee shop above Bloomsbury Books. Coming in the back door, they saw that they had lucked out— the two best chairs, comfortable wingbacks—were vacant. Lily threw her jacket across one and Aidan plopped his laptop case on the seat of the other. Both thought this marked an auspicious beginning. Love was hard to find and just as difficult to navigate; these chairs didn't come easily, either. Standing at the counter, ordering, they felt the energy crackling between them. It brought them pleasantly close together and just as surely kept them apart. It was frustration they felt, yet not of the unsweet variety. Sitting down with their drinks, Lily waited and Aidan did not disappoint. "Tell me more about your work," said Aidan. "You told me a little about it at the post office and I've been thinking about it, and you, ever since."

She began to tell the story of her lifelong love for Manga and the work of Arina Tanemura. She was describing Tanemura's emphatic yet lyrical line work when Aidan's phone went off. His face coloring, he apologized and took the phone from his pocket. Nervously glancing up at her, he was soon engrossed in texting back and forth with whoever was on the line. Lily waited. Five minutes later she was still waiting. "Are you going to text all through this?" she asked. Aidan furiously finished a message and sent it. Then he made sure that she could see him turning his phone off.

"There!" he said. "I'm so sorry! We're opening a new show this weekend—paintings and sketches of the Bloomsbury circle—and the logistics and arrangements have been crazy. Sometimes I feel like a mad top, spinning and spinning. Do you like paintings?" Lily gasped. "Is something wrong?" Aidan asked.

"Wrong? Oh, no," said Lily, "and yes, I love Bloomsbury, too. I suppose Duncan Grant is still regarded as their best painter, but I think it's a shame the way Roger Fry has faded from consciousness, don't you?"

Aidan was impressed. He felt lit up. This woman knew more than a little about painting if she could say that about Roger Fry, the older Bloomsbury member who really mentored all of them for a time.

"Maybe I'm sentimental," he said, "but I'm in love with Vanessa Bell's work. It fascinates me that she was the sister of such a great writer. But I think her work stands up quite well on its own without that connection. I adore her painting of the woman in the bath and the portraits she painted of Virginia, including the odd ones without facial features. She sometimes painted herself that way, too."

So he loves my writer's sister, Lily thought. *Promising. Very promising!* She couldn't help smiling, wondering how he'd react to her telling him she'd had tea earlier in the day with Vanessa's sister. She decided she would not tell him just yet, if ever.

"I'd love to take you to the opening!" said Aidan. He looked nervous, afraid he was being pushy. "I mean, if you'd like to come with me. If not, I can still get you a ticket, or two, if you want to bring someone else."

Lily liked this young man's confidence tinged with awkward humility. That was always a winning combo for her. Aidan knew how to handle himself in public, but he could falter in small, intimate ways, such as checking his enthusiasm about taking her to the opening and making clear his awareness that she might actually like to go but without him. Yes, she thought, she would like to go with him. "I'd love to go," said Lily, "even with you." For a moment, Aidan's face froze, blank, then they laughed together. Yes, thought Lily, we can joke around; we can laugh together.

One wave of patrons was leaving now and another was sweeping in, filling the small tables in the center of the room and the larger ones lining the three available walls. An artist's paintings—a series of cats—hung on two of the walls, but Lily and Aidan took little notice. Twenty minutes later, Aidan felt comfortable enough to ask Lily about her family and confident enough to stick with it when she began by telling him that they were dead, murdered by pirates aboard a cruise ship. Aidan reached over and took her right hand in his. "I'm so sorry!" he murmured.

Lily offered her soft, small tear-smile. I like how my hand disappears in his two big hands, she thought. *He offers me protection and commiseration.* She enjoyed the sensation of her hand nestled safely in the cocoon made by his hands until she needed a sip of coffee. Removing her hand, she apologized, explaining that her right hand was her coffee-drinking hand; with her left she drank tea.

It was nothing, really, this information, yet it impressed Aidan. It excited him. It's a small eccentricity, Aidan thought, meaningless to some, but it's one of the small things that makes Lily unique. Aidan thought of his own eccentricities and wondered how they might match up with Lily's. It was constant with him, but he didn't mind going out wearing mismatched socks. He followed the poet Robert Frost's suggestion to carry something in a pocket that reminded you of who you really are; lately it had been a thorn.

"I lost my father," he said, "when I was five. He and my mom were already divorced—about a year—and he was in some drying-out facility. He was doing so well that they'd made him a cook; he had car privileges. He could leave the premises and go shopping in town. What they didn't know was that he'd shop, but he'd also gamble at a Lo-ball parlor in Gardena. When he started to drink and lose, he'd write a bad check. I heard once he'd written bad checks for 18 thousand dollars, but who knows. Well, they got on to him, of course, but before the police arrived at the facility someone tipped him off. He stole the car and drove to our house. I'd seen him once in the past year. He went into a room somewhere and talked to my mom. My older brother and sisters sat together on the sofa in the den. They looked like they were waiting for a bomb to explode. My dad passed through the den and asked me to walk him to his car. Outside, he said he had to go away for a long time and would I go with him."

"What a question to ask a five-year-old kid!" said Lily. Her eyes were teary.

"Yeah. Suddenly I felt older, really old! I also felt how much he was hurting. Still, I told him 'I think I'd better stay here with mom and everybody'. Then I thought *he* might cry. He hugged me and held on; I held on to him. Then he was in the car. He started it and waved. He put it in reverse and backed up the gravel drive in moonlight. I remember that detail and one other. I remember the sound the tires made on the gravel. I never saw him or heard from him again. Years later, my brother or one of my sisters told me that his abandoned car had been discovered in the desert half-way between L.A. and Las Vegas. There was also a rumor that he might have gone to Florida and remarried."

"Couldn't you track him down through social security, marriage or death records? Lily asked.

"My brother became an attorney and he looked into it. Nothing. There was no record of him anywhere. He just vanished. My brother's theory is that he died in a ditch somewhere and was buried as a John Doe. My sister thinks he wandered off in the desert after the car broke down and died out there."

"Do you believe it?" Lily asked. "What does your gut tell you?"

"My gut tells me," said Aidan, "that if we keep talking about this we'll both be starved! Would you like to get some dinner?"

Now Lily touched his hand and said no, she couldn't, not tonight. But she added she would like to, later, soon. Aidan smiled. She could tell he was relieved and grateful. He asked about tomorrow and yes, she said, yes.

Eight

"You said Yes?" said Shaya. "That was quick! Wow, this guy must have connected."

"We'll see how tomorrow night goes," said Lily. "Something else happened earlier in the day that I want to talk to you about, but I can't now."

"I'm around," said Shaya. "Call me whenever."

Nine

"Is it not exhilarating," said Virginia, "to stay in a Bed & Breakfast together in this quaint little town? I drew the proprietor out and she told me there is actually a B & B on the coast with rooms named after us! Is it not fame when one's bedroom is replicated? We are here, alone this evening. You wish to write & I wish to ramble. I wish to haunt a library in the flesh again. So I'll leave you to pen and ink, dear L-Bug and lose myself in the stacks for an hour or two."

Virginia walked at a brisk pace along Main street through the town, taking in everything. She slowed down a little to enjoy the heady aroma pouring out of Standing Stone Brewery and the sweet aromas from Puck's Donuts. She feared that she suffered a stenosis of intellect, of empathy. She felt porous, invaded by thoughts and feelings behind the faces passing her. What were they thinking? What were they feeling? To the extent that she could stand the mental commotion, she was sedulous to tune in to as many as she could. There were the familiar feelings: Excitement, anticipation, anger, love, frustration and abandonment; disappointment, doubt and resentment. *Too much, too much,* she thought, the teeming tide of humanity on the pavement! They pass, they pour out of shops; young men crouch on benches and slump in doorways holding up signs begging for food and money. Five women all in black stand motionless, protesting war, ignored by the cars that hustle by, while across the plaza on the second floor the city council urges the cutting down of mature trees so that Ashland may double the plaza's parking capacity. So much and all a little frightening! I want to rethink this village into wild countryside again, she thought and walked faster, faster as her mind reached a boil. I must walk this over-stimulation out of me, she thought, as I used to do. There's sanity in movement, in physical exhaustion. I must walk it out!

"Because we are back in this World and she has been gone an Hour, an Hour of Lead," said Emily, "I miss her!" She sat at the ornate desk that was not unlike her own in her bedroom in Amherst and gazed at sunset bathing the Cascade Range in gold. "I wonder—was it always so? *Always*. Is that my word—or Virginia's? It must be Hers. Mine was *Never*. Never, never, never; how many times did I write it down like a block—a monolithic Structure designed to stop my frenzied pace, to give shape to a *reality* (that word again) that threatened to—fly off the page and out of my unanchored Heart? Without *Never*—I was lost, though what I hungered for was *Forever*. Ah, there's the Word! The key that turns the lock! It was also true—for Her. She desired it, too. She wanted Forever—but more than that—Billy Goat wanted—*Rapture*!

"Many were the moments she has shared with me of each day and night that destroyed her with rapture! Flowers opening in the garden, the scent of ripe apples, Nessa's children playing wildly, rambunctious, innocent and naked on the wet grass at Charleston.

"Rapture," said Emily. "That is a beautiful word! Yes—it is her word. But what was mine? *Ecstasy*. Thinking of Her—writing about Her—conspiring with Her," said Emily, "I see that I am coming close—to Her! I am taking Her on—and leaping away, Free—as I always chose to be. Oh—but my Freedom had consequences—as did hers. She needed—to be loved. She desired and demanded caresses, kisses; we both did. She yearned for but could not endure—the physical love of a Man. Thank Clouds and Bees! There is no Pain—in the world next to this one!

"But now we are back in the country of our old hurts—disappointments and Ambition. A woman meets a man on the street.

They board a bus and disappear—and my Goat makes a Story about them, about us making a Story—while I—make Verse. That is our reality—each moment a sacred Trust—never to come again—never to be replicated. We were separated—by years and circumstance, yet we're together in my thought, in hers. She's at my bedside—as I die; I am in the river—with her—'unvanquished and unyielding'."

Virginia thought it strange, over a library volume of Aeschylus, its pages open to the famous simile comparing Iphigeneia to a painting just before her sacrifice, that she could still so easily give in to her voyeur self and observe a young woman so earnestly trying to be... *her*. This anonymous young woman, rather like her Lily, was bent to her work, while Virginia saw herself shimmy down a tree or emerge from shaggy green grass or slip through muslin curtains or appear out of thin air, come again. *I will pass like a shadow on the waves*, I wrote that once, believing it. It is strange to discover, she thought, that my 'celebrity', my long endurance, has such legs. I thought that three or four of my books might last fifty years, she thought. Now she had become what she'd always dreamed of; I *am* my books, she thought.

Virginia watched the young woman read, her brow wrinkling with concentration. She stopped, slowly put down the book and took up pen and began to write in a notebook. When that thought had run its course, she leaned back in her chair and took off her glasses to clean them. When she was finished, when the glasses were back in place, she picked up another book, opened it and read.

My life and my books are inseparable. Virginia thought. Indeed, there on the table beside the young woman writing were copies of *Orlando* and Virginia's *Diary*, second volume. I so loved to be loved! Virginia thought. Still, she thought, it takes some getting used to, like acquiring one's sea legs while adjusting to another in close proximity, as in a marriage. She remembered how her own marriage nearly finished her in the first year. She had gone quite mad and any other man would have bolted, but not her man, not Leonard. She had chosen well. Leo stayed, and he saved her.

But now, *this* young woman trying so hard to be her fascinated Virginia. She watched the girl in her cubicle, writing, considering, scratching out words, sitting back, slumping a little (her posture is not as good as mine, Virginia thought), feeling a faint dawning, leaning forward over her paper and rapidly writing words, words, words. *Where are you going with them?* Virginia wanted to ask her, sounding to herself like her own mother. Indeed, she felt a kind of motherly instinct for her, she who lived childless in this realm, who now had so many aspiring daughters.

Like many of my little darlings, Virginia thought, writing, for this young woman, is a cocktail of passion and irritation. What drives her? She was as transparent to Virginia as the world seen through the wings of a luna moth. This clarity, this enhanced second sight, was one advantage of being dead! But the question of what drives *her* interested Virginia.

Like Lily, Virginia observed, she wants to matter somehow. She wants to be recognized, admired and praised for her ingenuity and hard work. She wants to please her mother, show up her sister and friends and seize her father's attention. She wants to tell a story that will change everybody, especially her; she wants to tell it in a new way. She wants to tell a story so that critics and professors will say, 'Yes, there is undeniable genius in her prose. She has broken new ground'. She wants to create amazement.

Yet is it enough, Virginia wondered, all these things that drive her? Does her pain motivate her? Is her loneliness up to the challenge? Virginia perceived her starting fast and bogging down, starting and petering out like the match that extinguishes itself between the tip and first joint of one of her cigarette fingers. Telling stories and writing novels are long-legged pursuits, Virginia thought. You must be built for them or build yourself up to them. You must become Odysseus on his ten-year voyage to reach home; there is no other way.

If there were some other way, Virginia knew that she would step out of the shadows and tell the young woman writing. She would put her hand on the back of the girl's writing hand, gently, as a mother guides her child's hand as she is learning to write and she would show her. Gently, she would lead her, and together they would do it. Together, they would tell the story she had dreamed of all her life.

But it's no good. It can't happen like that, Virginia knew. She cannot feel my touch, she thought. In reality, she cannot even hear my voice, but she can catch the sense of it from my own words written down, and that's the best I can do; for she must earn it, if she will, the story so hard to tell. She must sacrifice herself on the altar of others she will have to become if she wants to succeed at telling stories. She must do this over and over as she sits in her library cubicle trying with all her might to be me; for Lily it is much the same, except that our connection is deeper. It extends from her mother to Lily to me—and to Emily. She chose us and here we are.

The young woman's thoughts intruded on Virginia's thoughts. Virginia heard them as if they were boiling in the ancient sea of her old, earthbound head. The young woman was thinking, 'I am getting hungry. 'What's for dinner? I have another engagement, but I love this library! I could sit here forever, building higher and higher walls of books on my table here, disappearing behind them, making myself woozy from the smell of them, opening them here and there, though I never quite disappear into any of them. I know this is a serious flaw in my plan to become the next Virginia Woolf.'

There! Virginia thought. Her brain-voice has said it, my name. It inflames her and douses her all at once. Yet, she has no story she has dreamed of telling all her life, just pieces of stories, good beginnings all, but once she's written them down, then what? Lily has come much farther, Virginia thought. This young woman wants attention, not the solitude and drudgery and near-death experience of creation. This is her artistic Waterloo where her process breaks down, where she ceases to discover anything, where she gives up and admits defeat. Lily won't do that. She is already wrestling the death agony of creation.

I could spend all of time here, Virginia thought, observing young, earnest women just like this one as they grow weary and listless in the library trying to be other than what they are, missing opportunities to be what they could be. Or one might say that their efforts to be other than themselves are part of the long, wandering process of becoming. This one will become what she must and that is neither un-useful nor distasteful. She is one of the lucky ones. The butterfly is so diverse before the breaking free, the drying in the sun, the spectacular colors flashing as it takes wing, and the folding of wings at dusk. Ah, look! She wearies of her labors. She is packing up, making ready to go. But wait! Who scans a volume over there? She smiled.

My Lily, she thought, tuning in to her. Like me, Virginia thought, she needed a walk, time to move & think and it brought her here where she has pulled down a volume on Brigid, sweet mother guiding us. I could interrupt her with wild stories of Brigid, but I won't break in on her research and reverie. She is hitting her stride, taking her own fences. I will go quietly.

Virginia was so intent on stealing away without interrupting Lily and so deep in her speculative thought that she did not notice the spooky man trying with all his might to push over a tall library shelf. At last, it tilted and creaked, but too late. Virginia had moved to the door seconds before the shelf and its heavy volumes crashed into the aisle where she had been reading Aeschylus, observing the girl writing and Lily looking up Brigid. Shelf and books crashed with a bang that echoed throughout the library. Virginia, startled, jumped like a bird and looking back, glimpsed Dick bolting down another book row and out of sight. He was unaware, Virginia could tell, of Lily's presence in the library. He was after *her*!

❦

"You startled me!" said Emily, as Virginia whooshed into their room and slammed the door. Her brow wrinkled as she noticed the concern on her friend's puckered face.

"They were at the library, L-Bug!" said Virginia as she rushed around the room making sure the curtains were shut. "They're stalking us and getting closer. I was almost flattened by metal, by books!"

"You mean the two we saw in the park?"

"Yes, quite so. The man-beast tried to eliminate me in the library. Oh, his face was hideous in the library reading lights. His oleaginous eyes were a fright; they leered at me. He drooled. We must sleep in shifts tonight! We cannot let them find us both asleep!"

"There, there," Emily said, wrapping her shaking friend in a hug, but the shaking was contagious. Soon they were trembling together like agitated aspen leaves. The room darkened until Emily disengaged and thought to switch on a lamp. "There!" she said, "more light for the problem! Sit down—my dear, and have some tea." At table she lifted the pot and poured two cups. "Lemon for me—sugar for you," she said. They sat. They sat, deliberate and composed and drank and munched biscuits from a tin brightly decorated with a colorful farm scene. "We shall not—lose our heads," said Emily, sounding more like her sister than herself. "I do wish Lavinia was here," she muttered.

"And Nessa!" Virginia blurted out. "She's afraid of nothing!" Emily smiled, patting Virginia's hand.

"Yes, but it's just the two of us—for Now," Emily said, doing her best to sound like a stalwart mother or camp counselor.

"What shall we do?" said Virginia.

"We shall be resolute little beasts and do what is necessary!" said Emily. "I mean that we'll know what to do when the time comes—for Doing! And what can they do to Us—really? We're no longer of this Realm."

"Yes, but we are *in* this realm now. Doesn't that make us vulnerable?"

"Do you Believe that?" said Emily.

"Don't you?"

"No," said Emily, "I don't think I do. They've come for our young lady—our Lily; we know that. We're here to thwart them—and We shall."

"But," said Virginia, "suppose they do have some power over us; suppose they enchant one or both of us instead of Lily? In addition to Lily?"

"Impossible!" Emily said, though in her heart she acknowledged a wedge of cold fear. To be taken by the De la Nuit—what a terrible, unexpected Fate! But no! Mother Brigid would never allow it. She was quite sure of that.

"L-Bug is right, of course," said Virginia, sounding as if she were trying to convince herself. We have a plan to save Lily, don't we?"

"Our plan will evolve as we proceed," said Emily. Thinking of Brigid's example, she said, "We will Know what to do—when the Time comes."

Curled up together in the Queen-size bed, a thick comforter pulled tightly under their chins, they listened to each other breathe. "Dear Goat," said Emily in a sleepy-soft voice, "did you know anyone who was taken by them—the De la Nuit?" She waited for what felt like a long time, but then came an answer.

"I've always suspected they touched my idiot half-sister," said Virginia. "I could never discover a better explanation for how an imbecile child could be a part of the Stephen family. Oh, I was awful to her; we all were. We didn't know any better. We might have been living in the Dark Ages for all the progress medicine and psychology made to that point. But yes, I always thought they must have taken her. There might have been others. My half-sister, Stella...surely the doctors killed her at the age of 23. My brother, Thoby, the Goth, his friends called him, he was taken so unexpectedly, too, so young; and my nephew, Julian, who was blown up in Spain. Nessa never really recovered from that. He was so loved, so full of promise! And one other, dearest, my Kate, Katherine Mansfield. Have you read her? No? She is worth it. She was the only one I truly regarded as my rival. How about you, L-Bug?"

"I must have—Known—many," said Emily. "Death surrounded me— Death—Death from illness, Death from War. Yet, the Deaths that haunted me most were—my young friend who loved poetry and died in the war—and little Gib, my beloved nephew—Austin's son. Oh, I adored him! He was the Sun and Moon to me—he was taken while still—a Golden Child! They both were. I never recovered. It made my own Transition—easier. So, yes—like you—I have good reason—to defeat these evil—soulless Meddlers. Well, there's nothing more to be done Tonight. Remember the Deliciousness—of sleep—when one could find it? Let's revel in it—Now!" And they slept.

But as they slept, a pocket of shadows—human shapes, animals or some kind of dust devils stirred by wind—wafted across their private porch and seemed to hover for a moment at the door before suddenly climbing up the frame, crossing the top and dropping down the other side. A sound like labored breathing, like sawing came out of the shape and broke up in the wind. Were those eyes at the window? Did a hand reach out for the windowsill? Was an indescribable thought like a net penetrating the walls of the room and the shell of the women's sleep? Had snares been set on the porch floor? Was their bedroom inviolate? On some levels, in each of the women's dreams, these questions and possibilities swelled and eddied, came close and moved off, dangerous and far away. They had their own considerable resources keeping them safe, and both dreamed that energy from Brigid, and other allies, would also keep them safe. So, at last, they slept unimpeded, completing their first long day of return with rest and renewal. In the morning, they would be ready; they would get to work.

Ten

The soft restaurant lighting encouraged easeful conversation. Aidan had done well, procuring a discreet corner booth with a window. They sat on the same side of the table rather than across from each other. They tracked the moon rising and noted the occasional passersby. Lily and Aidan ate with discretion but talked eagerly. Their buoyant energy extended through the first glass of wine (Aiden knew about wine, Lily noted), the salads and main course, yet somewhere in the midst of the second (or was it the third) glass of wine and the delicious but too-rich dessert, the tenor of their talk shifted. What was it? That they were more comfortable with each other and so began to sound more self-reflective? That was true. What else? Were they also retreating, succumbing to the residue of past failures that threatened to leach into the ground they were sowing?

"I've been hurt," said Lily.

"It's your passion and empathy that I could fear *and* love," said Aidan, blurting out the words before he could stop himself. He tried to recover. "I'm ashamed of my tongue-tied mistakes," he said, as in calling an astrological House by a planet's name."

"What did you say?" asked Lily.

"I called the 12th House Mars."

"What an idiot!" Lily said. She laughed. "I'm pulling your leg," she said and they both laughed.

"Well, I stupidly did that once at dinner in a crowded restaurant and was loudly upbraided by my date," said Aidan, "which of course reduced and rendered me, stunning me, shutting me up in an inarticulate gloom. Rendered is a good word. It has 'rend' in it.," said Aidan. "Yet, we may resist, little by little, thought by thought, deciding no, today, at this moment, we'll refrain. We won't tear each other to pieces. We'll choose mercy and moderation and create a modest, safe space for self-discovery. In that way I receive all that I desire. In that way I win."

"In a competitive world, if you win," said Lily, "I lose. If I win, you lose. Competition does that; it separates us, one from the other, and smacks us both in the head."

"Competition, winning and losing hurls me into a pit of sorrow, guilt and loneliness," said Aidan. "Competition drives us off track. I can't be with you, or you with me, achieving our highest selves, as long as we're competing. It grinds us up. We rage, breaking; we rage, cutting others to pieces. We run, we hide; we break any pact we make."

"We smash it," said Lily. "We tell ourselves we do not care, that even though we cared once, we are well past that now. 'We do not need the aggravation,' we say. 'We will be better off apart, alone, or with someone else. We must separate,' we say, 'or we will die,' we say. 'I am tired,' we say; 'I am quitting. I have had enough of you. Go away now even as I go away. There is nothing left, nothing you and I can salvage or nurture. We have killed it. We have murdered each other's love. We have blackened the moon; we have put out the sun!' Lily took a deep breath. "Ok!" she said, "I just realized that relationship 'voice' sounds a lot like my coach in the head." Aidan brightened up.

"You have a coach in the head? Me, too!"

"Always barking?"

"Always! Once," he said, "as a teenager, I crashed headfirst into a brick wall during a basketball game. I crumbled to the floor. When I opened my eyes; I was lying flat on the bench and the concerned faces of my teammates and coaches were bent over me in a claustrophobic circle, a net of intense eyes and sweaty, fleshy faces and nostrils. As my head cleared, I looked up at the clock and asked how long I'd been out. About five minutes. Five minutes! I searched my memory for any recollection, for any shade or dreamy shape I could call back from the nothingness I'd suddenly become. But there was nothing. Nothing at all. Then the coach in my head started in on me, yelling at me to man up and get back in there! But where had I been? It was nothing, nothing, nothing. Won't it be the same when I die?" His eyes were wide open and he wanted Lily's response.

"No," was all she said. He waited. She saw him gathering himself behind his eyes, up from his heart. Then she said, "You did not go anywhere because you did *not* die. You were disconnected in your body for five minutes, but you were still *in* your body. Do you understand the significance? It makes all the difference that you do, because we make this mistake all the time about unconsciousness and death. They aren't the same—not at all!"

Aidan was impressed. "How can you be so sure?" he asked and thought of the summer he joined a ride-share from Los Angeles to North Carolina. He told Lily how he, his friend, Andreas, and two guys they'd never met agreed to drive a Chevy 2,400 miles across the U.S. in three days. That meant non-stop driving, with three sleeping while one drove. The plan worked smoothly through the first day and deep into the second. It was the middle of the night of day two and Aidan was driving the vast, empty Interstate while Andreas slept in the passenger seat beside him and the other two were out cold in the back seat. Aidan felt good driving. He liked driving. He was thinking of something—he never remembered what—but he was suddenly startled by a jolt. It was more than a jolt. The car was actually bucking like a wild horse. That's when Aidan saw trees in front of him, trees to his left and right—there were trees everywhere. Terrified, he steered through the trees in disbelief. What were all these trees doing on the Interstate? Why wasn't he hitting some? The car bucked and charged on through the trees until an inner signal told him to jerk the wheel to the left. As he did so, the car dodged more trees, shot up an embankment and skidded to a stop on the gravelly shoulder of the Interstate. Aidan sat stiff-backed above the wheel, which he white-knuckled as he struggled to breathe. Beside him, Andreas woke up, stretched and said, 'my turn to drive?'

'Uh huh.' That was the only sound I could make."

Egged on perhaps by Aidan's story, Lily decided to raise the stakes in their conversation. "What would you think if I told you," said Lily, "that I know without a doubt that ghosts—spirits—come to help us. Suppose I told you I had tea with two of them yesterday, before I met you for coffee and that they happen to be two enormously important people to me—Emily Dickinson and Virginia Woolf. How would you react to that?"

The first thing Lily noticed was that Aidan stopped chewing. He forgot to swallow, or so it seemed and Lily hoped he'd remember to do that soon. He did, gulping his last mouthful with effort, then slowly lowered his fork to the table. Thoughts cascaded through his mind like a massive, fast-moving weather system. What did he really think of this beautiful woman's confession? That she was crazy? He felt crazy himself even thinking that for a moment. Excited? Yes, he felt that, as if the whole world were suddenly, deliciously on edge. Why not? "Emily Dickinson?" he said. "Virginia Woolf, Vanessa's sister? Do you think we could get Vanessa to come to our opening?"

He wasn't teasing her. Lily could see that. She could hear it and feel it, his willingness to believe, to climb out with her on this limb and accept what comes. "Vanessa's not here as far as I know," said Lily, "but I can ask—why not?"

Aidan had always known that he'd cheated death in that car; they all had that night. He'd assumed his guardian or guardians were watching over him, but recently the thought had come to him: what if it had nothing to do with him; suppose they'd been saved by Andreas's guardian, or the guardians of the guys in the back seat? But if that were true, his life, and saving it, amounted to nothing. How could that be? Maybe it made more sense to accept that several guardians could work in concert and actually collaborate on a dramatic rescue. Aidan felt stupid thinking like this. Obviously, he'd been involved in some pretty important way. After all, he'd been the one driving. That had to be significant. It had to count for something that was not haphazard. He had been the best athlete in the car, so maybe he had to drive because his reflexes were better than anyone else's. It embarrassed him, this back-patting and he suddenly felt tired.

"I vote that we lighten up," said Aidan. They looked at each other, startled. Then they were laughing, bursting like liberated seed pods, relishing the soothing sensation of laughter, that great doctor that costs nothing. When they settled, breathing evenly again, they gazed at each other, smiling.

In the kitchen, Dick, dressed as a waiter, hustled back to the stoves where Ula stirred an immense pot. "Bad news," he said, huffing, out of breath. "They're sharing 'hearing voices' stories and guardian angel stories."

"Then it's worse than we thought, Blotch-Face," said Ula. "We must isolate this impediment right now! Here. Sprinkle this on his dessert. She'll have nothing more to do with him after he's puked all over her. Get going!" Dick hesitated but didn't want to risk a screaming match with Ula in public. Besides, he had yet to win one. Meekly, he took the vial and returned to the dining room.

In the dimly lit room, Dick observed the young couple. They were too engrossed in their conversation to observe anything, dumb bunnies, he thought. As he fussed about them, refilling their water glasses and collecting spent dishes, he had no trouble at all sprinkling, undetected, the contents of the vial onto Aidan's last bites of dessert. How sad, Dick thought, that this budding romance will come to nothing. Something in him wavered, but his bitterness and numbness overwhelmed it. He retreated to the shadows, watching.

Meanwhile, Lily and Aidan were separately beginning to imagine the couple they might become. Strange that they should have the same vision, but it was so. They imagined two people in their own boats on a lake. They tested the waters, tentatively nudging their little boats closer and closer to each other's. They floated out, new and shiny and hopeful; they drifted, they dreamed and suddenly one's keel bumped against the other's prow. Startled, they woke from one reverie to merge into another. They looked up; they laughed; they steadied their boats, holding them close together as they talked. What stirred in them charged the water, turning it a deeper blue and green. The sun dazzled. It sparkled in the leaves of the elm and maple trees. It turned the dust into pillars and dancers. It streamed down and connected with the fire in their eyes and that fire flared.

They were shy and almost speechless. They were self-conscious, but that faded as they talked. Their heartbeats quickened, their breath, too, as they leaned closer, closer. Aidan in his vision saw little beads of glistening water on Lily's brown forearm and his breath caught. She admired the musculature of his bare chest as the boat rocked. They talked, they laughed. They made plans to row their boats to shore and go on together, perhaps for a drink, for lunch. Side by side they rowed, stealing glances at each other. The paddles dipped and sometimes clattered. More laughter. Her laughter to him sounded like music; for her, his laughter was the sound of a safe room.

They neared the shore, he slightly ahead of her so that he leapt out first, and in a graceful motion, pulled his boat up on the sand and hooked hers with his free hand. He pulled her boat ashore. He took her hand, thrilling to touch, and steadied her as she stepped out on the sand. So it began, the great adventure that cannot be stopped and who would want to? (Ula peered through the kitchen curtain into the dining room, impatient to see what was going on.) Lily and

Aidan emerged from the past, or pushed away the present, gambling everything on a new thing. But none of the details mattered. Nothing ever mattered once the cover opened and the story began and two people accepted each other. They were guileless. They were vulnerable. They surrendered their defenses and invited another to destroy the thing they'd been. *Destroy*—the word in this sense, Lily knew, came from Virginia Woolf. Somewhere she'd written that she accepted Leonard's marriage proposal 'because he destroyed my loneliness'.

They were talking, Lily and Aidan, about what Aidan called those inevitable moments when the man 'disappears' into deeper silence, brooding, semi-braindead. Lily laughed. She told him women knew that one of their jobs is to try again. Women patch things up; they sew. They make the incomplete complete. Women comfort the weeper. They dry the tears of the world. Women create bridges that unite and bring others closer together.

Aidan, smiling, imagined needing *her*. It was pleasant, but he needed more water, too. Suddenly, he was sweating. He was sweating a lot and the back of his head throbbed. The waiter, Dick, appeared and filled their glasses. Aidan drank off half of his immediately, and Dick refilled the glass again. "Are you all right?" Lily asked. How pale he looked! It alarmed her, but Aidan shook his head and insisted he was fine. He complained about the room temperature, which seemed normal to Lily. He suggested they pay the bill and go, that he just needed a little walk and fresh air.

In the kitchen, Dick huddled in a corner with Ula. "He ate it," Dick said. "It's working."

"And the girl?" said Ula.

"She's leaving with him."

"What good is *that*!" Ula hissed. "You idiot! We don't want them to leave! We want to take him to his place or the hospital, then drive the girl home—*our* home! What kind of serve-monkey are you? Get back out there and *do* something!" Dick's hand twitched as he thought of grabbing a saucepan within reach and braining her, but the action he did take, slump-shouldered, was to turn around and trudge out of the kitchen. But when he returned to the dining room, Lily and Aidan were gone.

As they walked, Aidan felt worse and worse. He wanted to say things to Lily and tried composing them in his head, but his head hurt too much. They walked until he had to sit down on a bench beside a lit up basketball court. Aidan leaned in to Lily, sweating, breathing irregularly. He took her hands in his. His hands felt clammy and again Lily asked, 'Are you all right?' 'Yes', he said, but with less conviction than before. They sat there watching and listening to the boys playing two-on-two—*back door, back door! Crash! Outlet!*—and she observed the boys' girlfriends on their cell phones, their long fake nails clicking, clicking, like the clattering sound of thousands of cockroaches that surrounded her motel bed once as soon as the lights had gone out. Someone switched on a lamp and they froze; a foot swung out of bed to the floor and the insects retreated to the floorboards from whence they'd come. It had been an unforgettable, creepy bug ballet. Lily wished she could shine a light on the girls and stay their nails, but they were oblivious to her. Aidan, leaning on her, groaned and muttered that he feared he would be sick.

It was difficult, but she lifted Aidan to his feet and with the help of two of the basketballers, got him into a cab one of the girls had called on her phone. Lily told the driver to take them to the nearest emergency room, and five minutes later, Lily and the cab driver steered Aidan inside where he was taken by wheelchair to a back room. Apparently, he was sufficiently endangered to merit immediate attention.

Lily paced in the ER lobby like a troubled cat. What happened? Food poisoning, she thought, but what if it were something worse, something darker? What had her new 'aunts' called those people, the bad people from beyond? Oh, that was just paranoia, she thought. It was something he ate, and I was lucky not to get it, too, she thought. Lily made herself sit down. She drifted in and out of the pages of *Oprah*, advice on weight loss, a review of a book about the sexual and spiritual language of love, but mostly she was thinking about all that they'd said to each other. They had found words in each other.

A doctor appeared beside her. "He's spending the night," the doctor said. "We pumped his stomach, and we'll do tests, but it will be morning before we have the results."

"Food poisoning?" Lily asked.

"Poisoning almost certainly," the doctor said, "but I suspect something other than food. Because of that, we've had to alert the authorities." As if on cue, two uniformed police, a man and woman, entered the ER, asked at the desk, and walked towards them. The doctor stood up and met them half-way across the lobby. They spoke briefly, then the doctor walked on; the officers approached Lily, introduced themselves and sat down on either side of her. They asked her about the restaurant, the food, the service. Lily was surprised at how little she remembered. She did recall at least three things that Aidan had eaten that she had not—the sourdough bread, Brussel sprouts and the crème brulée. After jotting down her contact information, the officers thanked her and went away.

There was nothing left for her to do. She got up and checked her watch. It was after two and she felt exhausted. At the desk, she asked if she could look in on Aidan before she left, but the woman told her that Aidan had already been transferred to a bed upstairs in Intensive Care. She would have to wait until 8 a.m.

Eleven

Dreamily, Lily fanned herself with the shiny copy of *Oprah, the Magazine*, that she had absentmindedly lifted from the ER waiting room. The act of fanning herself with such a substantial and highly regarded journal of health, beauty and wellness made her feel, for a moment, healthy, beautiful, even well. Then she remembered something Aidan had said about people, how you could tell a lot about someone's character by the magazines they stole.

It was generous, as always, of Shaya to rush to her side first thing this morning. She had made tea and listened; she had cuddled up with Lily on the bed and told her everything would be all right. She felt sorry for Aidan but stayed positive. It would turn out to be nothing, she'd said. Something else she'd said was even more important. "If it's true that your visitors are the real Emily and Virginia," Shaya said, "why not ask them about your parents? Ask them if your parents can come back!"

"I'm working on that," said Lily.

Shaya stayed as long as she could, making herself late for work at the architect's office. She promised to call later.

Lily wished for protection. She wished she was at the park where she could sink into the roots of the grasses while Emily and Virginia watched over her. She wanted to go down into the topsoil, eyeballing grubs, and they her, as they passed one another going up and down. She would forget herself in the soil. She would be bold and fearless and give no thought to the plump robin plummeting down to spear her for the wailing, open mouths in the nest above. She wanted her mother. As this thought took hold, Lily admitted how happy she would be to swap that sudden, functional fate for this awful anxiety and yearning. What else did she want? Was it Aidan?

As Lily stared at her drawings, dimension flattened out. It was late morning, the apartment still cool, the outside temperature rising. Feeling a sudden urge to get out, Lily dressed in a hurry—black tee shirt, yellow shorts and socks, Asics running shoes that had run their last mile months ago. She held on to things. With people, with memory and things, she did not part easily.

On the street, she made her way at a brisk pace to the organic grocery store half-a-mile up Tolman Creek Road, delighting in the rapidly growing goslings at the pond across the blacktop. How many were there from the original hatch? Four, five, six, she counted—thirteen, fourteen out of the original sixteen. Good! Nature can be kind, thought Lily. She thought of Aidan and wondered how he was feeling.

A red Cessna puttered off the runway to the east. With wings rocking slightly to and fro, it climbed into a bright blue sky fringed with clouds and slowly vanished in the hazy distance lying due south towards Mt. Shasta and California. She watched the plane grow smaller until the haze seemed to fling out a shawl and cover it.

Lily picked up her pace, feeling a sudden elation at the depth of the shadows on the green grass and shade trees. She stalked the shade, crossing the road twice to prolong its embrace and arrived, almost prancing, at the automatic door admitting her to a refreshing blast of cooler air inside Shop N Cart. The perspiration on the back of her neck tingled as it turned to icy sparkles, deepening her delight, and she traversed the store aisle and ordered a decaf at the coffee kiosk. Waiting for the pour-over (no watery café Americano for her, not ever), she counted her steps as she walked up and down aisles, noticing three young women with their boys—each no more than six years old, all of them happy and eager, one boy looking smart in sunglasses, all in jackets, happy to be with their mothers on an outing, an adventure. She remembered her delight in common adventures with her mother when she was the same age as these boys.

She wondered what it would feel like to have a child to walk with, a child beside her, in her day, never far from her. She came right up to it, that gulf of sadness occasioned by childlessness that many women feel, she supposed, at one time or another. She observed one mother and son shelf-shopping, selecting a few items, heading to check-out, going, and she yearned to go with them, but only for a moment. No, she thought, she would not go with them. Impossible to be part of them, part of that social thing they made. Well, she thought, I will avoid for now that egotism of mothers, that talent for making things seem as they are not. No, her adventure was not theirs; hers would take her to the work that was waiting for her on her desk, always waiting, imperious, daunting, so standoffish and inviting.

Suddenly, in the dairy aisle, three glass doors startled her by puffing open as if blown out by a great-cheeked god, or by rowdy children from some other boisterous and lawless world. The sensation delighted the child in her. Feeling that child alive and well and responsive again, Lily defeated time, erased its tethers, tore down and burned its curtains and was scarcely conscious of which Lily she was or where and she did not mind it. But such moments never last. They disappear, *poof*, like the cold air cloud, so arresting one moment, so invisible and nothing the next. How to keep the magic prickling in the brain 24/7; that's what I want to know, said Lily to herself. *Can't be done*, an inner voice said. *You'll go mad if you try. It's fire playing with fire.* A fire sign, Lily liked fire. That thought, absurd in its timing, made her laugh out loud. *It's the only way to get to the truth*, another version of her inner voice countered. *You can't run away from a challenge and expect to accomplish anything in this world!* But, which world? Which one was the voice talking about? The doors puffed open and again Lily felt the pure elation of surprise, of being out and moving through the world on her own strong legs. She, too, experienced being magically puffed open, her spirit-breath visible momentarily in the aisle.

On her way home, Lily noticed two odd characters, a woman and man, sitting outside Martolli's and ravenously tearing through a large pizza. They ate with gusto. They ate as if the pizza had completely seduced them and they'd never eaten anything like it. Their concentration and zeal amused her, but the feeling faded quickly when the woman looked up and made eye contact with her. The woman stopped eating. A yellow pepper dangled from the corner of her mouth as she nudged the man and pointed at Lily. Why is she pointing at *me*? Lily wondered. Then she felt frightened. She quickened her pace. She breathed faster and harder. She almost skittered up the block, going through people on the crowded street like a seasoned, elusive halfback. When she stopped, looked again and did not see the woman or the man, she told herself what a paranoid fool she'd been. Most likely the woman had pointed at someone or something else.

"The trouble with saving this young woman," said Virginia peeling an orange in the sun-splashed sitting room of their B&B, is the threat of steering her off in some worse direction."

"Or overloading her brain," said Emily, "with—Circumference!"

"That's not helpful, L-Bug. Seriously, after last night's poisoning debacle, we must become more 'hands on' with our Lily. Yes, we must help her train her mind so that she will be capable of deftly maneuvering through all transparencies and transgressions, but we must, in the short run, relieve some of the burden of discovery and decision-making. Apparently, now we must do the same with her young man."

"Lest her brain—and his—Pop like ripe mangoes," said Emily, who admitted to being more than a little overwhelmed by the exotic abundance of all the fruit stands they'd seen.

"Precisely," said Virginia. "There are certain aspects of our Lily's head that have more than a little in common with an especially healthy cabbage. We must elevate her, so to speak. We must lift her out of the dirt, even out of the garden (bear with me, L-Bug!) so that she stands on her own stalks. Feet, I mean."

"Suppose," said Emily, "one woke & found oneself a Fraud.

> No Fear shall Idle be
> On Arctic ice—a Sled
> For feet—too blind to See—
> A mad frog-croak—
> But who will hear or bury Thee?"

"Clever, L-Bug," said Virginia, "but not terrifically funny."

"Dear Goat! Everything is *funny*—especially now. Who is left to Impress? It took each of Us time, me, especially, but didn't we do a fine job of impressing—Everyone?"

"Let's pack up your basket," said Virginia, "and pay our Lily an unexpected visit. Your lemon cakes shall brilliant emissaries be, more brilliant by far than this moldy brie!"

"Billy Goat, you Rhymed! For me? I Adore you!"

"It is better said with petting & kisses," said Virginia.

The treats in Emily's magical basket would have ravished the taste buds of the artistic, literate as well as the inarticulate and those that had always relied on *Cliff Notes*. Emily's renowned lemon cakes accompanied soft malt cookies with vanilla ice, delicate peeled quail eggs, Jamaican bananas and mouthwatering slices of Cornish game hen (the pieces separated from the bones, then pan-braised in olive oil and sprinkled with fresh garlic and basil), sun-and-poetry ripened Gala apples, which Emily brought through the portal in the large pocket sewn on the side of her dress (usually reserved for her writing notebook), juicy (but not overripe) oranges and (a touch of the Exotic)—marzipan! For drinks they packed six bottles of Emily's homemade lavender and blackberry tea.

"No chops?" Virginia asked.

"Sorry," said Emily.

So, off they went, catching the #12 crosstown bus to the south end. They exited and walked north along the creek, each alone, thinking their thoughts, yet quite comfortable in the close proximity of their physicality. Like sisters, Emily thought; we walk together like sisters.

"You're an excellent walking partner, L-Bug," said Virginia. "Not everyone can keep up with me."

"Billy Goat may have the longer appendages—but I'm made of the bee's wings & Intensity! We're a good match."

Twelve

Aidan woke from a nap feeling weak, feeling groggy. He thought about his first dinner date with Lily, replaying the moments he could remember. He must have made some impression! Too bad, because he liked Lily. He wanted to see her again, but he wasn't optimistic. "Fat chance," he said aloud. He thought of the police interviewing him in hospital, but what could he tell them? Did he think he'd been poisoned? What *did* he think? Yes, he'd been poisoned. Was it something he ate, or was it worse? He thought of Lily and the thought roused him, focused him. How much of a fool had he made of himself? What good impression can you make when you vomit on a first date? That line of thinking, of remembering, took him nowhere.

What, then, *had* he eaten? He'd been so absorbed in conversation and in looking at Lily that he couldn't remember. He couldn't recreate in his mind a picture of the table and his plate. The thought that someone might have tried to kill him, or wanted him dead, seemed absurd. He was just an assistant to an art dealer and gallery owner. Who would want him dead? He breathed deeply and came back to Lily. He wanted her.

As if in answer there was a knock at the door. It was Lily. And here I am again, Aidan thought, unshaven, greeting her in a ratty bathrobe. "Come out here," she said as soon as he opened the door. Aidan stepped into the hall. "Do you know what that is?" Lily asked. He shook his head no. "It's a bear trap," said Lily, "and it's set. That thing can break your leg or snap it clean off. Do you usually keep bear traps in your hallway? Are you that anti-social?" She laughed, but it came out strained.

"No," said Aidan, "I don't keep bear traps in my hall, or bears, either. I've never even seen a bear outside of a zoo."

"Really? I've seen a couple of black bears. There was a cub a year ago that walked up and down the aisles in Rite-Aid looking for its mother. But this trap here. We ought to do something about it."

"How about you come inside with me and we close the door," Aidan said.

"And leave it for someone else to trigger? That thing could kill a child."

"You're right. Well," Aidan said, "let's trigger it." He stepped into his apartment and came back to the hall with a broom.

"Stop!" said Lily. "That broom will snap like crazy. We might be impaled. Let's call 9-1-1."

Aidan groaned. "The police again? Lily, I really like you, but what's going on?"

"I'm not sure, Aidan, but let's go in and have a talk—after we call 9-1-1."

Over green tea with honey, Lily spent the next hour telling Aidan everything she knew about her strange visitors, her new 'aunts', and their grim warning about the De la Nuit. Aidan listened quietly. He listened well, not interrupting and waited until Lily was quite finished before speaking. Lily talked and talked, interrupted only for a few minutes when the police arrived and interviewed them briefly. When they left, they took the sprung trap with them.

"I think I've got this," said Aidan. "You are struggling to move on from the murder of your parents and you want to find deeper focus in your work—I'm remembering some of this from our dinner conversation—and you would like to be in a mutually sustaining relationship. You have a deep and abiding love for the works of Emily Dickinson and Virginia Woolf. Somehow, they have been watching you from the world next to this one and they've come back to help you. They're also here to save you because you are in danger from an evil secret society on the other side. How am I doing so far?"

"I know," said Lily. "You think I'm nuts. It sounds crazy, doesn't it. At times, *I've* thought I'm nuts."

"Well, you might be crazy," said Aidan, "but then I'd have to admit that I'm crazy, too, because I believe you." Lily's face relaxed in surprise and relief.

"You really mean it?"

"I mean it," said Aidan, "I've had spirit visitations before. On that long car trip, on a bicycle; an angel actually appeared and pulled me out of the Pacific Ocean. They saved my life. So, I'm down with your spirit friends, Lily." He wanted very much to kiss her. "May I kiss you?" Lily leaned in to him.

When she was gone, Aidan stretched out on the couch feeling exhausted and deliciously content. He felt happy until he veered off into memories of old relationships, not that there had been so many. Still, they counted as evidence. They ensnared him and made wriggling free difficult. He relaxed and went with it, the inventory. It was wise, now and then, to submit to one. What he needed to change, he would change.

No matter how his relationships with women had begun, Aidan thought, they often ended with a woman raging, a woman in tears, or both, and him feeling rattled and shattered, guilty or hopelessly confused. He once sought answers from a counselor; he studied Hinduism, Tibetan Buddhism, read the *Upanishads* and researched ancient matriarchal cultures. He was blessed with a few smart women friends. He adored women. He liked them better than men. He liked listening to them and looking at them; he loved working with them; when it was appropriate, he loved defending and supporting them. Most of the women he dated, after the dating ended, remained his friends. It was just those women with whom he went beyond dating to commitment—those seemed to blow up on him. What was it about him? What was it about them? "No," he told himself, "I am the common denominator."

Aidan also admitted to a near-fatal weakness for rescuing women, which meant gravitating towards women in distress—women who had been abused, treated shabbily and had poor opinions about themselves and men, generally. It was true. He had found victims inordinately attractive, even irresistible. Wasn't Lily in distress pursued by demons and inconsolable grief? No abuse issues, he thought; that was different, and he did not detect any hatred for his sex. He recognized in her a healthy wariness towards men, but that was no drawback. Aidan saw it as a sign of health, of street smarts.

Aidan also confronted his history of falling for narcissists, which he knew was so stupid he deserved everything he got. He had never listened because what do naysayers know about love and commitment? That's what the scrabbling voice on the other side of his brain said; when that voice got loose, it chattered like a monkey. It always irritated Aidan to hear the two voices from opposite hemispheres get into it in his head. Like any stage manager, he felt that he should be in charge of his own cranial theater, but how little that was true! Sometimes, he felt as if he were living with a borrowed head, as if he had no brain of his own. He knew some women who would pipe up on hearing this and heartily agree with him.

He used to suffer a recurring dream about a narcissist, Lolly, he'd stayed with briefly. In the dream, she'd remove his head in the middle of the night, suspend it like a piñata in the yard between two poles and beat hell on it with a baseball bat. Then she would stick the pulpy mess back on his neck just before he woke up. No wonder he felt inadequate, ugly and deformed! He would stagger to the bathroom, glance in the mirror and groan, *what the heck happened?* She would come in and look and play the innocent, hiding the bat blisters on her hands, and Aidan would think, *I am ugly. I am getting old.* Then he would wake up.

Like death, Aidan thought, the stages of a relationship are endlessly complicated, fascinating and mysterious. How to describe them? One seldom describes them adequately, though one tries, as he was trying now. "What is there to say about death, about relationship?" he asked aloud. The sudden sound of his voice unnerved him, but kept on. "One is born and all through life one works one's way towards the green grass beyond. Yet, there are all the beautiful (yes, beautiful, why not?) changes one goes through along the way. Oh, to be able to depict them or describe them with pure love!"

He felt his pulse. It was sluggish. He touched his forehead. It was clammy. He sat up and drank water and fell back on the pillow thinking of the flow and size of love. Is love too small for a compassionate song or the wrong comment, or the wrong look? A car horn honked somewhere close. Couldn't one lovingly share the intimate details of really messing up, then wake up in each other's arms in even greater love and forgiveness? A couple bickered about something down in the street. Is that the love that Jesus talked about? Let me wash your feet, your hair. Let me read you to sleep from a very old and sacred text. Come with me to Brigid's well, to the cairn atop Ben Bulben, to Paphos and the ancient temple of Aphrodite. The beneficial Daddy Long Legs spider curled up for the night in its corner of the shower. Sing with me on the summit of the Mountain of the Women.

He had always feared loss and abandonment, Aidan admitted. In his mind he parroted Yeats: He had sought perfection in a partner and sought for it in vain. He sought it nightly for a year or so, yet found that he equally desired release from seeking. He had been good enough creating a beginning, more than good. 'Have we met before?

I was certain I knew you! Well, I would like to know you! Can you help me with that?' Smiles. Unbroken, dancing eye contact; encouraging soft light and evocative shadows; music from somewhere, a caressing breeze; deep listening; all his senses on high alert as he leaned down and slowly closed on her. He felt the magic between them as her curiosity rose towards him, crashing in to him like a wave lifting him up in its spume and spray and splashing him, disheveled, onto a new shore—*her* shore. So it began, full of promise and laughs and light, yet he lacked—what?—some emotional adhesive that truly bound them together?

Turning on his side, Aidan remembered a tryst with a grad school lover in a New York apartment on Riverside Drive. They were awkward, he recalled, after the years and their happiness in seeing each other again. They nervously talked through old friends and teachers, incidents and hang-outs. As the sun dropped down, the shadows in the room grew longer, creeping over their stocking feet and up their legs; eventually the shadows covered them. When there was only a visor of sunlight across her green-gold eyes she said, 'what is it you want?' 'I want to make love,' he told her and they kissed. They did their best to devour each other as they kissed and undressed. Naked, they made love on the couch and on their feet; they made love as they staggered into the bedroom and fell across the bed. He was grateful, Aidan remembered, as she squirmed, sighing and groaning, saying at last, 'Oh, you've learned a few new things!', which spurred him on to show her everything he could have possibly learned in the years since they'd last been together. She was pleased. He was pleased. They crossed over. Through the body and their intensity of feeling and imagination, they left the restraints of the body, surrendering to each other, submitting as if they were the only lovers in the history of the world. When they came back to their bodies and parted, they had wanted only to come together and cross over again, which they did the next night standing up in a hotel room rather than go out to a party. They writhed in an inward dance. They became each other and so felt, as they never had before, the womanly and manly feelings they'd only known separately. They were wet in new places; They wept for different reasons and all of them thrilling and good as they changed, alternating being dominant and submissive until they collapsed on the floor tremoring in each other's arms. "That is my goal," said Aidan aloud, "but lasting much longer than a single day."

Thirteen

"A bear trap," Ula snarled. "I don't know why I ever listen to you, Wormy."

"Go set yourself on fire," said Dick.

"Did you ever," asked Ula, making an icky face, 'fall asleep tremoring in someone's arms'?" Dick did not answer. He was thinking of the smaller of the two women that had traveled through the portholes. "Hey! I asked you a question, you tub of goose grease!" Ula screamed. But Dick, silent, blocked her out. Smiling, he felt as if the top of his head were flying off.

Fourteen

Turning suddenly to Emily on the bus Virginia said, "Did you over-hear what Lily's young man just realized? He surpasses my expecta-tions! Perhaps he will work out after all. I wish *I* could have written about an experience like that, but of course I didn't. I knew passion-ate, physical love, but with man or woman, it was always challenging. And you, dear L-Bug?"

Emily was slow to answer. Her eyes, soft in the quiet act of remembering, reignited with pinpricks of flame at the center of her pupils. "There was a young man who saw me—First—in my win-dow—but He died—in the War. Rather late in life," Emily added, "the Judge and I—Loved like that—once in the Parlor—once in the Kitchen. He died soon after—I know I didn't Push Him! And—His Passing nearly killed me—too. And there was Sue, but that was so complicated."

A baby up front cried in its mother's arms until a breast quieted it. A shaft of sunlight through their window cast a horizontal pat-tern of light and shadow across Emily's face. "I almost envy you. I was always something of a sexual coward," said Virginia. "I deflected most advances. I hedged my bets. And yet, I was a terrible tease, an awful flirt!"

"Yours is a put-away—laid-to-rest Envy, dear Goat," said Emily. "I mean, we've nothing to Envy ever now—yet another advantage to being Death itself. It's best to flow with—What Is.! The great Tidal Basin collects—everything. We are here—and elsewhere—as Aidan shall be—as Lily shall be."

"Aidan is not thinking that far ahead," said Virginia. "How would you feel about him, L-Bug, if you were Lily?"

"I should be—Thrilled!" said Emily. "Are you Surprised? Honesty is Sweet—Liquor to Fantasies of the Rogue Bee! Only the delivery of Honesty—not the truth itself—Wounds the Listener. Aidan's words are Clear. They bear not a trace of—Malice. Lily will love him more for his Experience and Honesty. She will be *excited!*—She will say, 'I can look forward to—Ecstasy!' He will be attuned to her great feminine power and do anything to be with her. And we can help both of them."

"L-Bug, you *always* know what to say!"

"You don't mean that, dear Goat—but I love you for Saying it! I love You—for so many things."

"Oh, do tell. Please! I love to be told how much I'm loved and why."

"I love my dear old Goat—for her lanky, perfect posture & long Proboscis. You are tall—and I like that. You are quick of mind—and tongue—I like that even Better! Your fashion—Walk and Look are eccentric—as mine are—yet you can also look—a little—Slovenly. I adore that about you! Your empathy—and *your* love are precious—to Me. Though I missed connecting with you in this realm, yet I discovered you—we Discovered each other—in Eternity. It's so much the better—bargain!"

"To be sure, it is the longer one," said Virginia. "I love you in most of the same ways, dear L-Bug, except that you're shorter; I love that! How boring if we were identical in every way! I delight in your exquisite insect nature, the way you buzz and hum and dive and soar and come to rest against my shoulder, in my arms. Oh, I must be careful not to squeeze too hard and damage your delicate wings."

"Don't be fooled," said Emily. "There is sand in them, iron and fairy dust. They are also in your horns when you are on land, and in your gills and fin when you're cutting through the water."

"Now that we've confessed some of the ways we love each other," said Virginia, "what will you say to Aidan, to Lily?

"I thought *you* might speak to Aidan," said Emily. "Division of Labor—is Sweetest!"

"Oh, dear!" said Virginia, "I was just getting used to sitting back and enjoying the whole show! But I must take my fences as they come. I know that. So, what shall I say to our angst-endangered Aidan? Perhaps I'll begin with a personal anecdote, one that titillated critics and scholars for years. I am thinking of the summer night I swam naked with the poet, Rupert Brooke, who looked like a god."

"Oh—he died so young!" said Emily.

"Yes, at the time of the first War, but he was very much alive the night I'm thinking of. I was older than he and his set, and I was rather self-consciously visiting the 'younger crowd' as a Bloomsbury representative. We sat at dusk on the banks of Byron's pool at Cambridge—a lovely lagoon. As the moon came up, Rupert said, 'I think we should swim together, quite naked'. Instantly I threw off my dress and dove into the water, sleek and shiny, free and happy. He plunged in right behind me. Oh, it was lovely floating, swimming, talking, touching, splashing, flirting! Yeats called him the handsomest man in England, and I believe he was. We swam together that night just a year before my marriage. There is perhaps an important lesson in this for Aidan! What do you think?"

"Yes, and no—and yes!" said Emily. "Why not? We did not come back here—to do anything by—half-measures. We're here to liberate and expand, not make excuses, and to—encourage our young charges to—meet Life."

"That's my beloved L-Bug!" said Virginia. She threw her arms around the Amherst poet and clung tight as if she would absorb her. Far from alarmed or resistant, Emily contentedly settled into that ensnaring embrace like a monarch butterfly surrendering to an overly enthusiastic but affectionate wave of a net. As they left the bus to walk the last blocks to Lily's place, Virginia squeezed Emily's hand. "Oh!" she cried, "I've a splendid idea! Aidan needs a man to talk to. I know just who to draft for that purpose."

"Yes," said Emily, smiling, "it's so obvious. Why didn't we both think of it sooner?"

PART TWO

Time Returning

One

'What in the unholy dark did you hope to accomplish with that bear trap?" said Ula.

"Shut your gob!" said Dick. "I'll stay on my side of the cave and you stay on yours."

⤷⦿⤶

"Is your new man a keeper?" said Shaya.

"Too soon to tell," said Lily, "I have a bad feeling about the poisoning, but a good feeling about him. I want you to meet him."

⤷⦿⤶

"Leonard's acting the brat," said Virginia as Emily fussed with making breakfast, "but he'll show up. He always does."

⤷⦿⤶

"You're all impulse, aren't you," said Ula through the darkness of the thicket cave. "I mean, you couldn't follow a simple outline if it was stamped on the back of your hand, Gum-Rot! Where are you going!"

"Just stepping out for a moment," said Dick, "to get you a little bouquet of reddish oak-like leaves you can rub all over your body sores. It'll make you feel *real* good!"

⤷⦿⤶

"I wish you'd called. I could have gone to the library with you," said Shaya. "I want to know more about Brigid. Doesn't she have a magical white cow?"

⌒◌◌

I'm tired of being laid up, Aidan thought and left for a brisk walk.

⌒◌◌

"Why are all the lights on?" said Lily, pausing in the doorway. "I never leave them on."

"Forget it," said Shaya. "You've had a lot on your mind. Tell me more about your 'Aunts'."

⌒◌◌

"I wonder what Lily's thinking?" said Aidan, walking towards Lithia Park.

⌒◌◌

"Shaya," Lily asked, "can you meet Aidan on Wednesday?"

Two

So, the seasons, ever agitating, ever whimsical, sought compatibility in the Rogue Valley, where since the springtime of Native Americans, magic and mystery imprinted the landscape and enthralled people of like minds seeking the mysterious, the magical, the unknowable. On they came from all points of the compass, decade after decade, to discover their preferred tribes. The seasons matched the dramatic, changeable landscape and seemed to imitate the magic of the nation's oldest, largest regional theater, which called Ashland home.

Townsfolk, not just the actors, delighted in pretending to be other than they were. They were always dressing up. A mime covered in gold paint from head to toe handed out fortunes on the plaza outside Renaissance Rose. A young man or woman dressed as a yogurt cup walked up and down Siskiyou Boulevard giving away ten-percent-off coupons. A reasonable facsimile of William Shakespeare himself declaimed verse in Lithia Park's Japanese garden. Fearless fawns and their mothers grazed on Lithia's green grass, ignoring nearby humans as if the humans roamed the park for the amusement of the deer.

In this way, imperfectly harnessed by teams of human seekers, winter affirmed its normalcy and its infinite surprises. It was all perspective, this way of regarding weather, of seeing others, or oneself. An icy wind and slick sidewalks compromised pedestrian-and-car traffic. Here and there a walker slipped and fell. There were fender-benders. Car horns flared, their going off precipitating mild altercations or opportunities for locals to demonstrate their empathy and forgiveness.

For a moment, the gray canopy parted, and bright sunlight lifted moods, warming everyone up; just as suddenly, heavy rain fell, then stopped, then returned again. It was as if the weather were a stand-up comic with a ceaseless supply of jokes. No matter the circumstances, she could not stop telling them. So, prepared visitors dressed themselves in layers. The weather kept them on their toes. Longtime residents thought and dressed in layers, too, but they were deeper believers in infinite mystery and surprise. Like a water bottle or backpack, the weather came with them, accompanied them as they strolled in Lithia Park, or walked the length of Siskiyou Boulevard, up and down, up and down, ducking in and out of Paddington Station, Soundpeace, the Varsity Theater, bumping into someone on the street and stopping to chat, sitting down for a drink, coffee, a meal, or all three.

In recent years, the valley's winter and fall lasted longer than they used to and their extended collaboration produced what could only be called a hybrid of the two, a sort of lingering 'Falinter' that stretched from early October to mid-January. Had this season been a new 'planet', say Planet X-10, much more coverage would have been given it in the media, but as it was just a season and a local and ambiguous one at that, it remained (so far) a secret of the Ashland and Rogue Valley locals.

Even more secret was the town's ripeness for visitation. Local lore was rich with ghost stories, alien visitations, abductions and unexplainable revenge sagas that chilled young and old alike around campfires and at bedtime. There was the story of the prominent pioneer woman who hoarded silver in nearby Jacksonville. She married a much younger, charming boulevardier from the East and mysteriously drowned in the Rogue River. Her widower grew increasingly nervous, some said eccentric, and was found hanging in his attic three months after his wife's death. A circle of silver coins decorated the floor beneath him where his feet would have been had he not been dangling by his roped neck.

A teenage boy, the victim of drug dealers, was said to haunt a secluded bend on Ashland creek. Locals believed that one tempted death straying by this lonesome stretch of the creek at dusk or later.

There were the haunted houses, too, like the one on a hill across from the town on Interstate 5. In a hillside house on Suncrest Road, a young girl ghost, about twelve, had been seen several times playing in an alcove under a roll-top desk while an unhappy Native American man grumbled and shuffled up and down a hallway at the back of the house.

In Lithia Park in 1993, strollers discovered a skull peering out of a jagged hole at the base of an oak tree. Ashland even had its own harrowing version of the urban legend that is the tale of the hook, that perpetual warning to parked couples that something awful may be trying at any moment to get to you in your car.

Wherever one rambled in the Rogue Valley, but especially within the boundaries of Ashland's 6.59 square miles, one was fairly certain to be touched by...what? The supernatural? A concordance of seemingly contradictory phenomena that raised the hairs on the back of one's neck and spurred a quickened pace, or froze the wanderer in his tracks, forever changing his relationship to self and that place? Who could say? Some shamans and healers and self-help celebrities spoke of the area's energy vortex, of the powerful vibrations pulsing down to the valley from nearby Mt. Ashland and other volcanic peaks. Science confirmed that the energy waves in the Rogue Valley were especially permeable, deliciously supple and life-changing. Spiritual seekers moved to the area to deepen practice. Scholars and historians came to study Native American culture. Californians sold their lucrative properties and bought out cash-poor, land-rich Oregonians to create and enjoy the gentrified country/town life that looked so enticing during rush hour on the Santa Monica Freeway or Oakland's Bay Bridge. The well-rounded and the culturally elite gravitated to Ashland's bustling theater life and left-leaning politics. With a smarmy largesse unique to the village, the city council legislated against real estate development and rampant growth; if it was that kind of growth you wanted, you would find sympathy and more relaxed regulations in Medford a few miles north off Interstate 5.

It was strange that even in Falinter the weather could turn, suddenly, hot. So it came, swiftly. The sun glared on Ashland's rain-washed, festive streets as afternoon lengthened. The town and its residents squirmed like a large body caught up too tight in a warm overcoat. Capillaries reddened, swelling with blood. Perspiration popped out on the foreheads and necks of walkers and dampened the shirts of drivers in stuffy cars slowed by insidiously timed traffic lights. A wad of gum oozed on the sidewalk and stuck to the sole of a tourist's boot. The tourist walked on, taking another's inconvenience with him. A cabbage white fluttering across Main Street smashed into a Porsche's windscreen, annoying the driver and startling his passenger, a beautiful blonde half his age. His daughter? His date? A man at the curb, waiting to cross, observed it all and wondered, then forgot as the light changed and he walked back into his own life. The chunky parking enforcement man in shorts, sandals and baggy linen shirt prowled along curbs monitoring with his handheld device, pausing now and then to turn it on and produce a ticket and envelope, which he pinned to a car's front window under a wiper blade. His enthusiasm annoyed not only his victims, but everyone else that observed his ritual. They watched him as he issued citations with smiling impunity and felt the hopelessness and anxiety of future witless violators and victims.

Like all American resort towns, Ashland was zealous about its traffic. Walkers and cyclists were good, cars not so much. Those who disagreed and were foolish enough to say so found themselves subjected to the patented Ashland eye roll, the Ashland smirk, the Ashland holier-than-thou shunning of cultural, economic and environmental inferiors—and at the worst, the raised, emphatic Ashland middle finger.

This attitude might have been easier to take had it been nurtured by historical roots that ran deep. But it did not originate among Ashland natives, of which there were few (and they *were* far between). Contemporary Ashland smugness grew up in the gangs of affluent immigrants, most of them flush from California land sales who relished the carte blanche that greeted them. In yoga and Nia classes, in organic grocery stores and upscale shops they were not shy about expressing their views; they expected agreement. The new Ashlanders were a like tribe, a closed club. Admission was not impossible but could be strenuous and difficult. Even after a new arrival was, after many trials, admitted, she or he was encouraged to supplicate in numerous ways to club members of longer standing, and continued inclusion hung for a time by a thread beneath the pendulum blade of the ripest and most offensive snobbery.

Yet, no amount of posturing, no explosion of egoistic crowing silences bird song and bee hum and the susurrus of the trees. Nature overcomes. Ashland's alpine valley surrounded by woody mountain ranges—the Cascade Range to the east, the Coast Range to the west—forms a beautiful bowl. Giant redwoods are not far away; lakes and rivers are plentiful and the waters of wells and grottos burble everywhere in sacred groves. Their primal songs travel great distances and are always sounding in the inner ear. They make puny and irrelevant human noise and posturing. They endure and outlast humanity, which is something serious and restorative to consider.

Three

Leonard Woolf, who moments ago had emerged from the base of an oak tree in Lithia Park holding a tiny monkey in his arms, thought about the order that thrives in nature at all times. Once a successful administrator in the foreign service, he had trained himself in his own rambling Monk's House garden in Sussex, becoming over time a master gardener. His garden was practical and a little wild, a little shabby—like himself and his elegant wife. *Over time.* He thought of that expression, the convenient way it encapsulated almost fifty earth years and how it had all passed in the wink of an eye, in the falling of a tear.

Walking the downhill path from his tree portal to the town, he admired the park's exquisite architecture. This is gardening on a grand scale, he thought. It's closer, he thought, to Vita Sackville-West's gardens at her home, Sissinghurst, which he and Virginia had visited many times. Leonard thought of himself as a day-laboring gardener, a practical planter growing apples and vegetables, a stocker of canned goods—and only then a grower of flowers. He had kept fresh-cut flowers in the house because they cheered his wife, who always needed cheering. As he walked, keeping a firm grip on Mitz inside his shirt (the monkey, overcome by the urge to explore, made several efforts to bolt), Leonard thought of how he'd resisted Virginia's initial summons, telling her he had no desire to come back and join her adventure. He gave in, of course, gruffly, and as he walked he tried to conjure his initial grumpiness, but he had to admit, now he was back, that it excited him—the old sounds, smells and light, his earth body devoid of the aches and pains of old age, his body feeling as good as new. He anticipated seeing Virginia again in this realm and desire filled his thoughts. He recalled an afternoon when they were older on which Virginia asked, "Do you still find me attractive?" He ached remembering her vulnerability. "The most beautiful of women," he'd answered. They loved each other like that. Looking down at his dangling hand, he noticed that his tremor had also come back. He smiled.

I had the shakes all my life, Leonard thought. He remembered how the government would not take him into service in the first War because his arms and hands shook so violently. They were afraid he'd turn loopy and spray rifle shots at his own troops! He had feared the same thing and was glad when he was sent home to Virginia with a paper assigning him to domestic work. He grinned thinking of how she had been so relieved! He doubted that she would have survived had he gone to war and left her.

She had required a lot of looking after, Leonard thought. He became expert at supervising her ups and downs. He managed her schedule and diet so that her bad episodes did not escalate; when they did come, he watched over her day and night, protecting her from others and herself. He made sure she ate enough and rested enough. He had not always been right, but he was right more than he was wrong. Yes, even back on earth after so many years, Leonard still believed that his wife would never have survived for 59 years had she been left on her own.

Approaching the plaza, Leonard remembered coming up to Virginia's room on her birthday while she was still in bed. They cuddled, talking and he gave her a new journal, exotic inks and new nibs for her pens. Later, they strolled through town window-shopping and stopped for a treat—fresh ice cream and strawberries—a favorite of Virginia's. They walked all afternoon, holding hands, arm-in-arm, chatting up this and that, enjoying being in love. Her diary passage about that day comforted him all the rest of his life.

Strolling now, Leonard's memory drifted back to his civil service days. In Ceylon, he discovered and refined his talent for organization, for administration, for meting out justice. He resolved disputes. He granted reprieves and condemned men to death; yet, he also learned to love the Divine Feminine. He adored the women he loved in every possible way. He practiced patience and forbearance, compassion and love. He listened well; he argued skillfully. He was fortunate living in a late Victorian era in which even a woman as fiery and independent as Virginia Stephen would willingly defer to him on many occasions. Leonard wondered if today she would have been rather less agreeable, but he also suspected that he would have been calmer, softer, more flexible. He thought of his earth temper, how he stood his ground and expected to win out eventually, yet he was also tender and very much in love. He believed in her, his wife, yes. Looking back through the long years, Leonard could see himself, a man with a craggy face and thick, wild hair, impossibly thin, with a constant tremor; yelling at dogs he first met to teach them who was alpha, then spoiling them; abusing Hogarth Press staff with horrible tantrums; forcing his wife to eat when she did not want to eat; siding with the doctors; a man teeming with projects in labor halls, in Parliament, in publishing, in the garden, in the village, in their homes. They all might have profited had he developed a better sense of humor.

There was passion, too, Leonard thought. There was the body. Regarding the body, he thought, adjustment and accommodation always came into play. As a student at Cambridge, he had chosen a life of the mind, a select community. In Ceylon he studied in isolation and ruled in public. He took tea with proper young ladies and made love to prostitutes. He rode horses through the jungle and when he was not riding he hiked for miles and miles. He was always busy doing, moving, his body the most useful device he knew.

But on his return to England after seven years, there was less need for a useful body. Mostly he walked to catch trains, to go to and from train stations. He walked with his old friends as they discussed philosophy and politics, painting and writing. He saw Virginia again and pursued her. Strange how he was so in love with a woman who was not on the best of working terms with her own body. He loved her beauty and her mind, her voice and her laughter. Oh, she was bright! She was quick and wicked! He had loved her sister, too; in fact, he had loved Vanessa first, but she married Clive while Leonard was still abroad. His love for Vanessa was infatuation; no doubt, at first, his love for Virginia was as well. But the more time they spent together, the more they talked, he forgot issues about the body. She became perfection to him. In this realm, he thought, she was the only person he ever knew who was, he was certain, a genius. Yet she had chosen him to be her husband! He gave up his career on the chance that she would accept him. Even after she turned him down he resolved to quit the foreign service and remain in England to be near her should she change her mind. And one day she did.

That was the happiest of all days, Leonard thought. Nothing is sweeter than the word 'yes' on the lips of one's beloved, especially as those lips release it for the first time. 'Yes,' she said as they talked in her room at Brunswick Square, 'I love you and will marry you.' Instantly he was at her feet, covering her slippers with kisses as she leaned over his back and wild hair, laughing. He hugged her in her chair, kissing her neck, her ears, her lips, her brow and her amazingly sexy nose. They jumped around the room, wrote a cryptic postcard to Lytton and hurried downstairs to the London streets where they dashed in and out of parks and shops, lovemaking all day.

There is nothing more exquisite, Leonard reflected, than loving someone who has accepted you, who agrees to take you in, to take you on. It is the truest miracle that occurs between people. No matter what came upon them or passed between them in their twenty-six years together, he never forgot the tenderness and joy of those transformational hours in the Brunswick Square house. It had been as if

Virginia and I were both born a second time, Leonard thought, yet born fully conscious as we entered a new world.

Walking on in the old way, the rushing waters of Ashland Creek on his left, Leonard thought of the bad days, the terrible days of his wife's final illness, disappearance and the three weeks that passed before her body was found. It surprised him a little to find himself remembering that horrible end as she lay in the morgue, her body ravaged, utterly destroyed, yet after he died, she greeted him in all her ebullience and beauty! He had wept otherworldly tears. He had thrown his arms around her and held her tight and kissed her, so many kisses, thousands, because of course in the next world one can go on kissing infinitely if one wishes to. Even better, she returned his kisses with equal joy and ardor. She had shed her mortal guilt and fear of the body. She was free. He was free. At last, they were free together. How did it feel to see her again, he thought? It was a moment in which he knew that he in his life had achieved perfection. It was like that.

The sun warmed the covered and uncovered heads of coffee and tea drinkers sitting at outside tables, driving many of them indoors to air conditioning, but almost as soon as they settled in to their new seats, the sun plunged behind the mountains; instantly the temperature dropped fifteen degrees. Coffee and tea drinkers that had run for cover moments before reemerged, like moles welcoming the blessed dark, to claim their out-door tables. The gum on the tourist's sandal sole cooled and hardened; the liquidated cabbage white disappeared in a stream of washing solution and a scrape of new wiper blades. The town sparkled and fizzed as white evening lights winked on from every tree and building on the plaza. A festive nocturnal coolness suggested reprieve and romance. It was Happy Hour.

Four

It was hours since the theaters let out and No Lily had appeared among the theater goers. Ula and Dick slumped on a sidewalk bench in the shade. Dick belched and stared at the ground between his sandals while Ula mopped her neck and forehead with the sleeve of her robe.

"What *is* this?" she said in an exasperated voice. She meant the dampness on her sleeve and all over her.

"You know!" said Dick looking up. "It's perspiration. Sweat!"

"Really?" said Ula. "I'd forgotten. You know, we have to come up with a better plan. I just want to snatch her and get the hell out of here. I mean, I don't even mind if we kill her and drag her back that way. Do you think our leaders could revive her?"

Dick stared at her as if he did not quite believe what he saw. "I'm not going to ask if you're nuts because I know you are," he said. "Do you really want to take the chance that our superiors would be able to revive her and still make use of her? They never told us to bring her back dead."

"Ok! Smart guy!" Ula hissed. "You come up with something! Oh, why do we have to sweat in this realm?"

"What did you expect?" Dick said. "At least the commodes are a lot nicer in this time."

"You mean—that, too?" said Ula, screwing up her face in a look of disgust.

"Sorry. That, too," said Dick. "Just give all that pizza you stuffed in your face a little more time to digest. You'll see."

Ula involuntarily rubbed her tummy. "You make me sick!" she said. That made Dick feel like laughing, but the sound that emerged from him was more like a high-pitched mew or groan. Members of the De la Nuit were not accomplished laughers. But Dick, too, sweating, suffered in his cowl and robe.

"I'm going to get me one of those shirts," he said, standing up and pointing to a kid on a skateboard. "I heard someone call it a tank-top. No sleeves. I like that." Ula watched the lithe skateboarder zoom away in his black, sleeveless shirt dominated by an illustration of The Grim Reaper.

"Ha Ha," said Ula. "You're really going to uncover those white, spindly arms?"

Dick tried out a new expression he'd overheard and liked. "Eat me," he said.

Five

Lily and Shaya were fond of 'Falinter'. Aidan hadn't given it much thought. Emily and Virginia found it odd—curious but odd. They had no past reference to a climate pattern that blended fall and winter as they had always known them. Yet, theirs was a mild bemusement. In the world next door, one conjured and enjoyed the weather one wanted. For now, they adapted, happy enough with the novelty and the excitement of their adventure. Yet, Leonard, Virginia's husband, preferred spring and summer. He preferred not being here at all, but when his wife appealed to him to do anything, especially for her, he did what she asked. Always. This was no different. He insisted, however, on bringing Mitz along for company and perhaps, though laconic Leonard would never admit it, a bit of mischief.

Six

But what does the season or the weather have to do with anything except as signposts pointing here and there, resurrecting the past or confounding it? Lily considered this as she walked through town on Main Street. She had been born on a farm up north but had lived her whole life here in the Rogue Valley. She had missed the seasons of farming and always regretted it a little in the way that one thinks of a coveted sweater that had worn out or been lost. Yet she loved Ashland, too. She loved it so much that except for rare, necessary professional trips to Japan and New York, she never wanted to leave and moving somewhere else was simply out of the question. She could practice her art and do her work anywhere and she preferred here, exactly where she was.

Running these thoughts as she walked strengthened her. She felt lighter, happier walking confidently through her town. She loved walking (a happy obsession she shared with Virginia and Emily). For years it had been an essential part of her spiritual practice. Lily walked when she was troubled; she walked when she was depressed; she walked when she needed to tease out a difficult problem she faced in a drawing or story; she walked, too, when she was happy, to sharpen the sensation, to make more intense the delicious pleasure of joy, of no guilt, no sorrow.

So, she walked today through the odd weather with new things to think about, to sort out. She thought of her new 'aunts', Emily and Virginia—and she felt warm all over. She thought of Aidan. Yes, she admitted to herself, she thought of Aidan and felt excited.

She was still thinking of him when she saw something on the street that jarred her: a thin old man suffering such severe curvature of the spine that he could only stare down at his shoes stumbled by. As if a darkening veil had fallen across her world, Lily saw only signs of vulnerability and damage everywhere. Despite her shame, Lily stopped, turned and stared. What's it like, she wondered, to be *that* poor man? A beautiful blonde in a wheelchair zoomed past. Lily had seen her around town before. What was *her* story? A ski accident? A car wreck? She felt sympathy for these wounded people and apprehension about her own imperfect understanding and morbid curiosity. What was it really like to *be* someone so...damaged? Whenever Lily's mood turned contemplative, this was its primary question. Her appreciation for everything and everyone in loss and abundance, but especially in loss increased, and she walked as she imagined St. Francis and other contemplatives walked, slowly, not defeated, not worn down, but measured in step and breath. Contemplatives walked like that, gazing out on the world with the soft eyes of contented horses. So Lily walked, or tried to, until growing self-conscious about saintliness, she quickened her pace. She imagined trotting along as a dog rambles, ever wary and aware, eager for acts of loving kindness but not surprised when someone takes a shot at you or gives you a swift kick in the ass. *Ruff-ruff!* She heard herself barking in her head. Her dog-talk made her laugh.

On the plaza, a work crew rose into the air in the basket of a cherry picker to change the white lights that created such cheer in Ashland after dark. An accordion player with a two-day stubble and a cigarette dangling from a corner of his mouth leaned against a brick building and squeezed out Irish reels. A block on, a brother/sister act finished a song A Cappella, then the sister soloed a haunting melody on her flute.

Claiming the empty bench outside Soundpeace, an Interfaith book and gift store, Lily sat down to watch the passing show. As usual, theatergoers walked along in clusters that included couples dressed from elsewhere. It was a favorite Ashland game to people-watch and guess who were the locals and who weren't. It wasn't much of a challenge. Locals exuded an orgulous confidence. Ashland was a happy town, a Special town; one only had to ask a local to confirm it.

A gaggle of school children banged out of the ice cream shop next door and formed a writhing knot at the corner as they waited for their teacher who was taking too much time paying the bill. A man wearing a beautiful full-head wolf mask crossed the street and walked right through them, growling and yipping, as the children, delighted, squealed and broke apart to get out of his way. Lily admired the wolf mask and wanted to stop the man to ask where she could get one, but she knew he would not come out of character for her. If she stopped the wolf, she would get nothing but barks, yips and maybe even a howl for her trouble.

Now a woman passed by, walking a large poodle; her face looked as if it had made perfect peace with the word 'snooty'. Two fit, gray women in yoga pants followed close behind, chattering earnestly about what sounded to Lily like herbal treatments for diarrhea, while a gaunt man and woman, also pale and gray, walked very fast, hand-in-hand, as if, like ducks, they were needed somewhere. Lily remembered to look skyward in the direction of the railroad tracks where a magnificent hawk's nest crowned a tall cedar tree. She found the tree and looked up, but the nest was gone.

It was time to move again. Lily left the bench, the thought that someone might be following flickering in her mind and attached herself to the backdraft of four middle-aged women walking briskly uptown. It pleased her to follow close the attractive women who moved confidently and conversed with so much animation. They were talking about men and they were laughing a lot, which she also enjoyed. Women love overhearing other women laugh about men; she'd been told that men love it, too, as long as they're laughing about *other* men.

"He never gets it," said the woman with dreads.

"They never get it," the ponytail blonde agreed.

"Oh, they get it all right," said the one with the hair of confusing color and short asymmetrical cut; "it's just that everything they get is wrong!"

That got a big laugh, a group guffaw.

"Mine gets more than you think," said the gray-haired one. "He does a lot for me, but much of the time he's doing stuff that I don't want!" Their nods of assent matched their vigorous strides.

Lily peeled off and left them at the next corner, crossing the street and continuing on in the same direction. It was delicious, the way her mind was working; she savored the experience and wanted to keep it going. A child raced around the corner and ploughed into her, his lowered head connecting with Lily's abdomen. It hurt, but not so much that Lily couldn't manage a weak smile. Gallantly, she waved off the mother's apology. She'd come around the corner right behind the boy and looked appalled. Lily reassured them and continued on. She thought about how deep, philosophical thinking is no match for an out-of-control boy of seven or eight with red hair that is almost as fiery as Mother Brigid's. She laughed out loud at this small revelation and quickened her step.

Thinking again of an unseen enemy nearby, and the man in the wolf mask still fresh in her mind, Lily conjured her own wolf, her spirit animal, for protection. The wolf (sometimes it was a fox, sometimes a heron, depending on circumstances she could not fully understand) appeared, loping faithfully alongside her, ready to catch and devour any demons threatening to block their path. Lily wondered what happened to people who never connected with their spirit animals. Lily wondered, then caught herself. Was she walking through town with a real wolf? Was she daydreaming? Did it matter if the sensations and exchanges seemed real enough?

The wolf turned its red eyes on her, its tongue lolling through impressive canines and incisors and spoke in beautiful English. "They are not doomed," said the wolf, answering her question about people who do not connect with their spirit animals. "They're hollow, like certain reeds in the marsh, like receptacles waiting to be filled. They walk through this world out of step and unbalanced. They do not stride with confidence, but nervously prowl and are easily distracted. They wander off paths, rooting in brambles and nettles for something missing; yet their sense of it seldom brings them closer to the thing they seek. This makes them even more restless, more uncertain as they strive and strive but bump face-first into obstacle after obstacle. Theirs is a twilight of half-knowing in which, now and then, they catch a glimmer of that which they cannot know—unless they wake up to their guide or guides. But that is a great personality-flensing step. Who takes that step makes progress, may even become whole; without that step, all progress is stunted," the wolf said.

Real or imagined, Lily was talking to her wolf and she liked it. "What happens to them," Lily asked, "when they die? Are they held back?"

"No," said the wolf in a raspy, guttural voice borne of mulch and tree roots, "but their crossover is different. They require the intervention of a family member or loved one, someone who must come to the threshold itself and help them through. That is why some linger here in the air, in the dirt, invisible, unable to transition. There is a saying among us of the multi-worlds: *Invisible here, invisible hereafter.* It means one runs the risk of being stuck *between* worlds—no longer part of this world, and unable to become completely part of the next one."

"But these souls can make it through with help?" Lily asked. She realized that she wanted to reassure herself that no one would be locked out.

"Yes," the wolf growled, "but family members or beloved friends on the other side are in no hurry sometimes to intercede. There may be unresolved issues with the soul in limbo. Sometimes, otherworld interventions must be done to encourage intermediaries to act." At this last detail, the wolf coughed or laughed, Lily couldn't tell which. As they came into the plaza once more, she was aware of her spirit animal receding into shadows. He was gone, yet as Lily tuned in to his absence, she sensed the wolf's eyes on her and it made her feel protected; she felt loved.

It was getting late. Playgoers scurried to restaurants for pre-show suppers. Car and foot traffic packed the road and sidewalk around the plaza as those understudies of the sun—streetlamps—began to wink on. Evening street musicians appeared to take the places of the musicians who busked by day; even a changeover in the stray cat population had taken place, and here and there couples entered or emerged from the park, which was supposed to be off limits at sunset, though people ignored that edict. Lily looked up at the warm, buttery lights pouring out of the big windows of The Brick Room and Granite Tap House. By concentrating and looking closely at the Tap House's corner window closest to the park, she could just make out the worker bees coming and going to the hive that had long resided inside the building's façade. When Lily ate there, she sat in that corner booth whenever she could and watched with delight the departing and returning bees. The bees energized Lily and she entered a state of mind in which the moment was all and it was quite enough. She settled into herself. She observed.

That couple turning into the doorway of the Black Sheep maintained a physical distance between them. They were rather too separate to be complete, Lily thought, while that couple leaving an outdoor table at the corner coffee shop did so arm in arm; they looked into each other's eyes and smiled. But how long would it all last? Who would endure? Would this be the final evening for the first couple? Perhaps their time together would be excruciating tonight, light years away from their beginning when they could not stand to be apart. Would the second couple, apparently so happy, turn into the first couple in time? Didn't every couple? Lily thought of her parents. No, they had never turned to darkness.

Lily thought of Aidan, of their dinner and the poisoning and anxiety returned to her. Fear returned to her. her breath grew shallow; her heart quickened as a third couple strolled by. Hand in hand, they walked with more serenity than the others. Lily struggled to tamp down the uneasiness that threatened once again to engulf her. She concentrated on the serene couple, telling herself that wherever these two were going, they would be up to navigating the storms behind and ahead of them. Theirs was the peace *she* wanted. Preoccupied, Lily did not notice the two odd figures loitering outside Martolis, the woman with Medusa hair, the man in the tank-top sizing her up as she walked by.

"It's the girl!" said Ula, scrambling to her feet, pulling her ragged coat around her.

"Huh?" said Dick. "The girl? Really? Where?"

"There!" Ula hissed at him. She glared, making him feel like the most embarrassing creature that ever lurched and crawled from primordial matter into a human form.

"Where? *Where?* "Said Dick, who realized his nearsightedness had returned with him.

"Over there, whey-face! Come on! She's getting away!"

With a bee's focus and effervescence, Emily buzzed around the corner and ducked into Mix coffee shop, but Lily did not see her.

Seven

While Emily flitted in and out of shops, humming, buzzing, Virginia visited a hospice house on the pretense of finding an appropriate final destination for her aging older sister. Dead herself, naturally drawn to the dead and dying, herself a former invalid who had spent whole seasons in bed and in institutions, Virginia found the hospice movement bizarre but also somehow sweet and charming and necessary. How different life might have been in her own time, she thought, if this option for caring had existed. But in her time families stayed together in ways they did not now, or so it seemed to Virginia and Emily. They had talked about it and the thousand little things that challenged their perception in this different age, things like impossibly fast cars, handicap zones, processed and packaged foods and a scourge called social media. Everybody pecked at little devices they held in their hands. There was so little easeful quiet time! They were blessed, though, Emily and Virginia, because they both had the habit of quiet.

Virginia enjoyed her tour of the house, a stately Victorian within walking distance of her B&B. She noted the pleasant dispositions of the caregivers, two middle-aged women whose faces showed the wear of eventful years. The women took care of four residents, all in their eighties, three women and a man, the man in the late stages of dementia. A resident named Sita was in fact in the closing stage of dying, and after her formal interview, tour and Q & A, Virginia made use of her power of invisibility to observe, unnoticed, Sita's transition.

Nestled in the shadows of a corner of a room, Virginia observed the old woman in the bed; she noted the television, the caregiver and the shadows. Virginia watched as Sita met the onset of dusk through cloudy eyes. She looked a little like a dusty, faded doily she was so small on the bed. The telly went on and on, but the woman neither saw nor heard it. The caregiver kept a respectful distance. When she spoke to Sita, the old woman ignored her. When Sita did speak, was it in a voice that grumbled or growled. Was she angry? Did she want something? She was happy and unhappy, or she was neither one. She was twenty and falling in love; she was 87 and preparing to die.

When you have time, Virginia thought, it's hard work, dying. One needs to go inward, inward, and then deeper still before all past experiences and submerged lives line up. Only then does one hear the tumblers click into place; and the great door soundlessly swings open.

Until then, one worked at it as Sita was working. If she had worry beads or a rosary, she might have been rubbing them smooth between her ancient fingers. The caregiver anxiously looked at her, now and then sounding her out, but heard no coherent response. Sita had no time for courtesy though she was not unkind. Never a verbal person, she did not have the words to describe what she was doing, but at some unconscious level she knew what she must do, and she was working, working. Though she had been through this many times, the caregiver was uncomfortable. Who wouldn't be?

Thinking of the aftermath of her mother's death, Virginia remembered how she described the image of a rain god desiring unrestricted rain for everyone: '...let all breathing kind, the munchers and chewers, the ignorant, the unhappy, those who toil in the furnace making innumerable copies of the same pot, those who bore red-hot minds through contorted letters, and also Mrs. Jones in the alley, share my bounty.' She had written that long ago, and now this old woman, Sita, became Mrs. Jones; Mrs. Jones was Sita. They became each other and everyone else. As identity shriveled, as dreams flickered, as individuality was squashed like a fly that a moment before had been dancing with sunlight on a sill, one was entombed in the dying husk of Sita, in the endless sweeping of Mrs. Jones.

Virginia quietly observed, excited and exhilarated by the miracle that was taking place in that room. Transitions never got old for her. She thought of how Emily performed this work all her life, caretaking her mother, tending to the sick and so was well prepared. Emily was composed. Her end connected as a piece with her life and work, Virginia thought, in contrast to her own, which was more violent. Virginia thought how she went swiftly, passing like a cloud over the waves. She thought of how she had intervened, how she slapped Death's face. I was unvanquished and unyielding, Virginia thought. I chose my time.

Sita was doing *her* work. Virginia knew it was harder when one has put off preparing for most of one's life. Sita's work had to be crammed into a fist of hours, but she was doing her best. She was already partway there. Virginia saw how she teased the veils, drifting in and out of her body by tiny stages. In a moment, she would slip away like a rush of wind through a tunnel, like a silverfish down the vortex of a shower drain, like star-stuff bursting in the night sky, and her little life would close with a click, the sound of a lid shutting on a perfectly made box. The poet, Yeats, said that a well-made poem was like that. Virginia had known him. Yeats was right. Working out one's death was just like that. There! Virginia thought. A bird hovered over the bed, its beating wings making a lovely sound like a breeze rustling leaves. Sita's spirit animal had come into the room; it was a meadowlark, whose song is sweetest of all the fields.

There! The old woman had done it. She had crossed over. Virginia wanted to speak to her, but Sita was taken up by family, by friends and by some who were not such friends—all on equal terms now. If I did speak to her, Virginia thought, I would say to her, '87!

Well done!' Or I would say to her, 'Now you are ageless, Time's yoke dissolved'. And she would say to me, 'Did I know you? Should I know you?' I will leave her to her circle till our circles intersect, Virginia thought. Oh, I never get enough of this, she thought observing others, making up stories, fantastic stories. She had peeled and peeled the onion and the fig to discover what was invisible and essential at the core. That was *her* method. Oh, the bother and the joy!

"Don't be hard on yourself, my Billy Goat!" said Emily, who had whisked in unseen during the last stage of Sita's journey. Virginia smiled, relieved to discover her friend beside her.

"I'm afraid death and dying have gotten no easier or less mysterious in this time," said Virginia.

"Did you really think it had?" said Emily, then to ease any unintentional accusation her voice might have conveyed, the poet went on about her own earth relationship with death. "I grew up with Death," she said. "My father on his travels collected magazines—for Girls and Boys. They were delightfully—Macabre! Story after story—told of James or some other star-crossed village boy skating on a Winter Pond and falling through the ice to an agonizing Death. Or little Amy and her sister—caught the Cholera or Whooping Cough—and faded like bright, pink roses and Perished."

"Each alone!" cried Virginia. "I survived whooping cough!" she added in an almost hushed voice.

"I'm glad, dear Goat," said Emily, suggesting they walk out what they'd just witnessed. A couple of blocks away, Emily picked up the thread of her recollection. "My mother, after endlessly heroic and energetic service, found one morning that she—could not rise from her bed. Thus—the Deathwatch began! On and on—the hours darkened until the Spirit in the wasted body suddenly flew away—the breast relaxed, the face beatified, as if kissed by—Immortality!

"I Saw so many faces, young and old, Kissed like that. Between epidemics, illness and war, I saw so many—called back—before their

ripening. I watched them laid to rest in the Cemetery below my bedroom window. I loved the funeral processions—like black-clad circus
trains parading through Town! At times I grew quite agitated—with
Joy!

"Dusk, thine cloudy Eye
Like sunset ribbons—Eternity
Not with gold but silver—almost bright!

The clouds attach—each to each—
Then helter-skelter, fly,
Obliterating light.

Letting go, oh who will teach
My Death—sobriety?
What will set my soul a-right?

The clouds swing Open—a loving reach—
As one who Thrills in gay society
With unexpected Love, release—and Light!"

Eight

So, as day transitioned to night, as Sita and some others crossed over, Emily and Virginia, visible once more, walked back to their B&B. They shared their quiet thoughts without speaking, feeling by the minute less and less bewildered by the sights and sounds of this strange age on earth. There are no bombs falling, Virginia thought, at least not here in this part of the world. Emily glanced at her and smiled. Outside a dress shop, across the street from Pony Espresso, a large hanging planter exploded two feet above Virginia's head.

Nine

Bits of crockery and the blasted colorful flower arrangement showered down on them as they instinctively hunched their shoulders and froze.

"Are you hurt?" a man asked. It was a policeman walking his beat who just happened to be there. Emily and Virginia checked themselves; they checked each other.

"We're fine—fine," said Emily.

"Such a strange occurrence," said Virginia. "Do the flowerpots often explode for no reason?"

"That was a shot, lady," said the officer. "I'd like to think it's an accident but..."

Two blocks away, Dick sprinted through the park entrance and did not stop running until he burrowed, panting, into the thicket cave. Concealed, safe, he hurled the rifle in his hands into a shadowy corner and sat down, shaking. From the shadows, Ula's strange cackle tormented him. "What did you do, Stinko?" She stepped into the half-light filtering through the cave branches and leered at him.

"I tried to frighten the do-gooders with this rifle," said Dick. His voice sounded hollow, resigned. "It was stupid. I regretted it even as I was doing it, but in this place it's so easy to get a gun!"

"Of course, you flubbed it," said Ula, "just like you botch everything. Did you screw up your whole life here? Your death, too? Why did they team me up with you? It would be funny if it was happening to someone else—but it's happening to me!" she screamed.

"Shut up, you revolting tub of guts!" said Dick. "If you don't stop, I'll..."

"You'll what!" said Ula. "Curl up into a ball, suck your thumb and cry? Oh! Ouch! Stop hurting me!" Her sarcasm dripped. Impotent, trapped, Dick ran out of the cave.

Still shaking, back at their B&B, Emily and Virginia sat on the divan together. They held hands, patting each other, fretting. Immortal, they couldn't really be killed again, so why worry? Yet now that they were back in this realm, they could feel the fear and fragility of existence here. They might even fail their Lily mission. Brigid's warning that this would not be a simple stroll in the park came back to them and they yearned to be home again with the Goddess of the well and the forge.

"Let's fortify ourselves with Brigid's sacred milk," said Emily, taking a bottle of milk from the little refrigerator and pouring two glasses. Handing one to Virginia she said, "The Goddess is with us, we who adore Her." They clinked their glasses together and drank.

Both ladies knew their own power and the power of each other. Both reasoned that their fear of the De la Nuit, if it was fear, was a good thing. It kept them on their toes. It motivated them. It pulled them back from distractions that might dissipate the energy they needed to succeed. The De la Nuit must be faced and thwarted. They knew that. Strengthened by renewed resolve, they promised each other that they would be more vigilant. They would be ready. They would watch each other's back.

Dick skulked around the duck pond five times, cooling off, and returned to the thicket cave. "We have to work together," he said, "so that we can get this over with and go back." Ula was silent. Dick was grateful for that, but he wondered if she was asleep.

"I'm awake," she said, answering his thought, "but I'm so depressed I can't talk, especially to *you*."

Ten

Aidan stared, surprised by the man standing at his door with a tiny monkey on his shoulder. The man was shorter than Aidan, not taller than 5' 10", perhaps a bit less. He was thin, bony, and dark with a thick, unkempt hedge of black hair. Aidan liked the man's long, dramatic nose and his blue eyes deep-set and searing. His hands looked like those of a gardener or printer. Something about the man's head made it seem too large at first, but the more Aidan looked, the more normal the head became. It was the thatch of hair, Aidan decided, not the size of the skull. The man wore a rumpled linen suit, and his right hand trembled. Rather than move, the two men froze in the doorway, as if the next step flummoxed both of them.

"I'm sorry," the man with the monkey said at last, and stepped forward as Aidan waved him in. "Thank you," he said, glad to feel the warmth of the apartment envelop him once Aidan shut the door. "You must be Aidan, of course."

"Yes," said Aidan, "I *am* Aidan. And who are you?"

The man chuckled. The monkey ran down his leg and darted into the kitchen. "Truly, I am out of practice," the man said. "I haven't greeted anyone like this for decades. Forgive me!"

"I forgive you," said Aidan, "but what shall I call you?"

"Call me Woolf. Leonard Woolf," and he held out his hand.

Aidan stepped back and laughed. He thought of making a nervous joke but remembered from somewhere that there was little in the historical record to suggest that Leonard Woolf had much of a sense of humor.

"You've a strong grip," said Leonard, "like the handshake of my co-translator of Gorky. He was fond of saying, when he encountered the genuine article, 'you are a real person!'"

"Are *you* a real person?" asked Aidan.

Leonard sighed. "Do I look and feel like one to you?" he asked. The monkey darted off the chair and scooted up the man's back to its perch on his shoulder. From there she grimaced and chattered at Aidan, who found it unnerving.

"Yes, you look real enough," said Aidan. "I can't deny that. That you are actually Leonard Woolf is more problematic."

"Directness is the best approach" said Leonard. "My wife asked me to come. Not that I couldn't have looked in on you on my own, but I've been preoccupied with work on a treatise about Divinity and its problematic role in the Hereafter, a subject I pooh-poohed when I resided in this realm. Now I find it fascinating, especially working with my fellow unbelievers, Mark Twain and Dot Parker. She's a cut-up, that Parker! Only Virginia rivals her."

Aidan watched the monkey going through his pen and pencil jar, making a mess of order. He thought of complaining but let it go. It's useless scolding a monkey, especially when it's some kind of super-natural monkey. Aidan wanted more clarity and he asked his visitor for it. After all, being poisoned makes one suspicious.

"It's just as I said," said Leonard. "Lily's 'Aunt' Virginia is my wife, Virginia Woolf. She and her friend, Ms. Dickinson of Amherst, Massachusetts and the Hereafter have come back to help Lily...and *you* now, I suppose, because you're also in danger."

"This would be too much," said Aidan, "if Lily hadn't shared so much with me just before I got sick. In hospital, I thought of how I'd met a beautiful woman by chance, saw her for coffee and dinner and wound up in hospital getting my stomach pumped. Digitalis, the police said. I could have died! Who would poison *me*? I hope it wasn't Lily because I might already be falling in love with her." Aidan stood before the man and monkey, temporarily out of words. Awkwardly, he managed to lead his guests into the living room and wave the man into a comfortable chair.

"Thank you," said Leonard. "I wonder...do you have some assorted nuts? For Mitz." Leonard nodded at the monkey.

"I'll check," said Aidan, and he went to the kitchen where Leonard could hear him opening and closing cupboards. Leonard could also hear him thinking and felt sorry for him. Success! He heard Aidan getting out a bowl and pouring nuts into it. As Aidan came back apologizing because the nuts might be old and stale, the monkey approved with emphatic chatter and gesticulations.

"That's an interesting monkey," said Aidan. "I mean, it *is* a monkey, right?"

"Yes, she's a marmoset, a gift from someone who couldn't keep her. It's almost too much to process, isn't it," said Leonard.

"I'm sorry?" said Aidan. "Oh, you know what I'm thinking before I say it." Leonard shrugged, his lips forming a tight smile.

"It's one of the perks of death," he said.

"It compresses conversation," said Aiden. "You *are* dead, yet you're very much alive, apparently, as are Virginia Woolf and Emily Dickinson. They're here because Lily called them and she and I are in danger. You're here because we need you. Is that accurate?"

"You couldn't be more on point," said Leonard, "and by the way, Lily did *not* poison you."

"I didn't really think so," said Aidan.

So, the two men talked as Mitz tore through the mixed nuts and scampered around the apartment. They talked about ghosts and religion. They talked about horticulture and travel. They talked about art and books and the way great love fit or did not fit into all of it. The Divine Feminine, they agreed, was making a comeback. Men would have to grow big ears and bigger hearts, they agreed. Listening and feeling were once again pulling even and in some cases just ahead of doing, they agreed.

As they talked, Aidan rummaged in his brain for historical dates. Just how old would this man be, he wondered. Leonard supplied the answer—137; it also happened to be his birthday. He told Aidan not to be alarmed by Mitz, who enjoyed scampering up to perch on Leonard's head. With the monkey sitting there, making faces, Leonard praised Lily. He praised love in the air and pressing one's advantage. He warned against self-sabotage and said he would be around any time Aidan might want to talk.

As the light faded, Leonard insisted they go for a walk. He had done his homework and knew of a very old orchard nearby with some 60 apple trees. It had been many years since he'd sunk his fingers in earth dirt. He was eager to observe new cultivation techniques—and pocket a sample or two. He described how working in a garden, an orchard or walking on the moors had always cleared his head. "I've battered your ears with advices long enough," said Leonard. "Come along!"

Eleven

"Letting oneself in can come as a Surprise," said Emily, as the sun lit up the auburn of her hair. "Don't you love the Sun, the hare with its wet, streaked fur?" she asked Lily as they met at Dobra for tea.

"Yes, I love the sun," said Lily, "because night and dreams give me a break when it shines."

"Yet, there is really nothing to Fear—in Night, or Dreams," said Emily. "Bees pour out of the hive as the Sun warms the fields; see how they riot among the waving Stalks of the lavender—outside the window. There! And there! Do you see?"

"They are busy," said Lily. "They are neither happy nor sad. They follow an instinct about which one can only guess."

"I suppose so," said Emily. "What do they tell you?"

"The bees?"

"The Bees—the Lavender—the invisible wind whose presence announces itself in the motion of Otherness."

Lily wondered what Emily meant by 'Otherness' and considered what the bees, lavender and wind were telling her, if anything. "I don't know," she said. "Perhaps they say don't think too much; they may tell me to move in my body as my body desires, to do my work because it's the work I have to do."

"And?"

"Is there more?"

"There is always—More!"

"Perhaps, but is more ever enough?"

"You will know It if it ever is," said Emily.

"Then I will know it when it is," said Lily, "and not before. I will know it without forcing it, without insisting."

"Do you wonder if you and Aidan might live that way, sharing the more that is enough? Internal difference where the Meanings, are?

Is that the question I've been looking for, and the answer? Lily did not say this but thought it as Emily sipped her tea and watched the bees at work. *Yes* flashed inside her, yet she felt no need to say it aloud; she knew that Emily knew what she was feeling and thinking. She saw her doomed parents on the deck of the ship, and they were smiling at her, oblivious to the desperate men with their guns that also appeared in her vision. She watched them smiling, suspended in a moment in time, yet living in her vision as present and future. They were like bees, Lily thought, and the men with their guns—they were like bees, too. As long as the sun shone on the water they would all be working and when the sun dipped below the horizon they would rest. Lily wondered about the hive. Where was it?

"Wherever it needs to be," said Emily, "and always the Bees—return to it. Where do *you* need to be?"

At my drawing table completing my task, Lily thought. Perhaps with Aidan in the moonlight, cuddling on a park bench in the warm summer air after eating a meal we have made together at my apartment or his, or after sharing a glass of wine at a restaurant. It doesn't matter where we begin, she thought, enjoying this romantic diversion. We've already begun, she thought. We are swarming and soaring and resting like the bees, like my parents wherever they've gone to, like the men with guns.

"Then it's enough—no more. Let's finish our tea—and you can be Going," said Emily.

"There's one thing more. It's important," said Lily. "My mother, my father. Did you put the image of them smiling into my head to comfort me? Can you and Aunt Virginia bring them back?"

Emily rang the little bell on the table that summoned the waiter, and he arrived with two mugs of tea. "You can't go yet," he said cheerfully. "The couple over there wants you to have these." He put the mugs before them, and both women turned to look at their benefactors. Because they were not looking at each other, Lily missed the expression of alarm that clouded Emily's face. She herself looked bemused; she did not recognize the couple and she searched her brain for an occasion when she might have met them. Nothing surfaced. Meeting Lily's (but not Emily's) eyes, the couple stood up, smiling and approached. "Thank you for this," said Lily, raising her mug. "Have we met?"

"Our pleasure," said the man, who was dressed in a tank-top, paisley yoga pants and sandals. He ignored her question. "May we join you?" the man asked. He pulled back a chair and sat down before Lily or Emily could say anything. His partner, a woman draped in blowsy linen that looked more like a tent than a dress, sat down, too, and watched Emily from the corner of her eye. "My name's Dick," said the man, "and this is Ula." Ula nodded but did not speak.

The smiles left neither of their faces, yet Lily felt for some reason she couldn't explain that they did not belong there. It was as if the smiles didn't match them, as if in a photograph you might put a different nose or mouth on the subject. Lily tried again. "I'm sorry, but I don't remember meeting you."

"You haven't," said Dick, who tried to stare at her but kept glancing at Emily. His smile neither flared nor flickered; it stayed just the same, which looked a little creepy.

"We knew your mother and father," said Ula, speaking for the first time. "We were all friends before you were born and when you were a baby. Sitting over there, we talked about how much you look like your mother. It just has to be, I told Dick. It has to be—what was her name? It was a flower—Rose? Jasmine?"

"Lily," said Lily. "Dick and Ula," she said. "I don't remember those names."

"Oh," said Ula, "kids don't know much about their parents' old friends before they came along. It's that pre-Copernican thing at work, you know?" No, she didn't know, thought Lily, but she did notice Emily rolling her eyes. Ula's voice sounded as if it had been roughed up by sandpaper.

"Anything wrong?" said Dick, looking at Emily and finally holding his eyes there. His smile dropped off his face as if someone had just slapped it.

Emily recognized the familiar look of the De la Nuit, that look between brain-death and malevolence, and she saw out of the corner of her own eye that Ula's expression was exactly the same. "Wrong? said Emily. "Nothing that can't be remedied by my friend and me—going on—our Way."

"Is that friendly?" said Ula, whose voice, Lily thought, changed from that of a choking bird feigning cheerfulness to that of a rattlesnake. "Maybe we should see Lily another time," she said to Dick, who nodded.

"I'd like that," said Dick, recovering his unnatural smile. "Wouldn't you like that, Lily?"

Lily knew the polite response, but emboldened by Emily's rudeness said, "I'm not certain that I would. Enjoy it, I mean. I don't know you. I don't recall my folks ever mentioning you."

"What if we showed you a letter from your father asking us to check up on you should anything ever happen to him and your mother?" said Dick.

"That was a bad business, that cruise," said Ula.

Lily faltered, her bravado melting like a Boardwalk ice cup on a blistering day. She no longer saw the shifty strangers so near, but watched in her head the familiar sequence of her parents' disaster. Emily touched her arm.

"Yes," said Lily, "I'd like to know more about your friendship with my mom and dad. I'd like to see that letter."

"Excellent!" said Dick. "Do you like pizza?" The smile faltered once more as he looked at Emily.

"I wish we could invite you, too," said Ula to Emily, "but you're probably busy and would find our conversation boring."

Leaning closer Dick added, "and we're on a tight budget. You understand." Dick sat back leering. "We have much to talk about, Lily," said Dick. "Tell all the truth but tell it slant, that's what I always say," said Dick. "Oww!" Someone had kicked him under the table. He glanced at Ula, who glowered at him. She had done it. She had kicked him! Just wait till I get her alone, he thought.

"Really!" said Emily. "That's what *you*—always Say? How clever. I might add—'Success in circuit lies'."

Dick's eyes looked like a possum's in a flashlight's beam, or a child's, his hand still in the cookie jar when the kitchen light blasts on. He'd been found out. He'd been caught reciting a line from one of Emily's most famous poems. How could he forget that? "Time to go," said Ula, poking Dick's arm. She stood up. Dick followed, rubbing his sore shin.

Lily felt an oppressive heaviness settling down on her. She roused herself, looking at Emily. "What do you make of *that?*" she asked.

"That was a smart-guy thing to do," said Ula out on the street. She slapped Dick so hard on the back he staggered and almost fell. "I always suspected you had a thing for that little insect-crazed enigma!"

"I dunno what you're talking about," Dick muttered.

"Really! You spout a line from her poetry and you don't know what I'm talking about! You clown," Ula said. "Now she and her scarecrow friend will be extra-vigilant. We'll have to go and get the girl. Time to wrap up this little comedy and beat it out of here—before you fall completely for that verse-spouting trollop."

Eleven

What does Mitz make of it all? Virginia wondered. With Emily and
Lily off together for tea, she waited for Leonard to arrive and give
her his report before skedaddling back to the portal. He had so many
next-realm things to do, he'd told her. He always did. No matter the
realm, Leonard prized meticulousness, schedules, order, attention to
detail.

Waiting, Virginia realized that she was feeling rather lonely. It
was an odd sensation after so long and she noted its presence almost
as a guilty pleasure. But there he was, there was Leonard tapping at
the door. No. It was Aidan. She waved him in, pointed to a chair and
grabbed a biscuit tin from the kitchenette. Aidan sat down and started in on the cookies, explaining that Leonard had come to see him,
Leonard and his monkey and that Leonard would be along later.

"Yes, Mitz!" said Virginia. "How did you like Mitz?" Aidan admitted that the monkey had made him nervous. He would have some
messes to clean up later. "There are always messes one must clean up
later," said Virginia. "What was your impression of my dear Leo?"

"I suppose I was also won over by his intensity and bearing. Was
he ever lighthearted in life?"

"You met Mitz," said Virginia, "and you ask that?"

"Yes, I'm sorry. The more we talked, the more I warmed to him."

"That makes me happy," said Virginia, "for I love my friends
to love each other. Of course it doesn't always turn out that way.
I couldn't stand Middleton-Murray, Katherine Mansfield's priggish
husband. An awful man and a Nothing writer. There were so many

awkward occasions with him! I remember once he ridiculed me because I was writing at my standing desk. I explained that it made me feel more like a painter to work that way and it kept me on my feet. I also loved stroking its smooth slanted surface."

Aidan had heard the same thing, that standing at a desk is better for your circulation. He remembered from his reading that Virginia had always been tactile, that she loved writing with a fountain pen but was always challenged finding the right nib. The wrong one, the wrong feel, could spoil her day and all her work. It was part of her 'illness' or her genius. Today, doctors prescribe a pill for it. Aidan wondered if Virginia ever thought how she might not have been mad at all had she been given lithium, but no one had heard of it in her day. By today's standards, her treatments were barbaric—rest cures, no reading, no writing, extended bedtime, unnecessary tooth extractions.

"I don't even want to recall the teeth I lost to nothing but a medical whim, a dental capriciousness," she said. "I know, I know. They felt they had to do *something*. I was sensitive to paper, too, to its texture, to its weight and color; sheets of paper had to be just so, and I had great trouble finding the right ones. But I succeeded sometimes! It must sound beyond finicky now, doesn't it? Remember, though, I was a woman that was devastated for twenty-four hours because my brother-in-law, Clive, once made fun of my hat. Life assaulted me and it romanced me. I was equally repelled and enchanted by life."

'Equally repelled and enchanted'—Aidan was finding that out. Past relationships could haunt one forever. Self-criticism could tear one down unless it was balanced with self-knowing. Sometimes it's hard to get used to these multiple lives we all have, Aidan thought. He thought of a balance in relationships and he wanted that. Yes, perhaps he could help Lily with these questions; maybe she could help him.

"Yes," said Virginia, "you can help each other."

"We can hurt each other, too."

"Of course," said Virginia, "but you can choose to hurt each other non-fatally. There will be arguments, fights, disagreements always, but you can hold on to the pact between you that says you shall endure together no matter what comes. You can always make up after a row."

"Easier said than done," said Aidan, staring out the window at the houses across the leafy street. Sunlight was harsh on them now, flintier than the light in a painting by Edward Hopper. It suited his mood.

"I said nothing about it being easy," Virginia said. "However, it can and ought to be graceful and kind. What is there to gain by going through it any other way? I still marvel at the fact that my marriage lasted through its first year. I was quite mad! They sent me away and confined me for many months. I said awful things to my husband; the worst possible things! I assaulted the nurses. I even attacked my beloved sister. Yet, my love for Leonard grew and he proved steadfast. He did not desert me. I wrote him love letters from the loony bin!" At this she threw back her head and laughed a deep hooting laugh until the tears came to her eyes. Regaining control, she continued. "He loved getting those letters, said he knew then that everything would be all right and for all of our marriage, which stopped, sort of, as you know only when I died, everything was better than all right. We weathered every minor and major crisis because we loved each other. There were no tests. We just were...together. Inseparable."

Aidan listened, still looking intently out the window. He thought of the people living alone and the couples living in those houses below. Here was one now. A cab pulled up in front of the grey four-square with the white trim and a middle-aged man got out, then reached back with extended hand. With it, he assisted a plump, modestly dressed woman from the taxi. They smiled at each other and walked up to the building. They paused, kissing. The man inserted a key in a door, opened it and followed the woman inside. There, thought Aidan. There it is.

"There it is," said Virginia, watching the same scene over Aidan's shoulder, "through time immemorial. One leans back, holding out a hand and helps another across a threshold. One second to another, one moment to another, one century to another, one world to another, hands are extended, help is offered; the offer is accepted or brushed aside or blindly missed."

"The hand is accepted or batted away," said Aidan, "just as a kiss is shared, or rejected by a lowering of the head that takes the eyes and lips out of play. I have lost kisses like that and potential lovers with them. And all the while, one's pathetic little heart-battered, spirit voice puffs up heroically and proclaims 'No! I will *not* be hurt again!'"

"But one *is* hurt again," said Virginia. She had often felt a suspension and release of feeling after an eight-mile jaunt through fields and marshes and hills; she would come back to herself damp or drenched, shivering, her clothes torn and muddy, her hands and arms scratched and bruised and bloody, with twigs and burrs and more than once, small pieces of barbed wire stuck in her thick, disheveled hair.

Every day, she remembered, she would write from 10 to 1, but the writing would not leave her there. Throughout the rest of the day and night, she worked out passages in her head, composing scenes, chasing after her own voice, *stumbling* is the word she used once to describe it, and the voices that came to her, always flooding her with words so that they often seemed not her own. There are so many clinical words now for what she was, she thought. But then they had so few, and none of them fit.

"Without Leonard," she said, "I would have disappeared beneath the waves much sooner than I did. I would have blown apart and never finished half of what I managed to do. He took charge of me, of my health. He studied my mind until he possessed a fine, intuitive grasp of it. He understood better than anyone (except, at times, Vanessa) what I needed in order to go on. Rest, milk, food, a regimen that kept me steady, though some part of me was always itching to break free, to break out of a normal life. I was never like the others. I lived on a taut tether between sanity and insanity and four times in my life I crossed over. The last time, I met my death, the one event I said I would not describe, though lately I've had a go at it! It's such fun to die and come back! What a delight! But I am going off again, even now; I am going out too far and in danger of losing sight of my raison d'etre.

"Have you ever noticed," said Virginia, "how we start out on some great expedition with a goal, only to discover new goals along the way? It's like that, always, as long as consciousness turns its wheel in us. I can't be content with this result or that. I must be moving forward, always forward to some new discovery. That's what I am made of. I think it's true for everyone, though we each creep along in our unique ways. Do you feel you are creeping along, Aidan, or leaping like a water strider across vast stretches?"

"Definitely creeping," said Aidan.

"Well, then," said Virginia, "calm your mind and ask me what you came here to ask me."

"You and Emily," he said, "you have...powers we don't. I know Lily is chafing to ask you about her parents and I thought..."

"You thought you might ask about your father. Oh, Aidan, there is no easy way to break this. I asked sweet Mother Brigid about him. She looked into it and informed me that he is among our enemy. Not by choice and maybe not forever, but there it is." Virginia was silent, giving Aidan all the time he needed to process what he'd just learned.

The cookies were gone. Aidan fingered the crumbs on his napkin, his face cloudy. Compulsively, he hugged Virginia, thanking her. She held onto him, rocking gently. Separating, she saw that his eyes were moist. "Aidan, this has been the great mystery of your life. As often happens when we find an answer at last, we realize even that lacks closure, yet it also opens new doors to greater mystery—and Hope—as my dear Lightning Bug would say."

"So," said Aidan, "you're saying that at some point my father may still be redeemable?" Virginia smiled, petting his hair. "Go home now and get some rest. You're still recovering. And don't forget! The four of us are having dinner in two days.

But what *about* Mitz? Virginia wondered, reboarding the train of thought she'd been on before Aidan's unexpected visit. Now he was gone she could parse it out, the mystery of Mitz.

As long as she was with Leonard, Virginia knew, the monkey would not fear going back and forth through the portal. Leonard was Mitz's anchor, her kin, her guide. In many ways, Virginia mused, the monkey wasn't all that different from her in her own relationship with Leonard. But what was the monkey thinking? Did she think at all? Of course she must have some thoughts. Virginia remembered the times she asked that very question of her husband, who would respond by saying 'she thinks what she needs to think, and that's all; she doesn't make thinking as complicated as we do.' That had always satisfied her, but now? Weren't they all together again, here, in a new arrangement, on a different level of experience? Just what *did* Mitz know, and when and how did she know it?

By asking what she knows and when and how she knows it, Virginia thought, I am testing my own process of knowing and not knowing. Much of what I knew when I was first here I still know; and I know more. I know what everyone thinks and when they think it. I know many things I wondered about but could not know when I was here. I know the treacherousness of jealousy and greed, and the relief and expansion of the absence of both. But even now I do not know what an animal really thinks, unless, as I did with the spaniel in *Flush*, I make a person out of it. So, I do not know what the monkey knows, close cousin and housemate though she may be. But I would like to know. I am in the mood to know. What does Mitz think about Lily and Aidan? About love? What's her considered opinion about world-hopping? As long as Leo is with her, I imagine she is up for anything. Do we differ so much in this regard? It must be loyalty and love that keeps her near us, else why didn't she scamper to the highest treetop the moment the fog of portal travel cleared in her tiny head?

"I must conclude," said Virginia, talking to herself, "that she stays because she understands something, but what? I suppose I'll never really know and must be satisfied with Leonard's answers when I question him. It was always hard to be satisfied with someone else's answers despite the love that connected us, but it is less difficult now. Really, it's not at all difficult. Where before my question erupted with a certain desperate tempestuousness, now it comes on a placid cloud of benign curiosity. It would be fun to know what the monkey thinks of it all. It would be interesting. But it's not like I must know. There is nothing I must know; just some few things, some odd things, it would be fun to know."

"I'll tell you what Mitz thinks," said Leonard, joining Virginia at table, helping himself to one of his own biscuits and delivering another into the monkey's clutching claws. "Mitz thinks that wherever she goes, wherever she looks, you will be there vying for my affection and attention, stealing the lion's share of my love. She thinks 'I am cold, I am hot, I am hungry'. She claims her perch on my shoulder where she surveys her kingdom and pisses down my back when the urge moves her. I don't object. She is merely following her nature. She thinks I am always carrying her to food or to rest; every now and then to a bath, which she despises and against which she rages, sometimes even resorting to biting me. In these protestations, she is not unlike you at your worst when I overcome your resistance to feed you and keep you alive. Like you, after a blow-up she is chagrined, ashamed and eager to make it up to me. She thinks that I like it when she helps me during the apple harvest and I do. She climbs to the higher apples, plucks them from the tree and throws them down to me, or to the ground when I miss her toss, which is half the time or more. She thinks that we—Leonard and Virginia—worry each other so. When I look at you and think 'I would like to kiss her', Mitz interprets that energy in me and screeches at you. She does not understand all the talking that goes on between us. She does not follow it; it bores her. If she were human, she would not be much of a reader. I'm afraid she would not stand at Cambridge. She would, however, be tireless in her devotion to duty as she perceived it, as indeed she is. She would make an excellent civil servant. She is fearless in her way, and thinks the same of everyone, until one proves one can't be trusted. She is tender, and she believes we need tenderness. One winter when you were ill and confined to bed for a month, Mitz climbed the stairs every day to keep you company for an hour. Remember how she would bring you a piece of a biscuit, a tiny handful of nuts, a slice of fruit? She is always thinking of food, if there will or won't be enough and what she has to do to get it. Her thinking is elemental. She neither ascribes motive to another nor has any herself. In life and out of life, she is Mitz and nothing else. But if you insist, if you press me to say, I will tell you that her single most important thought is a question: *When do I eat?"*

Twelve

Leonard was gone. Aidan had come and gone. Lily was home, probably asleep. Emily and Virginia sat close together on the sofa gazing at the moon.

"Lest we forget where we're from now, our dear Sister above is always there—to remind us," said Emily. She had come back to their rooms troubled, and she dove right in, telling Virginia the story of the De la Nuit couple intruding, lying and baiting Lily. "There was something more—the man—if you could call him that," said Emily. "He did something I did not—Expect. He spoke a line of Poetry—*My* Poetry." Virginia pressed Emily's hands between her own.

"He knows you!" said Virginia. "Or he knows of you. Should I be jealous or relieved?"

"Don't be silly!"

"I'm sorry," said Virginia. "I didn't mean to make light of it. How awful it must have been! And how brave you were to stare him down. But, think. Did you ever know him?"

"That's what's been—Tormenting—me," said Emily. "I want to say—Yes—but I can't place him—Anywhere!"

"It's possible he is so changed, given the company he's kept, that you can't recognize him."

"I've considered that," said Emily. "It's true—or Not—I can't Tell! Did he love me once? Is he death incarnate? Do I sense Harm? Anguish?"

"Or both?" Virginia added.

"Nothing compares to love but—the formal feeling of Death," said Emily. "It broke me open—It remade me. I was never happier than when I followed the voices sweetly calling—'Come, Emily, Come!'

"The lead-up to Death—that was Hard. My lungs were not happy; my kidneys Groaned and Rebelled. My puffy eye—Stung—the Pallor of my Flesh frightened Vinnie and Others—attending me. The Doctors—in my time—as in yours—Dear Goat, gave my Illness their best guesses. For learned men, Doctors could be so very—Stupid! Even today, Doctors don't quite agree on what Killed me. Bright's Disease? That went on the Death Certificate. But a modern favorite—Extreme Hypertension—which led to high blood pressure and could have resulted in heart attack or a brain hemorrhage. Not that I cared. I heard Voices—and I was going. Nothing could have brought me back once I heard the voices and understood them."

"I left not knowing we would all meet again," said Virginia. "Leo was an atheist & such a cynic! Outwardly, I went along with him, but all through my writing I washed up many times on the shore of belief & did not always row away. You say that you heard voices, divine L-Bug; I heard voices, too, as I stood in the cold river with the water above my waist & threatening to tear my legs out from under me, which it did, eventually. The voices I heard—they sounded like fish & underwater plant & tree root voices—made it possible for me to let go, to sink & not fight back. I went under, deeper, deeper, & made my way towards the voices that soothed me, that kept me calm—if one who is drowning *can* be calm. The voices I heard helped me navigate the currents as I died; they guided me to the bottom & back up. They held my body back from the sea because Leo just had to know without the slightest doubt that I was destroyed. He required visible proof. He did not hear voices like we did."

"There are Voices—for everyone!" said Emily. But many block them out and deny them. The Voices are real—as we are! Through the Voices, all of us come together—again—and know one another for who we are. It was always so. It *is* always so."

"Yet how much less chaotic life would be," said Virginia, "if everyone listened and welcomed the Voices as they came, when and where they came."

"Yes!" said Emily. "The life of Inner & Outer—indistinguishable one from the other. Together Always—Linked!"

"It's good to feel & hear our old voices wrap around these words," said Virginia. "I have missed the sounds & sensations of that experience, the rhythm of fiction that is truer than journalism."

"For Us," said Emily, "yearning is a willow switch—a violation of Library! Yes. Let's agree not to speak of it to Lily, to Aidan. It would only worry and confuse them. Or—if we do speak of it, let Us do so—Carefully—Skillfully."

Thirteen

"How can you be hungry again, Blotch-Face, after all that pizza?" Ula wanted to know. Dick threw silent bombs at her and did not answer. They squatted in the shadows outside Lily's apartment building. They had been there, fidgeting, for a long time. They hoped that Lily would walk out alone so that they could jump her, subdue her and drag her to the portal in the park. Really, the plan in both of their heads was vague, haphazard. Confused, their reason was unreasonable, but try to tell them that. They were two Calibans, eternally pestered by Ariel's nips and stings. It was intriguing, being back and more or less on their own in this world, but they were frightened, too. Everywhere they looked there was change and the fear of having to think for themselves. They must have done so, thought for themselves, at some point in their earlier lives, here or elsewhere, but where, and when? Both of them stopped short of internal investigation. Perhaps they knew instinctively that it would only lead to unendurable agony. In this suspicion, they were right.

"Stop thinking!" Simultaneously, they both said it. They looked at each other, then burst into their versions, hideous though they were, of laughter. The sound was worse than the cacophony of passionate alley cats. Someone yelled for quiet. Frightened, Dick and Ula crossed the street, running.

Five blocks later, they stopped, looking at each other for an explanation, for direction, yet all they met were looks not unlike the expressions of sheep that can't recall the field they were in five minutes ago or how they ever got to where they're standing.

"You coward!" Ula hissed.

"You shrew," said Dick, spitting into the gutter. They knew that they had panicked, that they had to go back. It was going to be a long night.

Lily put down her pencil and pushed back from the drawing table. There they were—four pages impeccably drawn and inked, the story advanced, the characters deepened and shaded with greater complexity. She was tired, but the energy rising from the page felt good. Sometimes she knew when her work was good, when it wasn't; this moment was such a time. "I know these are good," she told herself. She looked at the dancing figures—one yellow, the other sea-green (sun & moon?)—in one drawing, their backs to us. In the center just above their heads, Lily had created a glowing third eye within an object that looked like a stretched, ripe fig. The fig pulsed with energy. She was pleased with the plant tendrils that joined the dancers together. The tendrils looked like musical notes, or letters in a mysterious alphabet and all of this movement, like wind, played against an almost mauve, anchoring background. Gazing deeply into her drawing, Lily perceived a fertility rite and an initiation into partnership. That was a good day's work.

Through her window, the setting sun drew buttery, gold bars across her finished pages and the tabletop; the gold bars crisscrossed her forearms and extended up and down the wall to her right and behind her. She loved how nature made of herself and everything it touched a painting, an empathic expression of art. That's what she was after! She realized she wanted the confidence that dared to see and express the connectedness of everything. That's what Vanessa Bell talked about in her articles and letters when she wrote about painting—the necessity of seeing the thing honestly and Whole. On this afternoon she had tapped into her courage and confidence.

One of Lily's Panels

Now, how to make an everyday occurrence of it? Soon the street-lights would come on. They would be virtually invisible for most of an hour in the natural light, but as the sky darkened the streetlights would assert themselves, glowing eerily yellow against the black back-drop of the sky.

"I could sit here all night watching the light change," Lily told herself. "I could lose myself in the changing light, sans thought, sans feeling, sans everything." What would happen, she wondered, if she lost herself and never returned?

Fourteen

"I don't see why I should have to wait," said Lily after introducing Shaya, whom she'd decided to include, to Emily, Virginia and Aidan. They were meeting for dinner at Porters in Medford and they settled in to a curtained booth that suggested one was dining in a sleeper car aboard a train. The booths were hard to get, and Lily appreciated Aidan's resourcefulness and timing.

"Wait for what?" Aidan asked.

"For you to forgive me after what happened to you the last time we went out to dinner."

"I'm waiting to see what happens after we eat," said Aidan, smiling. "I'm glad you like the booth. I thought your 'aunts' would appreciate the privacy. And Shaya, too."

While they studied their menus, Lily launched into the line of inquiry that most excited her. "Aunt Em," she began, looking across the bread basket and water glasses into Emily's eyes the color of the sherry the guest leaves, "shouldn't you and Aunt Ginny take me into your confidence about everything?"

"*Everything?*" asked Virginia, arching one eyebrow.

"Respect Circumference," said Emily, her voice rising in pitch and energy. "The Bee is always questing—within the parameters of the Social Hive! Happiest is She who emulates the Bee."

"And the butterfly," Virginia added. "Let us not, in our homage to bugs, short-change the butterfly."

Emily smiled. "You are right, dearest!" Turning to Lily she said, "do you Understand—what we're saying?"

"I think so," said Lily. "You're saying that you cannot, or will not tell me everything."

"Neither 'cannot' nor 'will not' are quite accurate," Emily said, "but they'll suffice."

"We want you to know," Virginia added, "that there is a sequence of events, a stream of information unique to each experience and every person. You must make your own discoveries without undue influence from the likes of us, or anyone. Otherwise, you will miss out on living your precious life. We will not encourage that!"

"But my curiosity..."

"Unnerves you! It could even kill You!" Emily finished, embellishing Lily's sentence and thought for her. Suddenly lowering her menu and locking eyes with Shaya, she said "what do *you* think?"

Shaya drew back, nervous, yet game. "I'm still trying to wrap my mind around the fact that I am sitting in a restaurant with..."

"It's all right, my dear," said Virginia, patting Shaya's hand.

"...Emily Dickinson and Virginia Woolf! I mean, it sounds absurd to say it and yet...here you are. I mean, if it's you, really. I mean, Lily says it's you and I love Lily but..."

"I want to vouch for their authenticity, too," said Aidan. Shaya looked at Aidan and smiled.

"So far so good!" said Shaya. "As for deeper questions, well, I trust a lot in letting things develop as they will. I don't think that we're ever as smart as we like to make ourselves out to be."

"Bravo, Shaya!" said Virginia. "You have more than a little philosophy in you!"

"Not that I didn't think, at first," Shaya continued, "that if you *were* real, you should be able to produce Lily's mom and dad. But now it seems natural that you have good reasons why you won't—or can't."

Lily absorbed the conversation and examined her feelings, concluding that she could not be cross with Aunt Emily or with any of them. Her aunts knew more than she did. For a long time, they would know more. After a long time, they would pool their knowledge. It would be a long time, but it would not be forever. Forever would be longer than the wait before her now and she knew enough to be certain that it would be worth it—the waiting.

"It's not really in our power to bring anybody back," said Virginia. "Good mother Brigid shoulders that responsibility. Where your parents are concerned, we can assure you that they are well but still transitioning. You can't see them now, but you will, someday. Until then you have dreams. You have seen them in dreams, Lily, and you will see them more often and you will talk to each other."

It was enough. Awareness would expand and envelope her. She would be content. She, too, might become an aunt to somebody, to many, perhaps, and she might come and go, a guardian, perhaps. She had many selves to learn about. She must recognize nearness even as she had far to go; and *stillness*—she had that to learn, too. "I have wondered," said Lily, "where the voices come from. Do they begin in an old and young place? A Before-Time? My voices are some versions of my mother's voice and father's voice when I am in my crib in a yellow room. They mingle with their altered voices aboard ship. They are older and raspier on the ship. Their voices are frightened on the ship. I am not with them, but their killer, a pirate, is with them. It takes an instant for him to kill them, yet even after that, their voices rattle on inside me. I hear them, their voices and the gunman's—the killer's voice. Also, I hear the voices of dogs we owned; their voices are guttural and curious, made up of rotting leaves and broken branches and wood smoke. I hear the voices of mentors, always teaching, always dependable, and friends and acquaintances, those dead and those vanished. The voices of the quietly dead are the calmest voices of all. I can fall asleep to them when I dare to sleep, when I take the trouble to sink down and go."

"It does not matter where the voices come from, or who they are, but how one lives with them, or chooses *not* to," said Virginia. "How these voices show off! They vie with one another for attention, for a defining moment when someone from this realm says, 'yes, I recognize you! *This* is who you are!'

Virginia explained that the voices do not intend an assault but assimilation. When she who hosts the voices goes awry, it's because the voices, feared and not fully understood, overwhelm her. "Do not fear, and let be," said Virginia. "This is the true method for living with and learning from one's voices. Linking these voices to characters is the writer's art; it's our art, Emily's and mine. Matching them to color and shadow and outline is the painter's art, the illustrator's art. That's you. That's your way as it was (and is) Nessa's way. Together, we create the epic of life."

Lily thought about how she had often been stopped by her voices because she did not want to see them emerge, change and evolve on her canvases, on her papers. She eluded them, and in doing so escaped looking into the eyes of her dead parents, her long-gone friends, animals she cared for and herself in the mirror. Well, she thought, I am feeling a new eagerness, a quick desire to listen. I shall invite the voices in and encourage them to make of us all what they will.

A plump middle-aged woman with short, dyed hair and irritated capillaries inflaming her cheeks stopped at their booth on her way through the dining room. She looked surprised and confused. "Excuse me," she said, staring at Emily. "I'm sure you get this all the time," she continued, "but you look so much like the poet Mary Oliver. You aren't Mary Oliver, are you?"

"No, I'm not," said Emily. "Sorry!"

"Oh, I don't want to bother you," said the woman. She hesitated, unable to go. "Ok, then. Uh...you're sure you're not? Because I love Mary Oliver's poetry! I've read everything!"

"Sorry," said Emily, clicking her tongue as she shook her head. At last the woman broke free of her invisible tether. Doubtful, looking back at Emily, she moved on. Emily looked at Virginia and said, "Who is Mary Oliver?"

"Never heard of her," said Virginia.

"She's a famous poet," said Shaya.

"Oh, *really*," said Emily. Was that indignation, Lily wondered? Could her Aunt Em be annoyed by a famous contemporary poet?

"Apparently, yes, she could," said Virginia.

"You may not be Mary Oliver," said Lily, but do you know, Aunt Emily, that you are the subject and star of a hit TV show?"

"On the telly?" Virginia asked.

"Yes, on Apple TV+. It was created by Alena Smith, has a terrific cast and stars the incredible actress and singer/songwriter, Hailee Steinfeld, as you. It's called *DICKINSON*. You ought to catch it while you're here."

"On the telly," Virginia sniffed. Was it her turn to feel a little off? Lily noticed.

"Don't fret, Aunt Ginny. Nicole Kidman won an academy award playing *you* in a movie."

"You say this actress plays me?" Emily asked. "Has *she* won any awards?"

"A couple," said Lily, "yet she should have won the academy award for her first film role. The show won a Peabody award."

Virginia decided it was time to change the subject. "On our way over, we were debating about what to do tomorrow. Naturally, I would prefer a trip to Mt. Ashland and a river walk, while L-Bug could spend all day wandering through local gardens and bakeries. What do you think we should do?"

"Split up," said Aidan. Like every man, he could be quick on the trigger, wanting to fix a problem before it grew a life of its own, before it expanded to become something too big for him or any man to fix. Isn't that really what men fear most? thought Lily. Good-natured, Aidan plowed ahead. "You could split up, or you could take two days and do both together."

"How practical you are, Aidan!" said Virginia. She enjoyed flattering him.

"Or you could explore Lithia Park together," said Shaya, who was very fond of it. "A couple of years ago," Shaya went on, "it was named by the American Planning Association as one of the 10 Great Public Spaces in America."

"Impressive!" said Emily.

"I didn't know that," said Aidan.

"Tell us more!" said Virginia.

"Well, the park is 93 acres of forested canyon land around Ashland Creek. Lithium Oxide—'lithia'—was found in the water and that's how the park got its name. The water is supposed to possess healing properties. John McLaren was the landscape architect for the park. He also designed San Francisco's gorgeous Golden Gate Park. I'd like to become a landscape architect," said Shaya.

As they talked, the meal had wound down. Beating Aidan to it, Emily reached for the check and slid it between Virginia's long, tapered fingers. Virginia did not object. She opened her bag, counted out the money to satisfy the bill, consulted briefly with Emily about a tip ("I'm terrible doing the math for tips," she said to Lily, Shaya and Aidan), and put money on the table.

"Give the Goat more sugar," Emily said to Lily, waving her hands in front of her as if she were a conductor orchestrating waves of her own sentences. "She requires a Liquor never brewed!"

One dewy pat of cold butter, launched by the catapult of Virginia's knife, shot upward, then plunged towards Emily's plate and landed nicely atop a buttermilk biscuit. Virginia's smile was sly, even merry, as she leaned into Lily. "This is the point," she said, "where Leonard would come around the table, lift me out of my chair and guide me upstairs to my bed before I lost greater control of myself. Then he would come back and scold our guest for exciting me. Look, now. No one comes!"

Fifteen

"No one comes," said Ula. "Mush-Face, we must do something about that."

Sixteen

The plays were over, the restaurants shuttered. Two open-late bars on the Plaza gently but firmly shooed the drunken diehards away, sending them out with designated drivers or calling for cabs. Late shift servers and bartenders gritted their teeth and told themselves they could bear it, that their agony was almost over. Two foot-patrolmen, one thin, one chubby, parked themselves on a corner, keeping their eyes on the bars and the entrance to the park. The thin one yawned and because yawns are contagious, his stout partner yawned, too. Down the stairs from The Brick Room, Dick and Ula stepped onto the street obscured by rising ground fog. "Our kind of weather," said Ula. Crossing the Plaza, they headed uptown. Brisk walking delivered them to Lily's door, which Dick boldly rattled with loud knocks.

Rousted by the racket from a deep sleep, Lily padded to the door, saw no one through the peephole and said, "Who is it?"

"Friends," Ula croaked.

"Friends," said Dick. "We met in the teahouse. Remember?"

Lily frowned, scratching her head. "It's late," she said through the door.

"We have important news," said Ula. "

"Emily and Virginia sent us," Dick lied.

Lily threw back the bolt and opened the door. "Come in," she said. "What's wrong?"

"Nothing's wrong, nothing," said Dick. "We just need you to come with us to the park."

"It's important; it's a secret, it's a breakthrough" said Ula.

"What?" Lily said. Part of her regretted opening the door and letting them in. She was confused and curious. Why would Emily and Virginia want her to come to the park in the middle of the night? It had to be serious. It had to be important. But weren't these two the enemy?"

"No, we are not the enemy," said Ula. "We're actually allies under deep cover. We're working *with* your aunts!"

"Will they be there, at the park?"

"Of course," Ula said, trying her best but failing to sound friendly and conspiratorial. "You'll see!"

"Ok, give me five minutes to dress," said Lily, and off she went to her bedroom while Dick and Ula sat on the sofa, nervous, fidgeting. Ula noticed that Dick was doing things with his hands.

"What are you doing with your hands?" said Ula. The words came out of her mouth like a hiss.

"Sorry?" said Dick, who wasn't sorry, not one bit. That the two of them constantly scratched at each other suited them. In this world, in the world next door, it made no difference. It would be hard to imagine them *not* carping at each other.

"Your hands," growled Ula through her ground-down, yellow teeth.

"I'm trying to make animals on the wall," Dick said. "Look." Ula looked, but all she could see on the wall opposite were shifting blobs made of shadow.

"You suck," she snorted. "Watch me!" and Ula pushed him over to work with the light. Instantly the wall came alive with an unmistakable giraffe. An impressive elephant followed, then a bear, and oh, what was that? How cute! A diminutive field mouse.

"Ok," said Dick, who almost shouted. "You do it better! You do everything better. Are you happy now?"

It occurred to Ula that Dick might actually cry, but that didn't stop her hands. She was enjoying herself. "Aww, poor baby!" she said.

"Are your feelings hurt?" Her snaky, snide tone whipped out and wrapped itself around Dick and squeezed. "Well," said Ula, "enjoy your *feelings* (she fairly spat the word); you'll be back soon enough where you won't have any." Putting an end to any further escalation of their repartee, Lily came back into the room.

"Ready!" she said, oblivious to what had been going on between them. Grabbing a coat from the hall tree, Lily cut the lights and they were off.

Virginia sat bolt upright in bed. She threw back the covers, leaped up and started dressing. "L-Bug!" she shouted. "L-Bug, wake up!" Emily stirred in the bed, turned on her back and stretching, opened her eyes. "Hurry, my dear, they've got her!" That was all Virginia needed to say. Emily was also on her feet, dressing as fast as she could.

It was just past two in the morning when they stopped at the entrance to Lithia Park, and of course no one else was there. "Let's go," said Ula, but Lily held back. She would rather wait there for Emily and Virginia, she told them. She was afraid of the park at night. Had they missed the posted notices of a mountain lion sighting just days ago? "Nonsense!" Ula snapped at her. "They can catch up," she said, meaning Emily and Virginia. "They'll know where to find us," she said, not meaning it at all. She signaled Dick, who stepped up close to Lily and gripped her arms above the elbows.

"Don't squirm or look away!" he commanded. "Look in my eyes! You shall soon be first among the Last! You shall lead our processions of darkness. With us you'll shun the light." Lily looked and suddenly she felt heavy, as if thick smoke were oozing through her body, clogging her brain. She wanted to protest, but she couldn't speak. She heard Dick's voice saying over and over, *you are needed, you are needed.*

Wait, who needed her? For what? She understood Dick's words, but what he said made no sense. She was only certain of Dick's and Ula's urgency. That was it; they were urgent. Rather than making her feel important, needed, it made her nervous, even frightened.

"Where are we going?" Lily muttered. The sound of her own voice surprised her. It was hers, all right, but it was also her voice in the process of becoming someone else's voice. She wanted to stop it, this confiscation of her voice. She knew she needed to stop it soon or lose it forever. Somehow, she sensed that losing her voice meant losing all of her. She didn't want that, but she felt powerless, unable to stop it.

"Don't try to stop it," Ula said. "Give in, child! Don't you want to see your mother, your father?"

But even this promise did not reassure her. It was the way Ula said it, sarcastically adding that of course she probably wouldn't recognize them or be able to communicate with them. What did she mean by *that*? Where were they going? Lily tried to ask once more, but her voice slurred, the words indistinguishable, like vivid dream-words forgotten in waking. Maybe that was it. Was she dreaming? No, she was walking, stumbling, rather, between Ula and Dick, who pressed close to her sides and held her arms tight. Ula's mouth was close to her ear, telling her she was a lucky girl, telling her it wasn't just any-one who was chosen to lead processions of the De la Nuit, telling her she'd love traveling through a portal.

The De la Nuit? She was chosen? What for? Lily wondered. They were going to do what? Travel through a portal? An image of Alice in Wonderland flashed in her mind but just as quickly vanished. She thought it would be good to get away from these people, to disappear and be by herself, but she was too heavy, too thick to move without them. She was able to focus for a moment, just long enough to know they were passing the playground. She was conscious of Ashland Creek rushing off to their right. She even fancied, for a second, that she heard the guttural cough of a cougar. Normally, the sound would have chilled her, but she was already frightened deep in her marrow.

Lily did not know when they stopped walking, or how long they'd been standing before the shriveled and scarred oak tree. Dick and Ula stared at the opening at the base of the tree and chanted words that were incomprehensible. Their recitation went on and it seemed to Lily in her stupefaction that a heavy brown mist swirled up out of the hole—the portal—at the tree's base. A foul, wet latrine smell filled her nostrils; she felt she was fighting everything and everyone just to stay awake. The chanting went on and on. Why don't they stop? Lily wondered, but she could not ask them to and they did not stop. They chanted. And as they chanted, was it true, Lily wondered, that they were all getting smaller? No, not smaller; less...substantial? Was that the word? There had to be a word, Lily thought, for what was happening to them.

"There are two words, not one." Lily heard the voice as if it were real, but no, it had to be a voice in her head, but it wasn't. The voice wasn't inside her. She thought that the voice came out of a tree, but she saw that the voice belonged to the woman who stepped out from behind that tree. Emily. *Aunt* Emily. "Hypnosis," Emily said. "Abduction," she said. "Those are the words—for Everything that is going on here."

"STOP!" It was Virginia's voice; it was Emily's voice and Brigid's voice, too. For there between Virginia and Emily stood a magnificent, glowing woman all in white with flaming, long red hair. The woman threw out her arms, the sky thundered and her aura expanded as a pillar of fire. Letters pouring out of her formed in the air, visible letters that joined to make words and animate the mist into a pool of circling waves. Words and ampersands swirled; dashes appeared and, elongated, encircled Lily, Emily, Virginia and the weird couple. They bound the couple to each other and Lily to Emily and Virginia. Emily stepped forward, reached into the cosmogony, found Lily's hand and drew her away from the wailing, terrified couple.

Lily's head cleared instantly, though she was still woozy. The chanting had stopped. Slowly, the mist began to clear and the stench to dissipate. The whirling letters, ampersands and dashes faded. Lily became aware of Virginia, *aunt* Virginia, standing close by her side and holding her hand, and Emily, *aunt* Emily, holding the other. But where was the bright, terrible, magnificent woman? She was gone.

"You rattle-headed, squishy-jointed, mush-faced mud blots!" said Virginia to Ula and Dick. Virginia's imperious tone and accent exquisitely skewered the cowering figures above the portal, which looked cold and remote where only a moment ago it had seemed so diabolically alive. "Now that you've brought down on yourselves the wrath of Brigid," said Virginia, "it looks as if you can't even go back. Look at that clogged hole. Ashes and cinders."

Dick and Ula looked at the base of the tree and quivered like aspens. Dick quietly wept. He wept with such silent force that Lily thought (and rather hoped) that he might actually choke to death on his own tears. Ula punched Dick's arm. "Stop blubbering!" she commanded. "Be a shadow-man," she barked, but it would take more than that before Dick's pity party spent itself. Ula gave up on her partner and turned on Emily and Virginia. "What about you two goody-goods?" she said. Her voice screeched from the higher registers, but her rage was impotent. "Someday," said Ula, "you'll both be as brain-dead as this little tootsie was, or almost was until you spoiled it! You spoiled it!" She screamed, a sound sufficiently alarming to provoke a response from a nearby screech owl.

"Be careful," said Virginia, "or friend owl will swoop down and snatch out your rheumy eyes." Ula instinctively hunched her shoulders and dropped her head as if the thing Virginia said would come true at once.

"Or the Hornets—Deep inside The Tree," said Emily, "will explode & cover—You—like dark buzzing Clouds." Dick's knees buckled. Moaning, he rolled back and forth on the ground in front of the portal. Ula shouted at him to stop, but he had crossed to a different track than the one she was still on. Bending down, she hissed in his ear to get up or else.

"Get up or I'll leave you here," said Ula.

With an effort that surprised them all, Dick calmed himself and stood up. His red, swollen face and grief hiccups made him even more hideous to behold. He wobbled, but he stayed on his feet. Lily waited. Emily and Virginia waited. Ula and Dick waited. There was a next move—there always is—but what?

"Then I shall tell you," said Virginia. That she spoke up first, she thought, added to her authority. "Scheme if you must, but now you two must find a way to go back without a mortal for your games."

"That won't work," Dick blubbered. "There's no way back if we fail."

"The way back," said Emily, "is Always Circe-certain—If—going Back is what you want. Or You may try—*Circumference!*"

"Wait!" said Lily. She already knew the answer, but she was compelled to ask. "My parents...they never knew them?"

Virginia smiled tenderly at Lily. "These savages lied," she said. "They do not know your mother and father and they were not taking you anywhere you want to go."

"Come"—said Emily. "Come Back with us."

So, they were left, Dick and Ula, to a feast of grubs and bitter roots, scrabbling to retrieve the shreds of Identity that clung to them like secretions of the Dutch Elm. Enduring the grinding sleep of rust-clogged wheels, their night would be bitter.

At the entrance to the park, Lily, leaning on Virginia, stopped for a moment. "That was Brigid!" she cried. Breathing deeply, she stood unassisted, herself again, awake.

PART THREE

Reunions

One

What did it all mean? Lily wondered. Rather than parse it out, she slept for what felt like days and days and all the while she dreamed. It was surprising. What was this dream of feeding the hungry? From where had it come? What were *they* doing here in her room? She knew about them—the sick and hungry—but her life was so busy she lived far from them, until now. She was among them. She remembered her brief reading of Buddhist literature. Hungry ghosts. Is that what they were, the Homeless, the De la Nuit? Without touching her, they pressed in on her from all sides, from above and below. Though they were insubstantial, Lily perceived their bodies. She bumped into and bounced off of their auras. Their energy mingled with and altered her own. She felt desperate. She felt hungry, sick and homeless.

"I know the point of it," said a voice from the deep well at the center of her dream. "It's Aunt Emily. It's Aunt Virginia," the voice said. "They're showing you how to observe, to open your heart and mind." *Caterpillar to butterfly*—this process flooded her mind as she awoke to her own metamorphosis from cozy, uninformed artist to besieged, compassionate agent of healing and goodness. In that half-station between dreaming and wakefulness, Lily felt an odd sensation. She hovered, as rigid as a plank, several inches above the mattress. She felt no fear, only awareness of the two worlds swirling their energy together inside and all around her. There was her mother laughing aboard ship, her father looking ruddy and happy in summer linen. They played shuffleboard with their pirate killer, who was also laughing and no longer weighed down with ammo belts and weapons. I wish, thought Lily, that we could laugh the guns out of everyone's hands.

Sounds like a great Tweet, Lily thought; instantly the sentiment went viral, reaching billions in both worlds. But would it make any difference? Asking if it would make any difference always made some kind of difference whether one could see it or not. *Keep laughing. Keep asking.* These seemed to Lily intelligent, optimistic instructions.

"Good for others; so hard to apply to oneself!" said the voice. Again, Lily laughed and this time it seemed that a vast multitude of laughers behind her and all around her joined in. Their laughter reverberated inside her and made her skin tingle; like a tuning fork, their laughter made her hum and vibrate, laughing even more, even longer and louder.

"It's all funny!" Lily shouted and woke up, exhilarated, even giddy in her own room. She sat up in bed alone, yet she had never felt so warmly included. What was it—the embrace of the two worlds? It had to be something like that. What else could it be? It was Aunt Emily and Aunt Virginia; it was her mother and father and their murderer; it was Shaya; it was Aidan. In the energy of the multi-worlds, there they were, all together.

Not even taking time to wriggle into her robe though the rooms were cold, Lily ran out to her drawings and scooped one up. Walking around her apartment to keep warm, she saw instantly what she needed to do to complete it. Just like that, she thought. After so many weeks of blockage, just like that! Once again she laughed out loud.

Down in the street a child scampered back to the curb, driven there by the loud blast of a car horn and the driver's shout. She watched from her window. Is that Dick's face behind the wheel? Lily thought. Then *Pop!* The car ran over the child's red rubber ball.

Two

Several days had passed since their late-night failure to abduct Lily, yet Ula and Dick had seldom emerged from the thicket cave they called headquarters. The damp floor was littered with empty pizza boxes and candy wrappers. After their defeat, keeping to their separate sides of the cave, they had barely spoken to each other. If they had talked, all of it would have been about what they should do next. Going back emptyhanded seemed impossible. Neither was sure what, exactly, would happen to them, but they weren't eager to find out. Lonely, frightened, nursing bellyaches, they shivered with despair. At last, a message came through to Ula and she spoke.

"Wormy!" she growled across the cave to Dick, "Did you pick that up?" Dick stirred but said nothing. "The goody two-steps are getting more help."

Dick sat up, looking in her direction. "What are you talking about?" he muttered.

"Your little darlings, the writers," said Ula. "They're going to have reinforcements."

Dick flopped back to the ground in the fetal position, his back to Ula. "Bite me," he snarled, brushing an inchworm off his sweaty forearm.

"Come on, Slime Ball, we have to move fast!" She crouched over him, shaking him by the shoulders. He jerked away from her. He rolled over and glared at her.

"What can we do about it, about anything?" Dick said. No one ever looked so miserable.

"Do?" Ula screamed. "We can do what we were sent here to do!"

"Right!" said Dick. "They've already beaten us. What do you think more of them will do to us?"

"I have a plan," said Ula. "Don't you want to know what it is?"

"You're going to tell me anyway. What's your stinking plan?"

"We stop tiptoeing around. We kill her! I don't mean just kill her. We pulverize her! It will be easier to take her back that way. We kill her, we take her back and we leave it up to our superiors to revive her or make a statue out of her or do whatever the hell they want. Pretty good, huh?"

"You should go down and jump in the creek because you stink," said Dick, "and so does your stupid plan."

"Ok, Light Bulb, you come up with something." Ula waited, but she knew that Dick would come up with nothing. Dick was useless, she knew, but she was stuck with him.

"Don't you think they'll destroy us if we come back with a dead body?" Dick asked. Ula shrugged.

"It's better than staying in this cave!" said Ula. She stood up and pushed her way through the cave entrance. Outside, she paused to say, "I'm going to get hold of a vehicle."

Dick scrambled out behind her. "Wait! How are you going to do that?"

"It's called hotwiring," she said. "A friendly carjacker showed me how to do it when you were off wandering around."

Three

Emily's sister, Lavinia—Vinnie—always the indispensable protector and companion shadowing the poet's life—had discovered the poems tied into fascicles in her dead sister's dresser. It was she who guided the first publication efforts to share the poems with the world. Vinnie had played as important a role in her sister's eventual fame as Theo Van Gogh played in his brother Vincent's celebrity. In fact, Vinnie and Theo discussed what her sister was up to, returning to their old world. Theo insisted there was nothing, *nothing* that could persuade Vincent to go back. Yet, he eased Vinnie's spirit mind, assuring her that all would be well. But her worry flared and burned brighter the longer Emily stayed away. Lavinia missed her sister.

Virginia's sister, Vanessa—Nessa—was not as inclined to chase after her sibling. Not that she didn't love her; she adored and worshipped her monkey, her Billy Goat, but she had always been alert to her sister's unstable personality and how it might overwhelm her own steadier, bedrock consciousness. Still, the more she saw Vinnie, the sorrier she felt for everybody. They consulted others besides Theo, including Leonard, who had already gone back at Virginia's request and returned; consensus held that the two time-traveling immortals would be just fine no matter how long they stayed away. That was comforting, but it was not enough for Lavinia. Her intuition suggested strongly that the opposite might also be true. Vanessa perceived that Lavinia intended to track her sister down and persuade her to come back. Her devotion, Nessa could see, was touching if somewhat overbearing, but she respected it. At times, she even shared it.

Still, Vanessa-Virginia was different from Emily-Lavinia. The Stephen girls had not lived together under the same roof all their lives. In fact, by their mid-twenties, they never lived together again, though their homes were always close to each other and they were frequent visitors and caretakers back and forth. Also in contrast to the Dickinson girls, both Stephen sisters married, though Virginia waited until she was thirty to do so. Further complicating their sibling relationship was the brief, dangerous flirtation Virginia carried on with Nessa's husband, Clive, while Nessa was focusing most of her attention on their first baby. Though never physically consummated, Virginia's dalliance with Nessa's husband strained the sisters' intimacy for years and by her own admission, caused Virginia the greatest grief of her life.

But that, Vanessa knew, had all happened long ago, an old world folly. They'd made it up to each other as best they could before Virginia, who went first, crossed over and it proved to be a non-issue when Vanessa joined her two decades (almost to the day) later.

Something about Virginia's and Emily's return, though, worried the scar of an old wound. Who would have thought that possible in a Hereafter, however it was constituted? As she often had in the before time, Nessa found herself in the role of moderate supporter of a more volatile and insecure sibling. Possessing a fiery temperament of her own, she smiled at the irony. She gentled Vinnie as if she were her own sister and tried her best to turn her back towards the barn, but Nessa was hardly put out when she saw that Lavinia would not be deterred. If she could line up a portal and persuade Brigid, the sympathetic portal-keeper, Lavinia was determined to go back alone. Yet she sweetly and urgently persisted in asking Nessa to come, too.

Well, why not? What was she feeling, Nessa wondered, for the first time in more than half-a-century: curiosity? That was fun! Though she, like everyone else in the next world, could feel everything, Vanessa did not feel everything all the time. Sometimes, as was the habit, now and then, of those who had been dedicated caretakers on earth, Vanessa delighted in feeling nothing at all. But finally, about a trip with Lavinia back to the old world, *why not?* She wondered how she would paint old world scenes now, if she would see and compose them differently. It was exciting to contemplate the discoveries ahead, the painting she would do when she returned. And she would see her Billy Goat, her sister who was such a part of her. She would see her, perhaps, in the old way. But was that really possible? Desirable? She was not unhappy where she was; she knew no one who felt unhappy. Unhappiness had been shed like dead skin cells in the transformation of physical body to spiritual body. She was still Vanessa Bell, née Stephen, eldest daughter of Julia and Sir Leslie, older sister of the famous novelist and critic and feminist, herself a famous painter and feminist, yet she was someone different, too. She was capable of so many more things than she was when she lived in that realm of flesh and bone. She was more beautiful than she'd ever been. She desired and was desired, but there was no desperation in it or in anything she felt. Desperation had died with her. Grief and grasping and disappointment had died, too. Resentment had not survived and followed her. When she saw Virginia again, when she met Clive once more, she forgave them; she loved them.

The love was reciprocal. It always had been, even in their earlier lives, though she could not always act on it then. She felt it but held it tight against her heart, allowing her resentment to flicker, consuming ragged edges of their love and hers. It had always been painful, and though all of them lived long enough to want to extinguish the resentment and bask in the love, they couldn't quite come up to the task. The job remained almost finished, but not quite accomplished. That awaited the great transformation, the crossing over, the discovery of life in death, life through death and love again after that.

Vanessa stirred in her airy garden seat, surprised that she had traveled back so far in memory and felt things she thought she would never feel again. She felt them almost analytically, not desperately, and she could smile at last as she felt them and thought of them. She relaxed even more, sinking deeper into her feelings, aware of the sweet fact that there was no person and no device measuring out her experience, no arbitrator saying 'stop'. She would stop when she stopped. Until then she would journey on, feeling, easeful in experience and repose, and when she was finished, she would find Lavinia, Emily's sister, and tell her yes, she would go with her through a portal if Brigid allowed it and see what they could do to help their siblings and hasten their return. Vanessa had to admit it: the next world was not quite as scintillating without her sister.

When Vanessa informed Lavinia that she would go back with her, Lavinia praised Nessa's superior beauty, charm and practical intelligence. She felt more grateful than she could say, though she enjoyed making diligent effort to try to say it. "Oh, I wish I had been more like you!" she sighed.

Neither woman suffered the least timidity about the adventure ahead of them. Lavinia secured Brigid's approval and was assigned a porthole in the same location their sisters had used. "That park is full of them," said Lavinia. "We'll have no trouble at all reappearing almost at the same spot where they met."

"Then it's time to grab the bull by the udders," said Vanessa.

Smiling at but not commenting on Vanessa's famous use of mangled metaphors, which had not found a cure in this realm, Lavinia said "Shall we go?"

They went.

Out of a gnarled oak stump bedizened with shimmering green moss, they emerged one after the other and stood together brushing leaves from their own and each other's dresses.

"How sharp the air feels," said Lavinia, taking deep, gulping breaths. Vanessa closed her eyes and felt her body swaying in a breeze that wrapped like scarves and shawls around her. She listened to the burbling creek water and saw light through her eyelids and screened dozens of thoughts and conversations that were not her own. That was interesting. That new talent would have to be carefully monitored and regulated. But I am capable of anything, she thought, and opened her eyes to see that Lavinia had run down into a deserted playground to swing. Higher and higher she flew back and forth with a child's look of sheer delight. Yes, thought Vanessa, remembering the magic of her earlier life. She watched and waited as Lavinia swung back and forth, back and forth and as her eyes adjusted and sharpened she observed small silver fish near the creek bed and orange and red leaves like little boats dashing along the surface and all around the long legs of a blue heron fishing. She spotted an owl on a high branch of a redwood, and over there were half a dozen deer grazing on the lawn opposite a narrow roadway. She felt a tug at her elbow. Lavinia, sated for the moment with swinging, pulled Vanessa down the path toward the Plaza. It's pleasing, Vanessa thought, to be led and she acquiesced to a simple sisterly devotion. Yes, she thought, this should prove to be a most pleasant experience, conspiring with Lavinia.

Lavinia and Vanessa made a plan. They agreed that they would split up and find their siblings separately, then reconnect near the entrance of the park. At the little duck pond over there, Lavinia suggested. "Yes!" said Vanessa. "I so want to paint that!"

Not even the decadent fragrance billowing onto the sidewalk from Martolli's Pizza could sidetrack Lavinia from her sister-hunt. The pungent enticement of the open-air coffee kiosk, which in an earlier life would have wooed and won her, delaying her arrival to wherever she might be going, could not lure her off course. She noticed the pleasurable scents as she marched by, mentally filing her intention to return at some point to explore them, but she had one goal and even as a returning 'ghost', she was linear in that regard. Regaining her earth legs, steaming uphill, she piled up blocks on Main Street and walked into Bloomsbury Books at the street's south end. She paused by the magazine rack, enjoying from inside the elaborate window display and the street traffic, then turned to see her sister sitting up straight on a chair in the corner. She was reading, as anyone might have expected she would be and remained oblivious to her sister's approach or the fact that Lavinia stood silently over her for a good two minutes before speaking. In fact, Lavinia thought as she stood there looking down at a small line of Emily's soft white skull, which the part in her tied up, auburn hair revealed, that she could pass the time like this forever. Nothing ever gave her more pleasure than observing her sister's rituals and practices, or aiding her in one project, scheme or another. She had always derived the same pleasure from watching her sister as birdwatchers get from their passion. That she loved her sister and was devoted to their family, all of eternity knew. Indeed, her admiration and love had been the only bridge between the great poet and a readership that almost missed her. Had Lavinia followed her sister's self-immolating instruction to burn all her papers after her death, there would have been no surviving fascicles on which to base the volumes of poetry that followed and changed literature forever. In the next world, Emily had thanked her often for being the wiser of the two and saving her poems. Lavinia loved that Emily knew she'd done the right thing—something she herself had always known. It never occurred to her to burn her beloved sister's poems! Now, the poems were loved all over the world; they were pretty popular in the next one, too.

"Vinnie!" Emily cried in a high voice, standing up so fast she knocked a book off the little table beside her chair. Had she been bigger, she would have squeezed the wind out of Lavinia with her hugs. She kissed her sister ten times, perhaps a hundred times, she was so happy to see her.

"I missed you so!" said Lavinia. "I thought you might need me, so I came."

"How dear! And how brave of you! Did the portal frighten you?"

"Not at all; I did not come alone. I came with Vanessa, Virginia's sister. I had to work to convince her, but in the end she was so sweet and supportive. I believe she is almost as fortunate to have her sister as I am to have mine. But we do want you back! Will you come soon?"

"Oh, Vinnie, where is she? Where is Vanessa?"

"I suppose she is with Virginia now. In fact"—here Lavinia tuned in to invisible frequencies—"yes, there they are! At the duck pond, the lower one in the park! Shall we meet them?"

Emily put down the book she was holding. It was about poetry and spiritual practice ("I have poems in here!" she said). They were leaving the store when Lavinia stopped abruptly. "Look at that beautiful woman!" she said, nodding in the direction of an office at the back of the store. The sisters observed the woman in profile as she sat at her desk writing in a ledger.

"Exquisite," said Emily, "the brightest Flower in a sacred garden!"

"Doesn't she remind you of someone?" said Lavinia. "She could be a sister of Vanessa's and Virginia's!"

"No, she's not a sister—an Ancestor, perhaps!" said Emily. "She co-owns—this Shop—many Hearts—too! And—She must be a Bloomsbury—Fan. In this community—She is—like Sylvia Beach!" The sisters admired the woman, whose profile really did resemble those of the Stephen sisters, then walked out onto the street.

Four

Virginia walked through town, moved by her contemplation of the yearning for closure. Really, closure is a made up thing, she thought, a malignant, ugly thing of the fainting heart. Yet she noted that the practice of closure had gained clarity in this 21st earth century. It made her sad.

In her time, nothing had closed until Death turned down the lamp, shut the door and stoppered the ears. We were not afraid, after great disappointment, of going on, she thought. We went on until we died, she thought, or until someone died. So Vita stayed married; so Nessa kept rooms for Clive; so Carrington and Lytton and others combined and recombined in sinuous if not always harmonious partnerships. We cut no one loose for long, she thought. What would have been the point of that? Were we not capable of shouldering our great, unexpected disappointments, our shifts of allegiance, as well as our joy?

Yet, she had to admit, everyone in her earth time struggled along in their inherited caste systems, the abysmal classes. When the world they'd known changed forever between the two great wars, they were unprepared. They struggled to rebuild their lives, their world, but of course it was different lives, a different world.

Is that what these earthers are doing? Virginia wondered. If so, they are going about it in an odd way. So much of what they're doing reeks of judgment and people on the attack. Virginia paused to observe a starling overhead pecking at a raven flying south. The image reminded her of the day before when she'd briefly glanced at a TV broadcasting a spectacle of people arguing. 'I have the right to speak my truth, to speak my mind,' someone said, and oh he said it in such pedestrian ways! They are not wise, these people, Virginia thought, or clever or especially smart. They blunder. They bump into things. They are clumsy, Virginia thought. They hurt one another and go on as if nothing happened. They 'make amends'; they believe in it, making amends, but...really? One cannot make amends by throwing a wall up between a grudge and a misunderstanding.

Nothing comes of the choked throat of communication, Virginia thought as she swerved to the candy shop and came back out on the street munching a dipped caramel apple. She had seen them, couples donning their running shoes and sprinting away from partners of long standing or briefly met. They ran, they ran, convincing themselves as they sprinted that something better awaited if they just started over with everything new and fresh. Soon they were running again, knowing less and less about themselves the more they repeated the pattern. Maybe the point in this world, she thought, is to wind up on one of those screaming, fighting TV shows where relationships disintegrate into donnybrooks, free-for-alls. One need not fear wetting one's ankles when crossing the deepest depth of *that* stream! Virginia thought. Yes, there is much to resist and reform in this time, Virginia thought.

What does the old goat want to resist and overturn now? Nessa thought, locating her sister by tuning in to her mind-play and energy pulse. She wished that her sister could have approached this adventure as a holiday. But she *is* happy when she's stirring a pot! Nessa thought.

Her own thoughts alerted Virginia at once to her sister's presence in Lily's realm and in the wink of an owl's eye they were side by side, downtown on the sun-splashed Plaza at the Lithia water fountain. Virginia threw back her head and laughed while Vanessa moved in to wrap her sister up in a tight hug. They laughed and kissed and looked like two people dancing who are not dancing. Virginia's voice climbed its register.

"My Dolphin! You're here! I knew you would come if I were gone too long. Has it been too long?"

"Sorry to disappoint you, dear," said Vanessa. "It revives me to see you and hug and kiss you, but I was pummeled into coming by the poet's sister, who worked every charm to achieve my consent. And here I am. I must say that the more she cajoled and wheedled, the more inclined I was to see firsthand what you've been up to. I'm just glad we got away before Clive found us; he would have insisted on tagging along."

"So smart of Dolphin! I'm glad he didn't come, too." Virginia said. "This is a woman's working holiday if ever there was one."

Keeping close, the sisters walked quickly out of the plaza to the park entrance and sat down on a bench bordering the lower duck pond. Anyone could see that these two loved and delighted each other. Each brought to the other greater balance and beauty. Separate, they were dazzling; together, they were exponentially shimmering. Even the ducks, with no promise of being fed, crossed the pond water to be near them. Together, their voices made delightful music. They talked low and they talked loud, Nessa sharing recent events in the other world and Virginia filling her sister in on all that she and Emily had accomplished since they'd returned to this one.

"Are you finished?" Vanessa asked.

"Not quite, but soon."

"Oh, good! I shall leave them a painting when we go."

"Brilliant!" said Virginia. "Will I be in it?"

"My furry Billy! Aren't you always?"

It didn't take long for the Dickinson sisters to find their friends. Virginia's hands darted up and down and side to side like barn swallows—delicate creatures Emily was fond of calling 'poetry birds'; Vanessa's body shimmered and vibrated as if she might get up and dance at any moment.

"Well, we've succeeded!" Lavinia said to everyone as Virginia and Vanessa scrunched together; Lavinia and Emily sat down on either side of them.

"Do you realize what we've just done by sitting down here?" Virginia asked; without waiting for an answer, she informed them. "We've greatly enhanced the value of this bench on something they call Ebay. One sells 'valuable' junk through the air!" she laughed. "Someone should take our photograph for certification!"

"Billy-goat, Billy-goat," said Emily, "the Bridges you spin—out of nothing!"

"The hidden something," Virginia corrected her.

"All right," said Vanessa, "before we pluck the last feather from the camel's hat, perhaps we can stay on task." Lavinia smiled, silently thanking Vanessa for speaking her thought. "Virginia tells me," Vanessa went on to Emily, "that your project is almost finished and soon it will be time to return. So the question is, what remains to be done and how, if at all, may we help?"

The recent arrivals looked at Emily and Virginia and waited. They waited for what felt like a long time before Emily finally spoke. "It's not Closure we need—but Truth—told Slant—the method of it, Anyway."

"Agreed," said Virginia. "A farewell—something—seems to be in order. I know! A party. A Bloomsbury party! Who would not love it!" This suggestion was not met with the immediate enthusiasm that Virginia had taken for granted. "What's wrong?" she asked, responding to their expressions.

"I want to do a painting for them." Vanessa repeated what she had said before.

"That's lovely, dear Dolphin," said Virginia, "but what of the rest of us?"

"Emily and I will bake them magical baskets of cookies and cakes," said Lavinia. "No one has ever met sorrow in our baking."

"If I were still alive," said Virginia, "I should be plunged to the depths of despair. What shall I do, L-Bug?"

Emily cast her eyes past them over the duck backs and the cold pond water. Her face brightened, her eyes wide as she replied. "You shall write them a Letter, dear Goat—just as you did once—for your young Poet—John Lehman. Remember? Only this shall be made of Purple Words—Blue Words—Yellow Words of the Hive! They shall be Words—of Bride & Bridegroom—or—at least Gold words of—Partnership! What more perfect Nectar—to drop in their Laps & on their Lips?"

The storm that had wrinkled Virginia's brow lifted and slowly she smiled. She reached out, her agitated hands acting more and more like the poetry birds; she took hold of Emily around her ribcage and scooped the smaller woman up to her. She fluttered kisses on the poet's neck and cheeks and danced her round and round. "Yes, yes!" Virginia chirped. "Oh, L-Bug, how did I ever live and die without you? But the party...can't we still have one?"

"Give in, Emily. Surrender. It's the only way," said Vanessa. "Well, that's settled," said Vanessa, getting to her feet and bringing her sister back to earth with a word and a touch. Lavinia also stood up and took Emily's hand. "Shall we go to your B&B?" Vanessa said. "But first, let's stop by an art store. I need canvas, paint and brushes."

"We'll meet you later," said Lavinia. "We'll collect what we need for the baking." And off they went.

Five

A battered white Prius squealed around a corner at the north end of town and rapidly closed on her. Lily, in the middle of the crosswalk, jumped aside at the last second, landing in the gutter. The Prius had just missed her. A dazed and wilted Lily sat on a yellow curb and was vaguely aware of her hands rubbing her torn knees through the rips in her black jeans. She hadn't quite recovered enough to ask 'what just happened?' But soon she was able and did and was astonished to learn that she had stepped into the street without looking and was almost run down. Tiffany, a barista Lily knew, saw the whole thing and ran out of the Pony Espresso across the street to help her. She offered to call 911, but Lily talked her out of it. "I'm just shaken up and scratched," she said. "Nothing broken, nothing terribly wrong." Tiffany said "wait', went back inside, then reemerged with a large glass of ice water. She sat on the curb with Lily, keeping silent watch over her.

"Did you hit your head?" Tiffany wanted to know. "Do you feel sick?" The barista obviously knew something about first aid and concussions; Lily said "no" and "no" again, and so they sat on as cars and busses rolled past. Lily was grateful for the ice water. She swallowed some; she dipped her fingers in it and tapped her cold fingertips over her face. The ice water felt good inside and out. Only as she finished the glass did she realize that the driver had not stopped, but she was too grateful to be alive to feel angry. Tiffany cursed the driver, though, saying she wished she'd gotten the license number.

"Do you feel well enough to stand?" she asked. "You can come in and get off the street. You can lie down if you want to."

Lily accepted Tiffany's help in getting up. She felt wobbly, just a bit, then steady once more. Still, she thought it wise to go inside the coffee shop and take some quiet time. What had she been thinking that her mind was so far away as she stepped into the street? How close had she come to leaving the world? The prospect did not fill her with dread as it once did, not now that she'd met her spirit 'aunts', but she did have unfinished business. Aidan appeared in her mind. She was happy to be alive with her story of almost being dead. Aidan would worry about her and love her all the more. Perhaps there were certain advantages to brushing up against death, to logging close calls. Everything collides with us or brushes by us for a reason, she thought. But was it really true? Suppose there was no reason to any of it, even to the appearance of spirit aunts, despite their claims. And why hadn't one of them suddenly appeared to keep her out of the crosswalk? Speculation. Endless speculation. What was the point of it? She had almost died. She had been careless, but she was alive; she was well. She had seen what the unseen could do to you, how it could change everything in an instant. Just as she had avoided death, maybe a woman on another street had met her own on the bumper and under the wheels of a speeding ambulance. Wasn't that woman's fate an inexplicable irony? Why was she, Lily, spared, while that woman a few blocks away was not?

She knew what she wanted. She wanted to walk home. She wanted to take her time and let her head clear. She wanted to walk home and go to bed. Yes, that's all she wanted, but it seemed an enormous task to explain all that to Tiffany, who had to get back to work. When I can stand without feeling woozy, Lily thought, I will go. Lily stood up, felt reasonably clearheaded and thanked her friend one last time. The barista kept an eye on her as Lily walked outside, then out of sight around the corner of the shop.

At first, Lily's steps felt funny, but she got her feet under her after a couple of blocks. She found their intuitive rhythm, and she had the funny thought that feet are the empaths, not people. Why did that seem so funny? She laughed out loud as she walked and a couple of passersby stared after her. For a split second, she caught a glimpse of herself from the eyes of others. It was only a glimpse, but it was enough to urge her to say to herself, 'get a grip!' She saw herself unsteady, on a slow boil. She needed the solitude of her own home, the security of her own bed and pillows and comforter. By the time she reached her door, she had fully regained her natural walking cadence, but still she felt sore and tired. She wanted her bed, and sleep.

Six

Ula burrowed through the entrance and crawled to her own side of the thicket cave. There she collapsed with a profound sigh. Dick, across the cave, listened to the sound of Ula's teeth grinding. He spoke through the dark: "Maggot Munch, I *told* you it wouldn't work."

"I wonder," Ula muttered, "would you grow a new asshole right between your eyes if you ever said one nice thing to me?"

Dick was about to respond with his usual defensive sarcasm, but something checked him. He wondered where that unusual comment had come from. It made him think of how they both had other lives long ago; they had not always been the creatures they were now. Surprising himself, he heard himself speaking across the dark. "Sorry you had a bad day."

Seven

The sisters Dickinson, in crisp, white aprons, might have been nurses, housemaids or professional bakers. Baking pans cluttered the kitchen island in Emily's B&B—nine inches for pies, four inches for breads—cupcake pans and cookie sheets. A sheen of flour coated the island's uncovered surfaces and in Lavinia's hands a flour-dusted rolling pin swiftly flattened and extended dough. Emily, decorated with spots of flower on her chin, left cheek and forearms, was herself decorating a layered lemon cake with butter cream icing squeezed from a frosting tube. A timer rang and Emily put down the icing tool. Briskly thrusting her hands into oven mitts, she opened the oven door and extracted a sheet of pungent cinnamon, nutmeg and ginger cookies. The sweetness of fresh baking was almost overwhelming but in a good way, the feeling evoked being one of bliss, of rapture. Emily gentled the tray onto a cutting board, escaped her mitts and took up her icing tool. She made beautiful yellow and lavender peonies with it and looked completely and happily engaged in her work. Meanwhile, Lavinia laid aside the rolling pin and transferred the dough to a pie pan. Emily squeezed the last flower onto the cake, then took up a bowl of sliced apples soaking up brown sugar and vanilla extract and ladled the contents into the pie pan. Lavinia applied a lattice dough cap, or top, to the pie and Emily slid it into the oven.

The sisters worked this way all afternoon. They worked as though they had always baked together, which for the most part they had. Still, it would have been extraordinary for anyone to observe them. They were efficient, yes; they were artful; they were cheerful, too, emanating a joy that is always rare to behold or detect in oneself, or anyone else, or anywhere. They baked together as if they were in perfect balance, sharing the same energy cloud and never taking a misstep. Watching them, one could see that there would never be mishaps small or large—too much vanilla in the batter or a cake slipping to the floor—like those that afflict bakers who are only half awake, whose minds stray. They were as natural in their movements as the moon in its monthly journey, as bees coordinating their activities around the hive, as mothers tending their infants. They were present in the way that water is present in a sacred well; they were free in the way of running water in rivers and streams. They were also uplifting, as clouds appear to be if one takes the time to look up.

At last, as the sun descended, filling the kitchen with a sepia-orange wash of light, their baking wound down. They believed in cleaning as they went, so there was little in the way of a mess to take care of. Once the substantial baskets with two wooden 'doors' were packed and shut, they swiftly restored order in the kitchen. They wiped down the double sink and central island. They hummed and sang snippets of songs they remembered from Amherst days and as she draped her towel on the sink edge, Lavinia wished she had a glass of sherry; the desire surprised and delighted her. Emily opened a cupboard from which she produced a bottle and two small glasses. From the bottle she filled them, then handed one to her sister.

"We have—Earned it—dear Vinnie," said Emily. "There is such Delight in baking—Together—again." She sipped from her glass. "Delicious!" she cried. "Like the nectar—of Bees—the liquor of Love!"

"I think I'll have another," said Vinnie. "Just one more, a wee snooty."

"No drinking Alone," said Emily, holding out her glass. Vinnie filled it, and they walked their drinks into the sitting room, where cozy armchairs and end tables called to them.

Only when Lavinia sank heavily into her chair and sighed did she give any indication that she might be tired from her exertions. She held her glass up to catch the last natural light and observed the liquid's honey-caramel color. "It's luscious," she said to the room and savored another sip.

"Wasn't it so like home?" said Emily. "Once or twice I fancied I heard mother and father in the parlor and Sue and Austin coming in and Gib bounding into the kitchen to steal cookies. It's a blessing to remember all that without sadness. They come to me now with joy. It is sweet to consider that momentarily we shall all be together again."

"Reunion—the peak experience," said Lavinia through enthusiastic sips of sherry.

"Yes," said Emily. "To my Sister, my Rock!"

While the Dickinsons baked, then drank, Vanessa Bell worked at her painting on the easel she had set up near the duck pond and grove where she had 'come through' with Lavinia. Virginia, seated at the base of an oak and pushing her back against the reassuring bark, read aloud from an anthology—*Best American Short Stories*—a gift from Emily. Wrapping up an improbable and unsatisfactory story about a child unwittingly switched at birth with another in the hospital and what becomes of the very different lives of the juggled children, Virginia put down the book with some irritation, lit a cigar, and got up from the bench to consider her sister's progress. Quietly, she looked over Vanessa's left shoulder, her right shoulder; she bent down and got close to Vanessa's ear, then stepped farther back. She came closer and smiled. "You have this place," she said at last. "I suppose that's me coming out of a tree." Virginia pointed to a dark, angular, faceless shape emerging from the base of an oak.

"Of course, it is," said Vanessa, who did not stop her brushwork to answer. "Emily is already out and sitting down here by the water."

"Yes, I see that now," said Virginia; "one's eye goes first to the portal"—a detail that pleased her immensely. "But where are you and Lavinia?"

"We will not be in it."

"No?"

"No. That would make for too many figures. Besides, this has been your project, yours and Emily's. Vinnie and I do not need to be in this painting."

"I adore the way you obtenebrate your canvas, dearest Dolphin! Oh, look what you've done!" said Virginia, discovering something that had at first eluded her. "Emily almost looks like a creek-side fern; and I rather resemble the slenderest of tree roots, or an artery from the other world."

Vanessa smiled. "You catch my intention exactly," she said. "You always have, my monkey."

"There is the owl," said Virginia, delighting in discovering another detail in the painting. "And...yes! That's a blue heron standing midstream, fishing and that is a lark above it. Is that meant to be Lily and Aidan coming up the path to the portal? Darling, this is exquisite! You are my first artist."

Vanessa smiled, keeping her concentration, assessing the architecture of her scene as her brush hovered in mid-air like a bee contemplating the petals of a flower, or a hummingbird demonstrating the almost invisible speed of stillness. Inspired, certain, she reapplied the brush to the lower right quadrant of her canvas and changed its reality with broad, colorful strokes. Laying her brush and palette aside, she rose and stepped back to gain a different perspective. Something new, something unseen by anyone else, opened up for her from that angle and swiftly she returned to her seat, took up her brush and palette and applied paint to the canvas. So she worked steadily until the light began to fail and the park weaned itself of warmth and sharpness. Shadows of blue and gray asserted themselves, rolling over the light like fog off the sea obscuring the shore. "Come into focus, all my dreams of thee," Vanessa sang as she packed up her paints and covered her canvas.

"What is that from?" Virginia asked.

"I don't know, dear. It came into my head and mouth as I gazed at the picture."

Virginia speculated, "Its diction suggests our childhood."

Vanessa agreed. "I'm sure it's a snippet of something we heard sung in the nursery at St. Ives. But everything else about it is gone now."

'That's the curse of this realm," Virginia said. "So much passes by without notice, and much that matters is forgotten and becomes meaningless."

Vanessa recognized the tone of Virginia's depression as it used to begin to take hold of her and she spoke right up. "You are past that, dear Goat. There is no reason to regret anything here, or to slide down in mood or belief. Let that go. You're here for a specific purpose. You've done well and soon you'll go back. Aidan and Lily will have better lives because of you and Emily."

The tension in Virginia's face eased ever so little. "Let's go find them."

"And perhaps we can pilfer a few goodies from the baking, "Vanessa said. "I hope they had the good sense to bake extra for all of us." Virginia gazed as deeply as she could into the deepening darkness before turning to follow Vanessa, who had already started on the path back to the plaza.

"Do you know what you're going to write to them?" Vanessa asked, as they walked together.

"I wrote once," said Virginia, "of the novelist Mrs. Ward that 'her imagination sought to soar, yet it always agreed to perch. That is why one never re-reads her books'. I want to leave Lily and Aidan with a sense of this: always soar; never perch."

Eight

After the initial giddiness of reunion with their sisters, Emily and Virginia tuned in to Lily's recuperative energy. Distracted, they had missed the entire incident and aftermath with the murderous car and it unnerved them. This lapse reminded them that though they were immortal, they were not omniscient. It was a small spiritual comeuppance and it irritated them. They were flummoxed but relieved that Lily was not dead or seriously hurt. They were also reminded that the De la Nuit was still a threat. So they arrived at Lily's apartment, chastened and eager to comfort her. Lily was glad. She was waiting for Aidan to come over, she said. She had been reading, she said. She had been thinking about circumference and the different meanings the two writers had drawn from it over and over in their work. Emily suggested that when Virginia used the word, she meant war, the second one; when she herself used it, she meant ecstasy, the circular region between herself and some other self that she could only half see from time to time. *My Business is Circumference*, Emily recalled writing once; she said it became her more and more as she ripened.

When very young, Emily speculated, an injustice takes root and unhinges some who are never quite balanced again. Their bodies swirl, faster and faster—down, down from bigger to smaller hole—and through! Once through, the body's flight assumes an almost unfathomable elegance. If everyone in this realm knew..."

Virginia cut her off. "Not everyone, dear L-Bug. Remember the Unmentionables."

"Quite so," said Emily. "I meant—If most people here knew what awaits them in the next world—vast numbers would choose to cut short their stay here. Still, one cannot turn away from the body's—Destiny. One must live—and suffer—and rejoice and die—and live again! Pain and joy, wounding and healing—a cornucopia of flesh and desire, of bones and dust overwhelms us. Then suddenly one grasps the expansive reality of—ongoing existence. That is what comes—as one leaves the vortex in a portal." Emily described how one soars in ever expanding, luxurious waves past crystal palaces and great halls of learning, over sprawling parks of brilliant greens and blues and flowers rioting on mountainsides and meadows. Just to help you with your bearings—there are impressive facsimiles of the places that meant so much in this lifetime—and just as you recognize them, those you loved and those you loved less well appear suddenly and you're no longer flying on and on alone. You go on together as you once did, but without the contention, anxiety and fear of loss. Loss is lost in that next realm.

Thinking that she would 'modernize' their talk, Virginia declared that she would have liked to jump out of an aeroplane. Not to die, of course, but to float down under one of those canvas umbrellas and land safely in a meadow among poppies, or in the middle of a river's lazy current.

"Dear Goat," said Emily, "it's always the river with you! There *were* airships in your day. All we had were giant hot-air balloons—and they were mostly reserved for the war. Why didn't you arrange for a ride—and jump?"

Virginia described their fear of the airships because of the wars. She shared what it had been like to lose a home in London to bombs. It was dreadful—the books damp and mildewed, glass everywhere, furniture broken to pieces as if a drunken giant had stomped through in a destructive rage. It had been horrible but liberating, too—forced to shed possessions. "Still," she said, "I would have liked to have jumped out of a plane and floated back to earth, I believe. But then Leonard would have had none of it." She imitated his voice. 'Too much excitement by far for you!' he'd say like a schoolmarm—dear man!"

"I should think he would have been keen on a ride and maybe a jump," said Emily.

"Yes, one would think so," Virginia agreed, "what with all his gallivanting and traipsing around the jungle in his civil service years."

Virginia smiled thinking of Leonard and how they adored each other's company. Our intellects and artistry checked our baser disagreements and distances, she thought. She felt grateful again, realizing that she could not have married anyone else. She had known that quite early in their courtship and still she made him wait. He suffered! But she was ill prepared, she remembered, for certain aspects of marriage and soon enough they came up hard against them, she thought.

"Are you drifting?" said Emily.

With a start, Virginia said, "Oh, was I? Probably! I was thinking of the meddling of my older half-brothers, their hopeless Victorian attitudes and abuse. I was remembering how I had openly raged against my doctors and the medical profession, generally. It was no friend or safe country for women. Everything the doctors thought they knew was wrong. Their prescriptions were disastrous. They killed mother; they killed Stella and Thoby. They lied when they did not know and when they thought they knew, they misdiagnosed."

Emily took Lily's hand. "Are we boring you, dear?" Emily's eye fixed on a tiny brass heron watching them from a high bedroom shelf.

"I could listen to you two go on forever," said Lily.

Emily, who sat closest to it, responded to the knock on the door by hesitating before opening it, then standing on tiptoe to peer through the spyhole. Smiling she said it was Aidan, who rushed in as she opened the door. Nodding to Virginia, he sat on the edge of Lily's bed. Though she had told him what happened on the phone, he asked her to tell him the details all over again and she humored him. She stepped off a curb, she said. She started crossing the street, she said, then she jumped out of the way of a wild car, she said. "Do you drive, Aidan?" she asked. "Do you have a car? Just kidding!" she said and laughed.

It's good that she's laughing, Aidan thought.

Nine

Aidan had to go to work, but the three women sat on, drawing suste-
nance from their shared space.

"Sometimes a man's fumbling attention is so charming and necessary," said Virginia.

But Lily was setting out on another journey. "Sometimes," she
said, "I dream the pirates come out of my head. I see them bursting
through my skull as if they're charging to the surface from a dark and
locked up hold; they've slain the cook below and the cook's helper,
the cabin boy and the captain who was taking a little rest. One wrung
the neck of the captain's parrot because....who knows why?

"Do you understand what that is?" Virginia asked.

"It's the mysterious, the masculine and unmentionable," said
Lily, doing her best. "It's what happens when....when...."

"When one acts—while Unawake," said Emily.

"When one acts like a man," said Virginia. "Oh, I know it's even
more than that. We're all, in part, bombs in danger of exploding,"
said Virginia. "You've read about good men going bad; that's the
story behind it. That's the story behind every war. One gets tired,
loses focus, drifts in thought, then settles in thoughtlessness; and if
profit is attached, off they go. One kills randomly, foolishly, cruelly,
stupidly, and so it's off to war we go."

"It's off to war, said Emily, "the young men—and now the young
men *and* women—Go—and die, so many—just as their lives Begin. Young
friends—shot to pieces or blown to bits for a cause—just Because. What is
a cause but an argument that gets Loose—and hides from compromise?"

"My parents weren't at war and they were old," said Lily. "They were on vacation. They wanted me to go, but I said no; I had better things to do."

"Would you like my handkerchief?" said Virginia. "It's quite all right to cry. I soaked a mill's worth of linen when I was your age, and after, too."

Lily burrowed into Virginia's shoulder and sobbed; Emily plopped onto the other side of the bed, leaned in to Lily's back and put her arms as far around the two of them as she could. There they rested as the sun dipped below the Coast Range and the room darkened.

Speaking at last Lily said, "My parents talked about that trip for years. They were going to Italy; they were going to Greece. They wanted to see the cradle of civilization; they wanted to see the great ruins. They wanted to dance and drink ouzo under olive trees. They wanted to walk arm in arm along a cliff looking out over starlight sparkling on the sea. They wanted the trip to be a celebration of my growing up and going away somewhere, anywhere to my next act, my first great solo adventure. I don't think it ever occurred to either of them that I would not want to go. Meet Lily, the daughter that sent her parents off to die so she could stay home and throw a couple of stupid parties, so she could make a mess of the place and not hear voices saying *wash those dishes, pick up this room, please!* There were boys, too. My interest in them lasted less than a week. I sent my parents off to die for what? How can I ever make it up to them? How can I forgive myself? Do I even deserve that?"

"Such contracts are null and void," said Virginia. "Lily, your parents expect no recompense for anything; they hold you accountable for nothing. I've witnessed so many shipwrecks on the rocks of one's expectations borne of that single sinister question—what do I deserve, or not?"

"Unanswerable," said Emily, "the question of the pilot light—the Straits of Doom, the woofing waves—a carnal Exactitude. What fills up the Space when we are done asking about what one—or we or all—Deserve?"

"Consider, dear girl," said Virginia, "your parents' feelings. Suppose you *had* been there on board when the pirates fired their guns. Think of how happy your father and mother must have been, in their last moments, to know that you were safe, that you would go on, that your young life would not be stupidly snuffed out by men with guns. Men cannot have guns without shooting them at something else that is living. Seen in this way, you *not* going was the greatest gift you could have given them. Perhaps your intuitive mind knew this even if your conscious mind did not. Our bodies tell us so many truths that we ignore. But sometimes we listen and we benefit."

"When you say it so, it makes sense," said Lily, "yet I feel such stabbing pain in my heart! Perhaps I could have saved them had I been aboard. I'm young, athletic and vigorous. I've learned some self-defense. I carry mace in my purse. The thought that I could have made a difference haunts me. What can I do with that?"

"When Julian, my nephew, got it in his head to go to war in Spain," said Virginia, "I did everything I could to talk him out of it. I reasoned with him; I pleaded and made promises that I would help his poetry career if only he'd stay home. I had a strong premonition that he would not come back. Bitterly, I was right. Less than a month, he lasted. Nessa, my beloved Nessa, never fully recovered; none of us did. He would not listen; he had that male war gene in his blood. How old one suddenly feels when another dies whom one has loved so dearly! We seemed to walk around forever in a daze until so much time passed that it got softer, if not easier, somehow. L-Bug, you said it as well as anyone. Remember?"

Emily began to recite and partway through the poem, Lily's voice joined hers.

After great pain, a formal feeling comes—
The Nerves sit ceremonious, like Tombs—
The stiff Heart questions 'was it He, that bore,'
And 'Yesterday, or Centuries before'?

The Feet, mechanical, go round—
A wooden way
Of Ground, or Air, or Ought—
Regardless grown,
A Quartz contentment, like a stone—

This is the Hour of Lead—
Remembered, if outlived,
As freezing persons, recollect the Snow—
First—Chill—then Stupor—then the letting go—

"Is that what you mean?" said Emily.

Virginia's voice softened as she answered; "yes, that's just what I mean. It's perfect, divine Belle."

"So many Deaths—produced that Poem—so many lost Friends and Friends of Friends!" said Emily; her voice challenged its higher registers, as if at any moment it might fly off and be lost on the wind.

"Lily, you knew this little poem of mine. I hope—it brought You—Comfort!"

"Yes," said Lily. "I read it aloud some nights when I can't sleep. My scalp tightened at the nape of my neck as you recited it; a tingling sensation trilled up and down my spine and I felt....joy! I felt as if my grief was understood; I felt that it might be bearable. That's... different!"

"That's art-in-life," Virginia said. "The word on the page, the sound in the ear, the song and the music, the line & color on canvas, the figure in the dance. Like company that makes pleasure or pain more bearable by increasing its surface, art transforms grief and loss into something bearable, even beautiful."

"How does art do that?" Lily asked.

"By helping us perceive our Sorrows—not as stones—but as Boats shooting rapids," Emily answered. "Nothing is finite! All of life, and everything that happens in life, is Mutable. Even when you feel paralyzed—bogged down or locked out, you are changing—Changing!"

"I hope my parents felt that at the end," said Lily.

"On fairly good authority," said Virginia, "we can comfort you on that score."

"I wish you would say more than that," said Lily.

"Ah!" said Virginia. 'That's exactly the admirable concentration you must bring to your daily work! But as for more I've said enough and no tsunami of this-world impatience will change it."

Lily knew. Everything Virginia said was true. Patience was a virtue and she must learn and practice it. She also had to attend to the responsibility of *Here, Now.* "You know, I don't think we—Americans my age, I mean—have ever really felt in any personal danger until recently. Does that make sense?"

"It does," said Emily, "but it's changing—Isn't it?"

"The war, any war, reaches everyone," said Virginia. "No one escapes, not my nephew blown up in Spain; not the charwoman crushed as the cellar collapses; not the five-year-old child who survives unscathed while his mother beside him is burned to cinders and ashes; not the farm woman whose sons ride a doomed ship to the bottom of the Irish sea. 'All are punished,' wrote the Bard, who knew everything. Oh, now that I've met him, I could tell you stories! I'd tell my dear Friend, Edgar, for instance, that the Rochester conspiracy is whimsy. *No one else* wrote the plays. Our Stratford William did. But that's for another time. We're talking about war."

"There is always an answer, Lily," said Emily. "Women must stand up and say No—to endless squabbles that Evolve—No to prevarication—No to Greed that tantalizes the Heart & Soul (the ampersand is for *You*, Dear Goat!). Oh, Women everywhere—must—Unplague this Earth!"

"Women have let men make war," said Lily, thinking; so, women can stop them. Yes, that makes sense, she thought. One woman at a time, she thought.

"It's the best way," said Virginia. "A few women step up; more inch forward and drag the rest along in their wake."

"And that," said Emily, "is Circumference—a kind of Progress."

Ten

"Mrs. Moffat will come and sweep it all up," Aidan said to himself, deriving great comfort from the image of someone removing all traces of a mess. He was reading Lily's copy of *The Waves* and he found himself engrossed in it, identifying with this character, then that one and then another still. Like the novel's Bernard, Aidan found that he was making up phrases to explain himself to himself. He thought of how Bernard 'stole' rhythm. Bernard, standing in for his creator, believed that writing was all about the rhythm. He made this discovery as he was 'getting' Byron's rhythm inside him. Aidan thought that he, too, had done that, but with living. Aidan absorbed and appropriated the rhythms of others, shaping them to his own purposes even when he wasn't sure what they were. Suddenly, he felt vulnerable and ashamed, measuring himself against the strengths and weaknesses of a fictional character like Bernard rather than a real woman or man. Then he heard voices saying 'what is wrong with measuring yourself against a fictional character? Some fictional characters make great mentors; others make great friends; the best make great lovers'. Who was speaking? How many were there? More than one, he was sure of that, but how many more? It could be any of them—Emily, Virginia, Leonard, Lily, Shaya—or all of them together. Aidan felt himself growing disoriented. He felt fatigued, all tuckered out. He yearned to be prone, to lie down on a bed or a couch, or in an empty office on the floor if neither a bed nor a couch was available. In his work life, he had skirted prolonged depression and revived himself with catnaps on the floors of many abandoned offices.

In the glow of this slight revelation, he knew he ran the risk of going on too long and spoiling it. Succeeding, Aidan thought, one inclines towards going on and on past the point of stark and simple discovery. One wants to prolong the ecstasy that seemed so remote, then so sweet in arrival. One wants the good times to keep on rolling and dreads the slip back into chaos and uncertainty, the dreariness of uninspired thought and cowed feeling. Now Aidan thought he would strive to avoid the dreariness. He would push on, but slowly, measuring progress as he measured his breathing—in, out, in, out.

I am glad that Aidan is reading *The Waves*, Virginia thought, for the revelation and relaxation. It's good that he came to the breathing, Virginia thought. There is always that question of the body, she thought, the fact of it and the projection of it by someone else. There is always someone looking, measuring, weighing, critiquing how another looks, moves, talks, laughs, slumps, sits ramrod straight, eats, or refuses eating. Is her makeup askew? Is she having a bad hair day? Critique follows critique. People couple. They walk together, sit together, dine together, talk and do not talk. And in their shared silences they might as well be on opposite sides of the planet. Their relationship to one another is intimate and distant in the same moment. And in their lonely, tortured journeys they are sustained by a moment here, a moment there, where they truly see the other one and accept each other without judgment and attachment to their magical thinking. Then there is the issue of sex, sex, sex. So much lachrymal hugging! Dogs rut. An exotic jungle bird hops on a photographer's head and beats his face raw with lustful wings, lashing his neck with a magnificent yet ill-placed bird pecker. A honeymoon couple copulates and the night crashes down around them, smothering their lovemaking in darkness. From there, where do they go?

Where, *is* hope?" Aidan thought.

"Hope is the thing with feathers!" said Emily, tuning in to Aidan's contemplation.

Virginia also shivered at the sound of that bell-like word. Up in the air or under the waves, she thought, hope is found in soaring, in diving deeper, always deeper. It's a never-ending process through particles of magical thinking until the magic is real, until the magic is found in simply being, in two people accepting each other for who they are, not some dreamy, impossible version of perfection. We destroy ourselves and each other, Virginia thought, by refusing to dive deeper, by surrendering to the magical waves of illusion and projection. By asking oneself these questions every day, a thousand times a day, one gradually learns acceptance, how to give it and receive it. One mustn't fear the depths. What lies beneath the surface, under the waves...that's the truth. It is seldom what one sees across a table, or in sidelong glances on a long walk, or out a train window. It is seldom in the words that pass between us as we make our way through the day, the night. There's a deeper conversation to be had, a deeper seeing. One must go there, and by going, one will begin to arrive. Virginia wondered if her thought was becoming pedantic.

Now and then, but not often, my life-addled Goat strays in that direction, Emily thought.

Virginia, undeterred, went right on thinking. It's a third thing that Lily and Aidan want, she thought. it's a third thing we all want—to add up to more together than we are alone. We yearn for it and we resist it.

There is another life under the leaves, Virginia thought. It's in a fold of wind, in the surge and swirl of the waves, in that infinitesimal second each day or night when the moon and sun run off together, leaving the sky vacant for the romping, rioting stars and souls, who are also stars. Time passes. In *The Waves* I created Elvedon where gardeners sweep the lawns with giant brooms and a woman sits at the window writing.

Eleven

Lily sat at her window looking down at the street. She was thinking about laughter, how it *was*, in fact, healing; didn't the new science say so?

"Yes, it does," said Virginia, who flitted into the room having let herself in. She joined Lily at the window, hovering more than standing, and peered down, unbuttoning her green velvet bellhop jacket. Turning away, she took it off and flung it over a chair-back to dry. Lily noted the jacket, the pale green cotton blouse and off-white linen pants. She approved.

"I love wearing pants!" Virginia beamed. "I was always stealing a pair of Leo's for a jaunt. I'm glad you like them!"

"I do," said Lily. "Where's Aunt Emily?"

"Oh, she found me a difficult shopper!" said Virginia. She accused me of quarreling with the sales people and so I lost her to the bookstore. Rather than join her, I decided to gallop over to see you, to tell you that we have a splendid surprise for you and Aidan tomorrow night."

Twelve

Before the Bloomsbury party could take place, there was business to attend to. There were celestial visas in the form of Brigid's permission to be obtained by invitees in the world next to this one. Friends in this realm needed to be invited and food and drink had to be arranged. Then the location itself must be staged.

"I love it!—the party, but not here!" Lily protested as Virginia raced through a description of the fete.

"Your apartment's not big enough?" said Virginia. "Oh, shwoo! There will be magic in the partygoers and in these rooms, too. You'll see! Now put that 'smart' phone of yours to use and invite your friends—only the closest friends! Shaya can help. I must go make it up with the Belle. The truth is, I love fomenting little squabbles with my loved ones because I adore the petting and the making up!" With that, Virginia whisked out of the room.

While Lily and Shaya chattered over the phone about who and who not to invite to the party, the De la Nuit agents, Ula and Dick, discussed their predicament in their hovel in the park. Having failed to kidnap or kill Lily and Aidan, what would they do next? Would they be able to return in failure, or would they be banished to an in-between realm, or someplace worse, shadows that did not belong anywhere?

The misfits could be heard by strollers on the footpath, bickering as usual, the antithesis of pleasantly matched portal pals. Having stayed up night after night blaming each other for their failure, they looked even more disheveled than usual. In truth, the pressure on them was unbearable and they were terrified. But at last they bravely (or brazenly) emerged, squinting like newborn ferrets at the sun. They crabbed down to the plaza, staking their claim to a well-trafficked corner and began to busk for their morning rolls and coffee. It took an excruciating hour to attract enough donations (most of them proffered with pity) and as they munched their rolls and drank their coffee at a picnic table outside Mix, Dick declared himself for the party. "I'm crashing it, the party. I'm going," Dick said. "I'm sick of the De la Nuit."

"Whoo—Whoo! Big man!" said Ula. She cackled. "Up yours!" she said.

"Come on, admit it!" Dick said, choosing to ignore her sarcasm, as if that were possible. As its object Dick always felt like he was being bludgeoned 24/7. "Aren't you sick," he said, "of all the processions, the marching around and the meaningless rituals?"

Ula looked at him with even more disbelief and disgust than usual. At his last words, she expected his tongue and face to burst into flame. "*Meaningless rituals*? You're a bigger Stoop than I thought," said Ula. "Aren't you afraid? What do you think the Chiefs will do to you? To me?"

"Up theirs!" said Dick, appropriating one of Ula's favorite curses. She giggled in spite of herself. She'd been so used to thinking of Dick as waste material under her foot that this different Dick, after the initial alarm, actually interested her. "If we don't go back, what are they going to do to us?" said Dick.

"Whoa!" said Ula. "You might stand up to the Chiefs and even get away with it, but we have to go back."

"Who says?" said Dick. "Don't you remember anything about your earlier life here? Wasn't there something to hold on to?"

"We're dead, you Dummy!" she shouted. "We can't stay here! Besides, I've got other-realm things to do."

"Like what?" said Dick. "March around forever like a zombie? Honestly, is that what you want to go back to?"

Ula had to admit to herself that she'd never thought about an alternate existence, or at least hadn't thought of it in a long time, but in the light of Dick's revolt, she suddenly thought that perhaps she could change her fate after all. "Ok, Bright Boy," said Ula, "how do we go back to the Community and escape a fate worse than double death?"

"It's simple," said Dick. "With sponsorship. We get the famous writers to plead our case to Mother Brigid. With her protection, we're in! It'll make a great story!" Dick offered this with much more bravado than he actually felt.

"So, you propose getting them on our side by crashing their party! How do you think *that's* gonna work, Gum Rot? They fear and despise us! Besides, we don't have anything to wear to a party."

"They have big hearts," said Dick. "I will tell them a good story. Don't worry about a party dress. It wouldn't help you, just as the spiffiest suit wouldn't do anything to improve me. There's not really much style in this town, though. Mostly, everybody goes to things as they are. We'll just look like two more style-stupid eccentrics."

Thirteen

A Day! Help! Help! Another Day!
Your prayers and critical eye
From such convergence   Fear & Bliss
Might date a—Victory!
From waking up and letting go
The obstacles that bind;
Steady—my soul: what Surprise will—Find
We questing two!

"I am quite ready to go, dear L-Bug, but tell me, why repeat the word 'help' in your opening line?"

"What? Goat the Critic disapproves?"

"Disapproves is too strong," said Virginia. "It's just that the repetition verges on the...histrionic? And so early in the poem, too! And four exclamation points; the sensation is rather like being slapped awake."

"There are advantages to abrupt transitions," said Emily. "Despite desperation in the waking moment, there is hope! There are important tasks to perform! Victories to be won!"

"Stories to be told?"

"To be rolled and unrolled," said Emily. "I'll tell you how the sun rose—a ribbon at a time."

"Enough, then!" said Virginia, rolling a cigarette. "Out of the trees we go!" And arm in arm, they went.

꙰

"The sun climbs higher and higher like a great fin slicing through green and purple waves," said Virginia. "It races on, on to us huddled on shore. The sun will engage then engulf us one by one, bringing each of us to our greatest incandescence, then burning us out as it consumes us in fire."

"I went home in the sweetness of spring," said Emily, who as usual was working harder to keep up with the long-striding, longer-legged Virginia. "All was blooming. But I most identified with—going home in Snow."

"For me it was water," said Virginia, "which was cold, so cold! So green and cold and violent, then peaceful like water fronds on the river bottom. I might have gone on to the sea, almost certainly would have, but my body hung up on a man-built impediment on the opposite bank. So my body made little progress until it broke away three weeks later. The sea was in sight, but boys at picnic discovered me. One even swam out to me. Imagine his shock! At first he thought I was a log!"

"You returned by water and fire," said Emily, with sympathy.

"Yes," said Virginia, "by water and fire, but not by spring or by snow. I imagine the journey by snow would be restful."

"It was," said Emily. "It is. But the illness beforehand harried me. Oh, Because I could not stop for Death – He kindly stopped for me. He stopped for you, too, dear Goat, despite your Bernard's defiant words at the end of *The Waves*. 'Against you I will fling myself, unvanquished and unyielding, O Death!' Death met you coming full force ahead and opened its arms to you and in you swam, like a river fern, like a fish."

"Like a spent fish, like a withered fern," said Virginia. "I was not well when I left."

"Of course not," said Emily. "How could you have been well? Striding into the river like that!"

"I forget that you saw it," said Virginia. "If only everyone on earth could learn what we know here, how that knowledge would rout depression! Imagine making peace with death. Imagine writing about the stages of death, the fading physical looks and abilities, the waning mind so like the waning moon, but writing about it with genuine interest and curiosity instead of morbidity or fear. Suppose everyone learned how to celebrate the journey to death, which I pointed out, after all, is an experience we enter more consciously than birth. Oh, to think about death as one thinks of love or marriage! Why not? Lily would not have suffered so about her parents if she believed this. Dying brings us to happy outcomes; we can thank the microtubules of our brain cells for it."

"Yes!" said Emily. "Let Us call it—the gift of universal sight!"

"I do love your company," said Virginia, slowing her pace and coming to a stop. She embraced Emily, holding her tight. Emily returned the long hug with equal spiritual ardor; they resumed walking, holding hands. The love of woman for woman is greater far than any other passion, Virginia thought, and suddenly she remembered Katherine Mansfield, who had died so young. I hated her and loved her, Virginia thought and I missed her so when she was gone. I would have felt that way about Emily, she thought, and Emily, tuned to the sweet, winding path of her companion's thought, squeezed Virginia's hand tighter and leaned in to her side.

"My L-Bug," said Virginia, "with a flour-smudged nose moving like a hummingbird from pan to oven to sink and back—how vigorously you work and shape the dough! I see you rolling it flat. You wield the rolling pin confidently, like a conductor waving her baton. Like the conductor and the musicians that follow her, my baker makes sweet order out of chaos. Now you are cutting the flat dough into fanciful shapes. There is a pony, beside it an elephant or a pig—I can't tell. Perhaps one shape is a motorcar. Is that a pergola and a porch swing with two young lovers snuggling on its seat? Ah, I recognize them—the dog, the cat. I see you scooping them up with a spatula, carefully, sure-handed, and arranging them on the greased

baking tray. A quick check of the oven and in goes the tray and cookies. Within minutes the kitchen becomes pregnant with swooning
smells from the oven. Soon, you slip your dainty hands into cooking
mitts, open the oven door to a billowing, invisible, aromatic cloud of
cookies and remove the tray. I see you setting it to cool on the wood
block with its sea-green legs. I see us walking out into the garden
together, mesmerized by hummingbirds and when we come back the
cookies are warm yet soft. We sample one, a duck, together, and my
mouth waters. The pleasured roof of my mouth sends up to my brain
messages of engorgement and delight, which fires nerves throughout
my body to spread the delightful news: this vessel swoons to the taste
and substance of homemade cookies! All that's left is to pack them
into the basket with the small cakes. Upstairs, in another room, I
see you tying a rope to the basket's handle. You open a window and
lower the basket like a slowly falling maple leaf to a little clamoring
crowd of children that have congregated, squealing with delight, like
trained raccoons as if on cue."

Virginia let go Emily's hand and threw her right arm around her
shoulder. Emily's left arm wrapped comfortably around Virginia's
waist and so they walked that way through the buzzing town.

Fourteen

People were coming. The fine, soft night meant that the windows
in Lily's apartment were wide open. The sky was clear, the moon
bright. Auspicious, thought Lily, as guests began to arrive after sev-
en. Lily's good-luck barista and bartender friends, Merron, Abby,
Kaydee, , David, Chelsea and Jason burst in, flying high on caffeine.
Their jackets and hats piled in the bedroom grew into a rumpled
pyramid that teetered, threatening to spill over the edge of the bed
and tumble to the hardwood floor. Just another hastily tossed coat
or two would do it.

In the living room, which seemed to expand (just as Virginia had
promised) as more people entered it, Vanessa's finished Lithia Park
painting, still drying on its easel, commanded attention. No matter
where one stood or sat, one's eye inevitably returned to the painting.
One could enjoy the smell of the canvas as well as the look of it. It
would be judged a success, Virginia thought, by anyone who knew
anything about art.

Aidan knew something about art and other than Virginia was
Vanessa the painter's biggest fan in the room. "Your use of light and
shadow, color and almost invisible formal organization are so confident. You are thick with the paint yet it acts on the canvas almost as
if it were dancing!"

Vanessa felt a hot spell come over her. Was she blushing? "It's
different painting back in this world than in the Hereafter and it's
different than the way it felt to paint here before I crossed over," she
said, almost apologetically, to Aidan. Virginia, knowing so well how

her sister worked, offered only unqualified praise and adoration; she knew and cherished the direct path to Nessa's heart.

People kept on coming. Patrick, the singer, arrived with his ukulele and tin whistle. Three attractive young women were with him. They had all dated at one time or another yet remained friends after their break-ups. After saying hello to Aidan and meeting Lily, the girls fanned out, laughing, singing bits of songs; two of them—Sapphire and Laurentine—clustered around Duncan Grant, easily the most handsome man in the room (Virginia reported earlier that, alas, Rupert Brooke could not make it). The third girl, Nasha, wearing dancer's tights and slippers and a bellhop jacket, glided over to the painter, Carrington, who smoked sullenly in a corner, and complimented her bobbed hair. Soon after, others arrived; Randall Joseph, an earthy, soulful young man sporting artful, literary tattoos; Bruce, the epileptic dog man; Lisa, the sparkplug and caretaker of ill and elderly people; Diana, the huntress.

Other visitors from the world next door included Lytton Strachey with his long, out-of-fashion beard and sharp tongue; an enigmatic Tom Eliot, the poet, who unmistakably wore eye make-up; the flamboyant Vita, Virginia's lover and model for *Orlando*; enthusiastic Clive; Thoby (whom everyone called The Goth) and Adrian, Virginia's and Vanessa's brothers, and of course, Leonard, with Mitz on his shoulder, which was stained pee-yellow by the monkey's answers to nature's calls. These luminaries, bowing to the insistent invitation of the Stephen sisters, dressed in their earth finery and lit up the Lithia Park portals with their rapid-fire arrivals. If the deer and birds could speak, if the other animals could make known their reactions, who would not believe that they were scandalized by the flagrant throwing aside of the veil between the worlds? The fact that animals more closely witnessed spiritual comings and goings than humans was generally understood when the subject came up at all, but the experiences also taxed their more delicate constitutions.

In the spare bedroom that could now be called a sitting room, or parlor, Clive Bell charmed a small, happy coterie made up of the bartenders and baristas as he lectured on the transparency of true art and schematics in the paintings of Roger Fry, whose work, alas, was now mostly forgotten, and who, for some reason, could not make the party. Others surrendered this room to the listeners and to Clive, who had a tendency to speak a little too loud. The last to exit the room was Lavinia, who wickedly mimicked Clive to perfection, setting off Virginia's hoots and howls of laughter. Lytton chose the most comfortable chair in the living room and sat down, showering Shaya with beautiful, indecipherable sentences about long-dead members of the royal family. Across the room, Patrick's ukulele leapt to life and the voices of singers began to overpower conversation throughout the apartment. Vanessa danced with Lisa, her brothers and Duncan Grant to the upbeat tunes; Virginia, who still did not care much for dancing, allowed Aidan to lead her onto the floor for one number, while Mitz scampered from chair-and-sofa back to shoulders and standing lights, screeching in rough time to the music and raiding the food table with rascally glee. With a handful of fruit or cake, she would hole up in a safe corner and chew the morsels at super speed, then begin her frantic rounds all over again. Fortunately, Leonard had long ago been successful teaching her not to throw food at people. It seemed a law of nature in this world, thought Lytton, that the most outrageous beings always grabbed the stage and the most attention. For a moment, however, he was distracted from the monkey by another peal of Virginia's wonderful, waterfall laughter, which just then followed something Aidan said.

What was it, thought Lytton, the nature of the thing that young man said? It didn't matter. What mattered was the feeling evoked by Virginia's laughter, a sound and experience he'd enjoyed, even thrilled to, for many years before his own premature death. He reflected on a truth he had needed to come back here to learn—that laughter in this realm was even more precious, because so necessary, than in the next world where everyone was happy. It seemed odd to him that he hadn't thought of this as soon as he'd crossed over. Even immortal, he felt a little sting of fallibility, though of course he would never admit it to anyone. Before this secret broke free, he turned quickly back to Shaya and resumed his spellbinding disserta-tion on the hygienic habits of Queen Victoria. More than a little star-struck, Shaya, who had read *Eminent Victorians* in high school (but, honestly, didn't remember a word of it) was all too happy to sit at the great raconteur's feet. Meanwhile, the party's dynamics, dramas and energy surged and swirled all around them.

Nasha plopped in a chair beside Virginia and said, "was it your idea to throw this theme party? Cool! You know, you even kind of look like Edna St. Vincent Millay. She was Bloomsbury, right?"

"Lily had a close call with that car," Chelsea explained to Duncan, who was only half-listening as he surveyed the young men in the room.

Laurentine, studying Duncan's baggy corduroys and flowing scarf said, "so, you've come as a painter?"

Tiffany greeted Emily at the door with "Oh," are you the one who is supposed to be here as the poet? Who is it, Mary Oliver?"

Bruce, intrigued by the two striking women leaning close togeth-er, smoking, against a far wall, angled over to them and listened in. The tall one, Vita, smiled at him, but Carrington went on talking as if he were not there.

Sapphire, cornering Eliot coming out of the bathroom, compli-mented him on his sparkly blue eye makeup. "So, Tom," she added, "what do you write about?"

Thoby stood out on the balcony with Diana, who was demon-strating how to shoot arrows at the moon. "Aren't you afraid your arrows will hurt or kill someone?" he asked.

She let loose another shaft and looked at him over her shoulder. "My arrows never fall to earth." She took aim and the shot arrow sizzled.

The music took a quiet turn as one slow, rich ballad succeeded another. Someone dimmed the lights in the living room. Eyes grew larger, rounder and some brimmed with tears; some shone like animal eyes in late night hedges. Lytton, noting that Shaya leaned more and more towards the singer, finally released her and sat back with closed eyes as the music transported him back to an over-achieving summer in boyhood. Clive's group was scattering, too, his audience drawn to and mesmerized by the music; slowly they made their way to the voice singing its mournful stories.

Clive plopped down in the chair beside Lytton and lit his pipe. The two old friends settled back, content. Even Mitz calmed down, happy to curl up on Leonard's shoulder and be still, her thoughts inscrutable, known only to those who dwelled in the kingdom of philosophical monkeys. Patrick and Randall, harmonizing, sweetly sang the last lines of *The Croppy Boy* and after the resonance of the sad song faded, Vanessa turned up the lights.

"May I have your attention!" she declared. If she'd had a crystal glass in one hand and a knife in the other, she would have urgently tap-tap-tapped for order; as it was, she relied on her bright, commanding voice. "Please!" she said, "a moment!" All eyes focused on Vanessa and happily, too. It was a gift she'd always possessed, the ability to ensnare people who delighted in her voice, her dancing, her gaze, her company, her beauty.

Spellbound, Virginia looked at her sister with awe and adoration. In Virginia's eyes she was always Nessa, her Dolphin, her flawless sister.

"Tonight, we celebrate goodbyes, new friends and going on," said Nessa, "and an adventurous future for Lily and Aidan." Vanessa paused. Some partygoers cheered, some clapped their hands; a few who had been drinking more heavily shouted huzzahs.

"May they nurture a deep and abiding friendship," said Lisa, "as the Irish poet, Joan McBreen, described it to me once."

Vanessa continued, "Of course, who among us does not hope that this liaison will also be seasoned and spiced with exceptional lovemaking." The tipsy euuwwd and ahhhhd; suggestive titters surged from others and swirled around the room as Aidan, blushing, swiped at his brow with a handkerchief; he folded it over and handed it to Lily, who seemed for a moment confused about what to do with it. So she wiped her brow, too, even though it was dry. Vanessa resumed. "By celebrating this moment, we pledge our psychic and physical support for each other. We are all part of the process which nothing can break. Lily and Aidan have entered the meadow where trust, empathy and love are as abundant as wild flowers. If they choose to do so, they can care for each other and nurture each other's work. They may heroically collaborate, and we shall gift them with a Book of Man-Womanly and Woman-Manly Expressions!" From the table behind her, Vanessa picked up a large, ornate leather journal selected from the well-stocked shelves at Bloomsbury Books. The journal included the store's signature bookmark featuring Virginia's likeness and her quote about reading and the Hereafter.

"Let me be the first," said Lytton, rousing himself in his chair and uncapping his fountain pen. Taking the book from Vanessa, he wrote, "Respect the love of man for man, and woman for woman" and signed with a flourish. So the book went around the room, filling with inspiration and play and love.

"To be or not to be, that is the question"—quoted Randall;

"Put down the toilet seat and close the lid," said Patrick, who had once composed, at his sister's request, a song about bodily evacuations.

"Meditate together and ride together," Clive wrote in his own hand, ever the spiritual outdoorsman, who no doubt felt a responsibility to elevate their sayings and the Group Thought, "and frequently travel abroad together visiting museums and galleries."

Laurentine uncapped a pen and wrote, "find a man who is as beautiful and empathetic as a woman."

"Dance as if your clothes are unnecessary!" said Vanessa, who had, on at least one occasion, famously danced out of her own;

"Walk and read as if your hair is on fire!" said Virginia, who was feeling hyper.

"Plant trees and speak French," said Shaya, who did both;

"Experiment with your hair and eyebrows!" said Britney, who wowed her admirers with scissors and colors;

"Dare to eat a peach," Tom wrote, "a canned peach." Immortal, he had at last, to the immense relief of his friends, learned to laugh at himself;

"Always have something sweet on hand", Duncan added as he swallowed a bite of Lavinia's almond scone, "especially after an argument";

"Be flexible! Travel abroad and assume other identities," Vita shouted. "Love is bigger than you think";

"Take care of each other," said Bruce in a quavering voice, "and be especially tender through illness";

"Look to your immune system!" cried Thoby, who had died so very young;

"Let your monkey *be* a monkey," Leonard wrote, who looked as if he were repeating the words that Mitz whispered in his ear, "and keep records! Write everything down. Impose order!";

"Don't forget to keep lots of sass and laughter in your hearts," said Lavinia, "and bake, always be baking!";

"Remember to tell each other that you love each other," said Lisa, who worried she hadn't said it often enough in her life;

"Think of your life together as rehearsal for old age," wrote Carrington, who had never known an old age of her own;

"Run with the wolves, just run, and do not show up with an empty quiver," said Diana;

"You're never too smart for therapy," said Adrian, looking up from the pages of Freud;

"Tell all the Truth, but tell it Slant," said Emily;

"Discover and live by a system," said Virginia, "that does not shut anything out;"

"Forgive your trespassers be they Boogie-men or Boogie-girls!"

The voice came from the back of the room, which filled with silence. Everybody turned and craned necks to identify the speaker, but most had never seen him before, in this world or the next.

"It's that awful Dick and Ula," Emily, whispered urgently in Virginia's ear. Virginia's first instinct was to run, then to confront them, but noting the sheepish way Dick hung his head and the resigned hopelessness behind the fire in Ula's eyes brought up some other feeling in her. Yes, she felt compassion and she was glad.

"You can breathe, but you can't hide," said Vanessa to the motley pair. Virginia felt the usual thrill at hearing another of her sister's mangled metaphors.

"We come in peace," said Dick. It sounded ridiculous, but most could see and feel that he meant it. Did his Harpy comrade feel the same? Yes, Virginia thought, she detected sincerity in Ula's haunted face, a tenderness that grappled with her bitterness. Where had she seen that expression before, she wondered. "We want to go back with you," said Dick; "we don't want to go back to those that sent us here."

"A wish," said Emily, "Is Ecstasy! Yet—how shall it be—Obtained?"

"Indeed," Virginia added, "for so long you have been like stoats nailed to the barn door. Now you ask for Rapture. Did you hear?" Virginia turned excitedly to Emily. "I capitalized Rapture just for you!"

"I have a story," said Dick. "May I share it?" Demonstrating agreement, everyone sat down on chairs, the sofa, the floor. Dick almost succeeded in smiling. "Once," he began, "I lived in Amherst. I was a sickly, shy boy, but poetry kept me company and poetry woke me up. I spent much of my boy-life in a thicket cave in a small but wild wilderness I found at the base of a hill and there I read:

O World! O Life! O Time!
On whose last steps I climb,
Trembling at that where I had stood before;
When will return the glory of your prime?
No more—Oh, never more!

"That's Shelley!" whispered Virginia to Emily, who said "shhh."
"I read by thicket light," said Dick, "and I soared; in mind currents, I took flight. I beat my wings beyond the sparkling web of the
fat, mottled spider and the skunk lair, past the transparent, abandoned shell of the snail and the old nest grown over with mold. The
words on the page became birds and other beings, their movement
the music of orchestras. I sang. I danced. I read on and on, crossing
the boundary of childhood, crossing the Hellespont and the Irish
Sea, leaping from century to century, rebuilding the forgotten future
and welcoming the past. That's what reading did for me. I accepted a
teaching position in Deerfield and moved away; when I came home
for holiday I saw you." Dick stared at Emily.
"After many years away, I saw you leaning out a second story window. You were lowering a basket to children in the garden. I paused
on the path, interrupting my conversation with an acquaintance,
Deacon Hazlip, to ask the identity of the woman in the white dress,
the benefactress of those clamorous, fortunate children."
"Oh, the myth!" he said. "That's mad Emily, Austin's sister." The
Deacon walked on alone a few paces, paused, and returned to my side
with a quizzical look. "What are you staring at?"
"Emily!"
You must have heard my outburst because you glanced once our
way and swiftly disappeared inside. My heart constricted; I winced.
My companion observed me with disbelief and mild irritation. Reluctantly, when I was convinced you would not likely appear soon
at the window again, I walked slowly on, aware that my carefree,

animated gait before my vision had become a gallows-walk. The conversation with my friend had gone completely out of my head. 'Why did you call her mad Emily?' I asked. 'Because she *is*,' my companion snapped. I pressed him. In what way? He gave a great sigh, tagged me with a glance of weary aggravation, and explained that she stayed in her home for months at a time. She was known to hide on the landing and speak to visitors out of sight around the corner. Rather than come out to the garden to greet children with her sweets, she melodramatically (and some said dangerously) lowered them in a basket, just as we'd observed. 'Doesn't that strike you as melodramatic?' he said. 'Suppose the rope lowering the basket were to break!' Everything you describe is eccentric, perhaps, I replied, but mad? That's extreme. 'She writes *poetry*,' said the Deacon, as if that fact explained everything about the woman's madness that I needed to know. He could tell I did not follow him and he sighed again. 'But have it your way,' he said dismissively, as if my opinions could not possibly matter about this well-known character of local lore." Dick paused to gauge the effect his story was having. So far so good, he told himself, and plunged on. Ula studied him closely.

"After this revelation and prickly exchange with my old friend," I lay alone all afternoon on a green hillside above Amherst. With calm heart and empty mind, I stared into a disheveled expanse of blue and cantering, fleecy clouds. Suddenly, I felt my spirit, my essence, pour out of my body in a great pillar of energy and light. It raced into the clouds and joined their own boundless energy that was suddenly clear to me.

Happily, I lay there, my face damp, my arms spread out, one with the clouds and the sky and the life force! And that's how it felt, Ms. Emily, in your presence from the first moment I saw you at your window. I contrived to meet you one day as you walked with Carlo, your Newfoundland companion, and we talked past your initial reluctance. So, we met now and then, growing closer.

"After my death, after yours, in a winter dream, I visited your grave. As I stood there, suddenly the snow collapsed under me and I sank with a shock to my knees in snow. I felt as if you were playfully reaching up, grabbing my ankles and pulling me down to you. I heard you laugh. Since then, I have held on to a dream of you. And now, here you are. Alone, I've felt you, Emily. I've danced you and sung you. I see bees and their flowers, bees and their hives almost as you see them. Because of you, words took on deeper meanings; words woke up and took me with them, and I never read or thought or talked or felt the same. It's this that allowed me, when two owls swept out of the barn's cupola at two a.m. one night and circled me, bouncing sonar sounds off of me, to answer them. Because of you, I was able to talk with spirits that lived in trees and the stars; because of you, I communed with the Divine in the eye of a cow, the eye of a horse. All this, and you, I knew before I fell. Don't you recognize me, Belle? I was Richard Jenkins. In our youth, we knew each other. We were friends and later more than friends. I attended the wounded and fell at Gettysburg. Done with this world, or so I thought, confused and passing badly between worlds, I lay mangled on the battlefield until the De la Nuit claimed me. I was chained and too weak to break free—until now. Do you remember me?"

"I *knew* he had a thing for her!" Ula muttered. "He tricked them into giving him this assignment just so he could see her again!"

"Hush," said Virginia, poking her in the side. "I've listened, rapt, and with more than a little jealousy to this tale of life with my L-Bug. How beautiful they both were in their purity and yearning!" Virginia leaned down to whisper in Ula's ear. "Yet, when I hear how my L-Bug tried to pull him down on top of her, if even in a dream, *well!* She's more a pixie-vixen than she lets on, don't you think?" No one answered. Emily looked and looked at Dick. The longer she looked, the more Dick's face changed. It was not a dramatic change but more like the gradual, gathering light on hills at sunrise. The longer she looked, the clearer she saw the young man he had been once. Yes, the wretch standing before her really was Richie Jenkins of Amherst. Oh, how I mourned his death! she thought. Oh, how I loved him with the love of true friendship—perhaps more than that!

> Conveyance—through the night
> To Elvedon—for you, Dear Goat—
> Where second sight
> Wakes Us—
> As veils brush the Dead
> Then—hang Still,
> Resistance & Reunion become One!

"Richie!" Emily cried, and hugged him.

"Well!" said Virginia, "a moment of friendship and liking!" Virginia took Ula's arm and led her to the other side of the room. "I'm going to introduce you to a new and far more congenial Hell," she said, laughing. They stood before the largest chair in the room and the acerbic wraith occupying it. "Get up, brother-in-law," she said to Clive in the other chair, "and make room for this poor creature. Lytton, this is Ula; Ula, Lytton. Lytton," Virginia said, "I've told Ula that you will be happy to escort her back when you go. I'll leave you two to get acquainted!" Exuding mirth, like happy water, Virginia almost skipped across the room.

"*There!* You have it now," said Vanessa, presenting to Lily *The Book of Man-Womanly and Woman-Manly Expressions*. "Consult it freely." Said Vanessa. "Ponder it often. Add to it as you will," she said. "Ask others to contribute."

"This is the happiest party!" cried Lily.

"Yes," said Aidan, as the music picked up and people were dancing again. In a daring fandango, Lisa's shirt flew open to loud huzzahs and hoorays. Soon, Virginia thought, Nessa's shirt would follow, perhaps Carrington's, too. Diana was already shirtless, wearing the skimpiest leather half-tunic. The dancing released the tension that had built up during Dick's story. The partygoers danced and danced.

"You and Emily don't have to go back, do you?" Aidan whispered in Virginia's ear. Her eyes fired with merriment and she laughed her infectious, symphonic laugh. She bent her head to one side, allowing Aidan to kiss her lightly once on the left side of her neck and she wondered afterwards if he had enjoyed it as much as she did. She heard his silent question about Vanessa and said "go ask her!"

Aidan did that. Fully re-clothed and flushed, Vanessa listened as Aidan begged her to attend the opening at the art gallery where he worked. It would be a sensation, he told her, if he showed up with the real Vanessa Bell!

"No," she said, "I can't come. I won't come. But I have something even better to suggest." Aidan's look of disappointment brightened just a bit. "No one would really believe it was me," she went on, "but suppose you showed up with a hitherto unknown painting of mine? Wouldn't that be sensational?"

"Yes, yes it would!" Aidan had to agree. "May I do that? May I include this painting?"

"Of course! It's yours now, yours and Lily's. Think you'll sell it?"

"No! It will have a prominent *Not for Sale* sign beside it."

Aidan thought what a coup it would be, how it would help his reputation immeasurably. He would have to come up with a plausible story explaining how he had it, the painting.

"But that shouldn't be difficult," said Vanessa, interrupting his thought. "You found it at a thrift shop, or it has always been in your family. You'll pull it off!"

Reluctant to go, everyone lingered even after the music and dancing subsided. A few told stories and everybody within earshot of them roared at Lavinia's hilarious impressions. But finally, slowly, one-by-one and two-by-two, the guests began to go. Those from this world left first because they were, after all, tired; some had to work early in the morning. Then the next-worlders slowly departed until the young couple stood close together on the balcony and Emily and Virginia sat side by side on the sofa.

"We carried it all off rather well," said Virginia.

Emily rolled her eyes and smiled. "There were many Nights—like this?"

"Yes, many," said Virginia. "So many I could not count them. Often we simply neglected to go to bed at all!"

"In my Time," said Emily, "I might have Died from—Scrutiny!" Virginia put her arm around her poet.

"Now," said Virginia, "what will you do after reunion with your Richie?"

An alluring, glowing light suffused the couch and suddenly, sitting cozily between them was Brigid Herself. Her flaming red hair cascaded over the couch back and cushions. She was so beautiful the women couldn't bear to look at Her, yet they stared.

"I suppose that whatever you're going to do," Brigid said to Emily, "it will involve me." Was she almost smiling as she said it? Emily hoped so. Virginia burrowed into Brigid's side cooing hers and Emily's love. "You are also loved," said the Goddess. "Rest a little, then it's time to go."

Fifteen

Lavinia and Vanessa walked through the park in the direction of the portal that had brought them to this world while Emily, Virginia, Sha-ya, Lily and Aidan lagged behind. "Some are curious," said Lavinia speaking to Nessa, "about what it was like to be the sister of a poetic genius. Unlike you, with your painting, I had no calling to nurture other than Emily and the rest of my family. She was my canvas, my easel, my palette, my colors. Yet, I never felt I lived in her shadow. I was always the one out front, in the public eye, at least to the extent that we indulged the public and its curiosity. When people called at the house, I greeted them. When Emily wasn't up to visitors, I made excuses and did my best to entertain them. When Emily spoke, concealed around a corner, I served the callers tea and sandwiches and cakes. I monitored Emily's level of excitement and brought a visit to its end when I sensed she'd had enough. Sometimes I reduced Emily to gales of laughter mimicking the guest that had just departed. I possessed a certain wick-edness and I had a mind of my own."

"My dear sister's mind was unhinged," said Vanessa, "just not all the time. She didn't just look at things; she looked in between them. Her genius elevated her and it laid her low." They stopped and looked down at the water. Vanessa pointed at the speckled backs of two rainbow trout scrabbling upstream.

"Emily's mind and body," Vinnie continued, "inhabited a Middle Space, too—what you call looking in between things, what she called 'internal difference'. It was perfect that she would come downstairs only part way and stop, hidden from sight, and sit down between two destinations. That became Emily's perch from which she experienced the world yet remained hidden. In her late twenties, she began to live, through poetry, in two worlds. She moved like the bees and birds she loved, skirting one reality or another, diving in and out of them. She dipped; she soared; she hovered and hummed. So I would be standing in a room with her—the kitchen, the parlor—and I would experience the oddest sensation! It was as if my sister faded in and out of view. Impossible, I told myself, but it happened so often I stopped questioning it. We would be talking, I'd be looking at her, and suddenly she would simply fade away, then surge back—like a firefly."

"Virginia picked the perfect animal name for Emily!" said Vanessa. "My sister was good at that—selecting animal names for people."

"I wonder," said Vinnie, "what name she would give me?" She pointed at two stellar jays chasing each other through the branches of a pine tree. "I know that when Emily or anyone looked at me I never went in and out of view. I was solid, of this earth, until I wasn't anymore; then, and only then, did I become a spirit like Emily. Before that, I was practical, a strong root, one of those people that live to stabilize the spirited and spiritual among us."

"Other than my children, my sister claimed the greatest portion of my love," said Vanessa, "and my hate. I was older, but not very. Many, including Leonard, said I was more beautiful, but that depended on the day and how one looked at us. When mother died, then Stella, I had to assume the burden of the household and the care of a grief-ravaged father, an unconscious bully. I comforted Stella's husband, Jack and briefly considered marrying him, as he wanted me to do. I was crushed by responsibility. But as soon as father died, I seized the opportunity to escape. I sold that house of many deaths, as Henry James called the Hyde Park Gate house and agreed to marry Clive." Vanessa paused, thinking of how Clive, such an outdoorsman, must have loved this park when he came through for the party. "Clive was no artist," she went on, "but he was robust and he understood us; he was more analytical about art than we could be. He was the best of allies. I did not fully comprehend the extent to which he would prove himself an abiding friend until later, of course, after he wooed my sister.

"He wooed my sister, and he was married to me! Our first child divided us. I doted on the baby and Clive resented it; he felt neglected, and he was. He was lonely and unhappy. Virginia also felt cut off, doubly so, by my marriage *and* the child. Her jealousy burned bright! She fought for my attention and my family was her battlefield. Oh, I know she never wanted Clive as he wanted her; she craved most a motherly affection. She always died a little without me. What she couldn't see until too late was how successful she could be at blowing up my marriage. My husband didn't just lust after her; he fell in love with her. Insecure as she was about spinsterhood, afraid of sex yet fascinated by it, she could not resist the allure of an accomplished man, any accomplished man, including my husband, desiring her. The two carried on their flirtation in private and in front of me and by the end of it, Clive and I had turned to other lovers." Vanessa watched a duck couple huddled together at the water's edge and thought how that was not an image of her in any intimate relationship.

"We remained married," Vanessa said, "on a basis of friendship that endured for the rest of our lives. And though I loved my sister with more love than I ever felt for anyone except my children, some piece of me regarded her warily after the episode with Clive; some part of my soul insisted on a free zone, a No Woman's Land between us. I imposed this zone and caused her greatest grief, but it couldn't be helped. It's a measure of her love for me and mine for her, that we overcame our mortal rift. We noted the small separation between us, like a stone on a path that neither of us could step over and we went on in so many ways inseparable, the envy of others, the beautiful, talented and outspoken Stephen sisters." Lavinia saw that there were tears in Nessa's eyes, but not tears of crippling sorrow.

"We never lived far from each other," said Vanessa. "We worked and sometimes traveled together. We played together. We supported each other and we nursed each other through tragedy and chaos. When Julian, my son, was killed in Spain, Virginia pulled me through. I would have died then without her. No one supported my work more than Virginia and only Leonard supported hers more than I did. That I outlived her for twenty years proved a grim sentence I served as best I could. But oh the joy when I crossed over and there she stood to greet me; as if we were children meeting in secret once again in the vast and mysterious kingdom under the dining room table. Even better, that small, troubled space, that scratchy zone between us was gone. Just like that, it was gone. Only my returning here, however briefly, brings back that feeling—so sad and so unpleasant. I look forward, once again, to leaving that feeling here when we return. Oh, what's keeping them? It is time for us to go."

Before the others could catch up, a strong breeze stirred the fallen maple leaves. An odor, not the scent of the musty forest floor, but a putrid smell invaded the air all around them. The odor was so powerful that it clouded their thought and vision. "What on earth *is* that?" said Nessa.

"On earth indeed!" said Vinnie. "I fear I shall be sick!"

Their vision cleared and they saw that they were surrounded by half a dozen De la Nuit wretches, their glowering faces hideous in moonlight. They wore their usual stinking rags and robes, and each carried a long staff that trembled and rattled; the cudgels seemed almost alive. One Hell-face, especially odiferous and hideous to look at, stepped into the circle and spoke.

"We've come to take charge of you Other-world meddlers," he said. "Since you've denied us the services of the young woman, you shall both stand in for her." The others shook their weapons. "Resist, and you'll feel the indescribable pain of our punishment sticks."

"Your plan puts the cart after the horse," said Nessa, defiantly.

"*Before* the horse," Vinnie muttered.

"What?" said Nessa. "Oh, never mind! We refuse."

"Yes, and not just you, my Dolphin!" It was Virginia's voice at a high register as she and her party barged into the circle.

"Oh, my!" Emily quipped, rubbing her nose. "Someone open the windows!" She saw that Shaya, Lily and Aidan were about to faint. By mental transference, she urged them to hold on. Like peeling an onion, she told them without speaking; breathe through your mouth, not your nose. The De la Nuit leader stood his ground, but his followers cringed and trembled.

"We will take you *all* into service," the leader said. "Beware the punishment sticks!" He thrust the stick at Virginia and shook it. Virginia staggered back, bumping into Nessa. The leader, sensing his advantage, lunged at them brandishing his stick, but Emily suddenly went air-born between them. Whirling completely around, she hit the leader in the face with her right foot and down he went. Emily snatched the rod from the leader's deformed hands and examined it. The dazed leader slunk to his former place in the circle. His cronies moaned and shook.

"Fiddlesticks!" said Emily, shaking the rod at the De la Nuit band. "It's nothing—but pebbles—and rainwater!" Taking the stick in both hands, she swung hard and shattered it against an oak tree, which shuddered with exultation. "So much—for your Punishment Sticks!" said Emily. Virginia leapt forward, grabbed another stick, and smashed it just as Emily had done. The others did the same.

"Empty threats," said Virginia. "You have no power here, and none where you're going. Now, be gone before you find yourselves trapped in some awful realm between the worlds. Go!" Shaking, bowed and howling, the beaten fiends plunged into the thickets, taking their stench and failure with them. "My brilliant, surprising Lightning Bug!" Virginia said to Emily. "What was *that*?"

Vanquishing the De la Nuit

"The night you walked to the library—and I stayed in our rooms—I watched a DICKINSON episode—on the television. Then I looked for the actress, Hailee, that played me and found her in an action movie, *Barely Lethal*, where she plays a child assassin, but not really—a roundhouse kick, it's called! She did some in the film—and I tried it—it was Fun! Besides," Emily added, "I remembered that you're a Pacifist. I'm not."

A full moon shone high overhead, lighting up the park walking path and dropping, like tiny glittering leaves, dancing reflections on the creek water. The party gathered around a hundred-and-twenty-year-old oak tree and skillfully practiced stillness. The dark arch opening at its base resembled a cave entrance in miniature. Instead of rocks or jagged cliffs around it, the opening was surrounded by moist and musty moss the color of dark emeralds. Aidan crouched to see if he could peer into the opening. He could, he believed, but all he saw was deeper darkness. The sisters exchanged hugs; Lavinia and Vanessa embraced Lily, then Aidan, then Shaya.

"Come along, Vinnie!" Nessa said. "I feel hearty and Hell-bent!" Virginia and Emily smiled as their sisters turned to the tree to go.

"Come along," said Emily to Virginia, Shaya, Aidan and Lily. Travel through a portal requires some privacy and so mortals and immortals retired a little way off and waited. They stood close together, sharing a wordless, woodland intimacy that warmed them. They bowed their heads. They felt the moon on their necks and shoulders, the breeze riffling their hair. A barred owl hooted from a high branch. A pinecone fell. Something unseen stirred in the brush. Suddenly, their small circle of contemplation flared up and glowed a bluish-green, then just as quickly went out again. They stood still, listening, hearing nothing but the sussura of wind in the trees. Emily broke the circle, looking back at the oak tree and moving towards it. Virginia followed, then Aidan, Shaya and Lily. The portal looked exactly as it had before.

"They're gone," said Shaya, as if saying it helped her believe it. Virginia said, "like that."

"It's that quick, that easy?" Lily asked. Emily looked at her and smiled.

"Shall we walk back into town?" said Virginia. She took Lily's and Shaya's hands and started down the path, leaving Emily and Aidan to follow. Moonlight and town lights lit up the park entrance and the vacant pedestal that had once supported a statute of Abraham Lincoln (the statue, repeatedly vandalized by decapitation, was not repaired after the last head-lopping incident). On a corner, standing all alone, a lovely, tall young woman sang, a cappella, a beautiful, mournful ballad. She looked and sang as if she belonged in some world other than this one. Transfixed, the five friends stopped just a few steps from her and listened. Lily's eyes dampened. Aidan kept down the lump that had risen in his throat. Shaya stared at the singer with rapt admiration. The girl finished her song and Aidan stepped forward to float a five-dollar bill into the hat she'd put on the ground for such a purpose. The girl smiled at them. She had a warm smile.

"Your voice is a Choir—a Cavalcade!" said Emily. Blushing, the girl lowered her head and murmured more thanks. Sensing her shyness and embarrassment and recalling her own shyness attacks when she was young, Virginia moved on, pulling Lily along with her.

"She sings as if she knows such pain!" said Lily. "And so young!"

"Pain has no age," said Virginia. "Everyone packs great loads of pain. In the next world, all of it vanishes. There's that to anticipate! But yes, this girl sings like a warrior-poet from some ancient matriarchal culture. Run back! Here's more money. Take some from your bag and give it to her!"

"I only had nine dollars," said Lily, rejoining Virginia where she waited up the block. "I gave it all." Virginia nodded and all together they walked on; Aidan and Emily trailed half a block behind. The girl's new dirge, as powerful as the song before it, floated up the street, following them as they turned to climb the hill past Bloomsbury Books.

Sixteen

"Just because you cannot see us doesn't mean we're not there," said Virginia. Aidan looked at her. It was late afternoon of the following day, and she had agreed to meet him to, as he put it, 'clear up a few things'.

"Is it a burden, always *being* there?" he asked.

"Aidan! That is a superior question," said Virginia, "which could only form in a mind that is almost savage in its desire to plumb its own depth. Now to answer: for me, personally, no, not at all. I was insatiably curious here, the same there. You might, however, get different answers from different sources; yes, I believe you would. No two are exactly alike."

"How would I know the difference," said Aidan, "between happenstance and intervention from the other world, or my own instinct kicking in and guiding me to a decision?" Aidan, Virginia could see, was indeed thinking deeply.

"Your thoughts are outstanding!" she said. "Even if I had no answers for you, though of course I do, you would make out fine. I shall answer your question with another: what difference would it make? What difference? As long as you advance, as long as you arrive at a next destination, a next step you can understand, why should the origin of insight matter? I will tell you this: there is no resolve that does not build on what is inside you. It all begins and ends there. Mentors and teachers exert influence, but they are like signposts only. They point the way," she said, "but if you veer off the path" she said, "it's your choice to do so. The point, my dear young man, is to be open and in motion; even when you appear to be quite still, be always in motion. It's a simple enough discipline, like meditation."

"When I listen to you," said Aidan, "I almost believe I could do anything. This must have been part of your magic. Didn't it seem to you that every man you met when you were here fell in love with you?"

"Once, Bernard Shaw said the same thing to me," she said, "but the truth is I could not bear to be looked at or talked about. By 1907 I'd largely gotten over it; now I am delighted by attention! I would say that the men in question appeared in bunches, so that only in hindsight does it seem like a lot. Then, too, some were not at all serious. Vanessa and I joked all the time that we were surrounded by lovable buggers and men old enough to be our father! We loved them dearly, but there was no future as lovers in them. In any event, I think that the accurate word for what you are feeling is infatuation."

"Not love?"

"Infatuation fans the flames of love," said Virginia. "Sometimes the desire one feels is more infatuation than love and it passes; it leaves one as a cold runs its race and leaves the body. Then you are free to become infatuated all over again, to fall in love again. Love, on the other hand, is an endurance swim in a deeper sea. One mistakes infatuation for love all the time. You are fortunate if you can tell the difference. I always could. It's why Lytton and I reversed ourselves only a day after we had agreed to marry. In our case, we were infatuated with the *idea* of being married to each other; we already deeply loved each other, but as brother and sister. Besides, Lytton is a narcissist, lovable, but all narcissists are utterly incapable of the love required by marriage. When I visited Rupert and his friends at Cambridge and we swam naked in Byron's pool—that was infatuation—delicious, here, then gone! Exotica is a key ingredient of infatuation. Admiration is the basis for deeper infatuation, but even that is not love. For example, you admire me, I know. You like my 'look'. I know this because I have heard you say it to others! To the extent that your admiration endures, to the extent that it deepens and grows, then you approach the condition of love. It may be that you do love me. Yes! I believe that you probably do, or will, as we continue together through the worlds. Yet, I know that your fate is also to love and adore Lily, and in doing so, to understand that what you feel for me, for Emily or anyone else, must not obstruct or conflict with that love, with that destiny. Do you understand?"

"I understand," said Aidan, "that meeting Lily, you and Emily changed my life; or, it changed me, and *I* changed my life." Virginia smiled at the subtle differentiation, which she deemed worthy of her own thought. "All of you raised me up," said Aidan, "in ways I had not thought possible. Because of Lily, because of you and Emily, I feel more confident. I appreciate Lily in ways I might have overlooked before."

"Sauce for the goose," said Virginia. "Tell me what you feel when she appears."

"I love assignments! Let's see, now. The horse nickers at the stall gate and clouds curtain and unveil the moon," said Aidan. "When Lily arrives, my chattering mind settles down. My joints and bones no longer ache. My imaginary people dance. I sing happily behind the wheel as I drive."

"I believe you," Virginia said. "And do you long to give her a flutter of kisses on her ears and nose and eyes, her neck, hands and elbows?"

"Yes, exactly!" said Aidan.

"Oh, good!" Virginia sat down on a bench, her back and long neck elegant and straight, her pianist's fingers deftly rolling a cigarette and affixing it to the end of a long, onyx holder. She lit the cigarette and dragged on the mouthpiece. Exhaling a plume of heron-blue smoke, she said, "When I decided to marry Leonard, I did so because I became convinced that he destroyed my loneliness. I realized the remarkable gift in that and I was not wrong. I was not always happy, but I was not wrong. You won't be, either, you and Lily. Tell me when you're happiest."

"When Lily and I are—how does Emily say it—humming like bees, I think that I could never be happier," Aidan said.

"That's part of it," said Virginia.

"And the rest?"

"That you feel exactly the same way when you think that Lily is at her absolute worst, or you are, or both; the moment you slip back yet feel the same upwelling of love for each other because you are human, because you're two and also One."

"When two are One," Aidan repeated.

Virginia smiled and stood up, glancing around for a suitable public substitute for an ashtray. Finding nothing at hand, she walked to the edge of the curb and squeezed the butt out of the holder. It dropped into the gutter, catching a meandering ride on a wee stream. Together they crossed the street, entered Bloomsbury Books and climbed the flight of stairs to the coffee shop where an animated gaggle of young men and women leaned over a gaming table. Their game and chatter caught Virginia's attention. "What are they doing?" she asked Aidan.

"Dunno," said Aidan; "let's stop and see." They hovered close enough to observe the table and all that went on there. The players were engrossed in moving tokens around on a gloomy game board. Aidan, aware of Virginia's weakness for muffins, left her on the periphery of the game while he walked to the counter and bought a fresh muffin from Dave, the proprietor.

Virginia smiled, snatching the muffin and taking a bite with a look of rapture. "Well?" she asked. "What is this game?"

"It's called *Foreclosure*," said Aidan. "One rolls the dice and goes around and around the board trying not to lose one's home or business or rental property, trying not to go bankrupt or wind up in jail or homeless...and one never wants to draw the Suicide card!" Aidan caught himself too late. Thoughtless, he had blurted it out.

Virginia felt for a moment a cloud knotted up inside her, but she pushed it away. "Don't be," said Virginia. "I got over the self-consciousness of killing myself, if I ever had any, ages ago. In the next realm, in fact, we throw *Who Offed Who* parties, gay gatherings of suicides, murderers and victims! One day you shall come as my guest if you wish! I remember how at my first, Socrates put me at my ease. 'Better to quaff the lethal liquor,' he told me, 'than to suffer diminished capacities.' What a darling old bugger! In many ways, he reminds me of my dear Lytton."

"Is it always a struggle, the dying—for everyone?" Aidan wanted to know.

"Not always, but often," said Virginia. Science is getting better all the time and helps one understand the process. But for many, transitioning is a terrific struggle because they resist leaving their bodies, or let go grudgingly. One must surrender! The ultimate act of surrender more readily opens the door to the greatest freedom. But no need to rush it, my dear! Everyone has a time that's coming. It ought to be anticipated with a great sense of fun! It is, after all, inevitable. After that, it *is* fun!"

"So, there is hope for my father?" Aidan asked. Virginia patted his hand and smiled.

Seventeen

It shocks me this morning, Lily thought, how my drawings seem so crisp and clear. My intention hums in every line, shadow and color. I could measure my breath with brush strokes. Isn't it true that one's work is much stronger when one is not thinking she's a sham?

What changed? Only everything. Lily felt like a world-class surfer atop a gigantic wave. She was perfectly balanced, her goals—work goals, relationship goals—were firm and clear. She felt a part of the wave. Her board was part of her.

She wondered what Aidan was up to. She wanted him. She wanted to share this breakthrough and she wanted to hear all about his own, which she just knew he was also having. She could feel him yearning to share it, leaning towards her even though they were apart. She believed that there was nothing so precious in either of their pasts that they would value more deeply than the new thing they were making together. 'How strange to be contracted by another person into a single being'—where did that come from? Lily wondered, then thought of how a person becomes someone else with the aid of Byron, with the aid of Yeats or Cezanne or Sappho. For her, for Aidan, it had been the guidance of her 'aunts', the divine response of Brigid to her prayers.

When Aidan arrived, Lily shared what she'd been thinking and feeling. Both could feel how they'd been changing, shifting, becoming. They reviewed the discoveries, danger and narrow escapes that had brought them closer together.

"It's true," said Lily. "We are of the same mind. Even when I sound a stranger to myself, my belief is unshakable. I have no fear! I

no longer care what anyone thinks of me. Yet, I think of you, Aidan!
I think of you."

A cloud blocked the sun and the room darkened. Lily's and
Aidan's disembodied voices sounded in the darkness as if they no
longer needed bodies to contain them. They could be trees speaking
to each other in the dark. They could be meadow flowers, bodies
of water, dust motes. They could be themselves, unencumbered,
always changing, always catching each other as they shape-shifted,
gathering unto themselves pieces of the great soul that made them
stalwart and unique, soft, forgiving and communal. In the deepening dark, their voices found each other and wove in and out of each
other, making music like the masters and the spheres. Even their
silences found each other and made music of another order, but
music still.

Softly, evening came on. Outside, under yellow streetlamps and
the sweeping beams of cars and taxis, couples and solo walkers felt
something odd as they passed by Lily's darkened rooms. They felt
a subtle pull in their chests, an ever-so-slight sensation of leaning
towards the building, a wing-like flutter of excitement for no reason
they could fathom. Yet they were communicating—Aidan and Lily,
the couples and solos on the sidewalk.

"It's all their doing, Emily's and Virginia's," Aidan whispered.
"Before they found us...."

"...*we* knew much less," said Lily, finishing his sentence, completing his thought. "Or we knew everything yet hadn't learned how to
find it in ourselves."

Disembodied, together, they dozed, then drifted into sleep in the
dark in each other's arms; they rested in each other's silence. They
slept in delicious moonlight jazzing the room and they shared the
same dream—that something was waiting for them, something full of
promise and excitement. It was something that was not all intellect
or spirit, not title or caste, not mood or physicality. Whatever this

something was, it would be expansive and empty of greed, jealousy, indifference, hate.

They shared dreams of portals and tunnels that wound past roots and waves and air currents, of libraries, stages and theatrical lighting, of high mountain meadows brimming with wildflowers, of goat girls and herdsmen and flocks of sheep, of happy dogs and wise, eloquent cats, of fish free of poison and bodies free of pain, of bombs in tightly strapped vests bursting into stargazer lilies. There were birds in their dreams, there were voices out of time.

Eighteen

While Lily and Aidan slept, Emily and Virginia checked out of their B&B and walked arm in arm to the park. They stopped at the bench beside the lower duck pond and sat down. They sat gazing and breathed in the soft night. Presently, Dick joined them. He looked so much better that Virginia almost didn't recognize him.

"When the time is right," said Emily, embracing him, "Everyone walks through sweet asphodels—to Coronation!—The Lover steps to the precipice's edge! She stands behind him—forcing him to lean over until he feels that he must risk everything—for Her—even a plunge into Ruin and Loss. Yet—she takes hold of his arm and pulls him back. Then he will be fire in her Eye—he will be Hers. He will arrive, safe in her Country. The Bees' alarm will awaken them—Time will drop into the Sea."

"It's time," said Virginia, "to give our mounts their heads and trust them to burn up the ground back to the barn."

The Letting Go—
The air that rushes past
Arrives at Pinnacle

Ascent of blossoms—Dominion
The bolt-breeder's Chair

And nostrils jetting Hot
As Volcano—reveals itself

Star hands conjoin—
Pull tight the Sky

"Well said, L-Bug! Well said. We managed," said Virginia, taking Emily's hand.

"The great Detectives," said Emily, "in ceaseless Pursuit! Be Aware, ever Vigilant," she said.

"Safe home," said Virginia.

The three walked into the park until they reached the oak tree that housed Emily's portal. "My dearest L-Bug," said Virginia, "we'll reunite presently."

"I will haunt you forever if we don't," said Emily. They hugged each other; they kissed. Virginia smiled at Dick. A swirl of rainbow light and mist enveloped the tree. Virginia stood back and they were gone.

"Called Back," Virginia said. For a moment, she felt crushed by overwhelming loneliness. Wasting no time, she walked to the oak tree portal nearby that would take her home.

But there was a commotion coming up the path. "What now?" said Virginia. In a moment, she saw it was Lytton and Ula hurrying towards her.

"I'm glad we caught you," said Lytton. "You oughtn't to go back just yet."

"And why not?" said Virginia, drawing herself up just as her beautiful, imperious mother might have done.

"Because," said Lytton, "I think you will want to take this woman to Brigid yourself. You know her." Virginia could see that Ula was changed and changing. She was a redhead and she did look familiar. "It's Sophie," Lytton said, "your cook from your family's long summer holidays at St. Ives." If Virginia had been a dry stalk, she would have broken at her base and fallen flat on the ground. Amazed, she stared, studying the features of the person by Lytton's side.

"Sophie! Oh, good," said Virginia. "For a moment, I thought you were Katherine Mansfield! But I see now you *are* Sophie. Mother Brigid will love this. You're Irish and a redhead—like her!" Lytton took the opportunity to exit and moved, unnoticed by the two women, to his portal.

"Do you think I will really be able to come back with you?" Sophie asked.

"Why not!" Virginia said. "Wait till you get to know Emily! You'll love her, too!"

"May we go now?" Sophie asked.

"Yes," said Virginia. And they did that.

Nineteen

It was the first day, Day One after Emily and Virginia's departure. They'd promised the travelers they would wait to read Virginia's letter until this morning, and now 'this morning' was on them. Full of anticipation, they rose, showered together and dressed; they made tea and shared a blended juice drink.

At ten, they were ready to venture out. They would walk to the park, to a small grove where some of the trees housed portals, or what looked to them like portals. Aidan had taken to remarking on them and both felt more connected to the next world when they passed by or stopped there. It would be the perfect place to sit down and share Virginia's letter. Aidan would read aloud, Lily insisted, and that made Aidan happy and excited. He wanted to speak Virginia's words; he wanted to feel them opening up in his mouth. Lily wanted to hear and savor them as they came to her from Virginia through Aidan. So they would all be intimately connected in the moment, the transformational moment that would remain in them all their lives and beyond them.

They were pleased that the path up through the park was deserted except for the occasional huffing jogger passing them after calling out 'on your left!' or 'on your right!' They passed the empty lover's bench and the deep pool where teens sometimes ignored the posted sign that forbade swimming; they passed the oak tree with the owl's nest high up yet plainly visible, as the owl itself sometimes was visible—but not today. Squirrels skittered in the brush on either side of the path. Walking single file, they crossed the narrow bridge and continued on through the redwood picnic area. They passed the one remaining historic cottage from the days when the park first opened as an auto park in the thirties; they walked by the ranger's office and the upper parking lot, but they passed on their usual routine of walking out on one of the bridges that spans the creek to look down in the water for trout and salmon. This morning, they would not be sidetracked.

At the grove, they stopped and stood quietly for what felt like a long time and no time at all. Lily stepped off the path and Aidan followed. At the base of a gnarled oak, a perfect, mossy opening beckoned. Lily fancied that she heard voices coming from it, excited, happy voices. Aidan imagined effortlessly shrinking down, disappearing into the portal and emerging—where? He looked forward to finding out some day, but not today.

They sat down on the ground, on dry leaves, and breathed in the musty scent of mulch. Across the water, a doe and two spotted fawns emerged from a leafy thicket; Lily pointed them out, then reached into her shoulder bag and brought out the letter. She handed it to Aidan. She waited. Quietly, he fingered open the flap, pulled out the robin's egg blue pages, unfolded it and took a deep, slow breath. He exhaled, gazing at Virginia's words in purple ink. Then he handed it back to Lily.

"Lily, it's you," he said. "You must read the letter, you the focal point, you, the catalyst." Lily looked at the letter and waited as the lump in her throat subsided. Looking up, she saw a heron hunting in the creek pools among the rocks. A lark's clear song shook the dilly air. She looked down again at the letter and began to read.

Dear Lily, Dear Aidan,

Now that L-Bug & I are out of your earth-sight, you will want to know how taking Dick back with us worked out & some day you will see. Dear L-Bug will have her Otherworldly hands full! Are you lonely? Do you miss us? Of course you must, yet there is comfort, inspiration & solace all around you.

Begin, my dear doves, by giving to each other. No kindness is too little. No touch is insignificant. I remember being sent in to my dear mother as she lay dying. I was there for a moment only, a kiss, a hug. Leaving, I paused in the doorway looking back & my mother said, 'Stand straight, my little Goat'. I hear that parting instruction, that sweet reminder every day & smile…& stand up straighter.

Years later, thinking of life, of work, I said to myself that it is useless to repeat my old experiments. They must be new, always new. In the same spirit I say to you—do not repeat my old experiments, or L-Bug's, but experiment yourselves. You possess all of the ingenuity you will ever need. 'A day's walk—a mind's adventure'—that's how I put it once.

Lily, Aidan, don't live together as one might write a memoir. Too many aspirants spin out & wreck their togetherness that way. The memoirist often gives scene after scene, fact after fact & leaves out the person that the scenes & facts are happening to.

Easy to say, I know, yet so hard to do! It gets easier when one dispenses with the negatives—resentment, anger, jealousy, greed, selfishness—that corrode the carrier & the one attached to the carrier. The trick is to be attached & remain free. Be generous with each other & love generously. Is there nothing you wouldn't do for one another? It takes just that to endure & be happy.

I remember a day, when Leo & I had been married a long time, that I recorded this revelation: "I was overcome with happiness. Then we walked around the square lovemaking—after 25 years can't bear to be separate. Then we walked around the Lake in Regents Park. Then…you see it is an enormous pleasure, being wanted: a wife. & our marriage so complete."

May you both live to know such happiness, to feel that powerful sense of belonging & enduring. That's it, you see! It's the knowledge that you belong to someone who loves you unconditionally, just as you love that person. I never would have accomplished anything without that awareness. So! I am a salesperson at last! For love; I plead guilty. L-Bug added this postscript. 'Wherever You are—Stars— have their Arms around You!' We are the stars.

Your Virginia

P.S. If you're ever up against it & need cash, sell this on eBay!

It was finished. Lily handed the letter to Aidan, who reluctantly folded and tucked it in its envelope. They were quiet as they gazed at the portal, listening. Their soft eyes wandered across the creek into the brush and the woods beyond. They breathed in, deeply and slowly, the woodsy scent of the park. At last, Lily said, "can we live that way?" Aidan took her hand.

A shaft of sunlight sliced through the canopy and found the portal. Green and golden, the sacred hollow shimmered and glowed. A breeze stirred green leaves overhead and dry leaves at their feet; out of the portal rose a faint humming sound. Was it the sound of bees or the sonorous swelling of a choir? Was it the sound of a silk scarf in a raven's beak as it wore away a mountaintop, or the sighing of wind through the trees? Was it the rustling of cicadas, the moon chorus of an otherworldly wolf pack, or waves rising and falling, rising and falling as a fin sliced the surface? No matter who or what made it, they agreed that the sound made them feel as if they were being touched by the music of equanimity and abiding, of peace and awakening.

Lily and Aidan leaned closer and closer to the portal and its gentle waves of sound. They sat in the lotus position and swayed from the waist up in time to the music though they did not know that they were moving. A yellow plop in the creek water hardly disturbed their reverie, though Aidan glanced in the direction of the disturbance—a leaf, a fish?—then just as quickly moved his eyes back to the portal. A squirrel leaping from branch to branch knocked loose an acorn that fell and plopped in the leaf mulch between them, its impact stirring up a pungent smell of earthy dampness. From somewhere, the elevated cawing of ravens tumbled, competing momentarily with the orchestral music beneath the tree. The music thrummed in their ears and moved like light and water, like air and darkness through their bodies. They felt what the tree felt. The music makers' sympathy enchanted them like a requiem and in that embrace they lost all sense of time past or time to come. There

was only Being as they listened and swayed and perceived dim im-
ages of those who made the music.

Was someone coming for them? Someone always came, though
usually when least expected. No one was overlooked or left out. If you
had been born, then you would be summoned. These were the inexo-
rable bookends with all the Being and Not Being in between. Like trillions before them and trillions around them, they had been born, Lily
and Aidan, in between, and someone would come for them, but not yet.

What came now was the certainty that Emily and Virginia had appeared to them as real as they were to each other and that Virginia's
letter was their visit's coda and the young couple's blueprint, their
plan, their intention to love and live at the highest Conscious level.
Aidan knew this to be true; Lily, hearing the music, knew it to be
true. This, then, was the gift of Emily's and Virginia's visitation—that
Lily and Aidan would wake to the knowledge that they could live
together in work and love and harmony, doing good and not doing
harm, Being more than Not Being, and visiting this sacred place now
and then to restore their faith and energy by tuning in to the music;
by settling in to quiet regard, by feeling, accepting and sharing each
other's wholeness and knowing the moment will come when they
enter the portal and go.

"We could live off the grid," said Aidan. "We could have land, a
garden, horses, mules, dogs and cats; chickens, a pond, fish, a good
place for foxes, larks, and herons."

"And children," said Lily.

"Yes," said Aidan, "and children."

"And we'll never take a cruise anywhere," said Lily.

"No," said Aidan, "never."

Aidan reached out and drew Lily to him. They sat close together,
rocking, rocking, as doors and windows inside them opened wide.
They were stepping into one wave after another, Aidan knew, and it
was good. They were together.

One day, near or far, they would be going. They would go separately, like Emily's young friend on the battlefield, or together, as
Lily's mother and father had gone. They would be taken far apart or
close to each other, or all at once. But circumstance did not matter.
Emily knew this and she had told them; Virginia knew it and she had
shown them. Both taught them how to live, how to go to death and
live again. Did they believe? Yes. Could they sustain it, their belief?

Nearby, closer than they could fathom, Emily and Virginia listened and observed. Their expressions were serene and lively, their
eyes bright as Venus low in the evening sky. Nothing they heard or
saw troubled them and as they tuned ever more crisply into Lily's and
Aidan's thoughts; the couple heard in their heads the women's voices
and sayings with greater clarity. So they were all together, across di-
mensions or universes, or whatever one called it. They were together,
here and in some other place where love pictorially composed and
brushed the canvas of life ongoing. Lily smiled and dipped into
the beautiful picnic basket that Emily had left behind. Undressing
a golden-brown lavender, vanilla and pine nut scone, she tenderly
broke it in half and handed a piece to Aidan.

The morning after they read Virginia's letter in the park, Lily woke
to a clear sky. Rain had fallen all through the night. The pavement
glistened with wet, yet the sheen dried rapidly as the sun rose. Throwing on her sweats and lacing up her boots, she pushed outside into
the crisp morning air. Her skin tingled. Surprising weather was coming. She could smell it and taste it as she walked, avoiding pill bugs
making their excruciatingly slow way across the road. She looked up
to the purple hills ringing the valley, clear and cut like crystal, shimmering as the sun climbed higher in the eastern sky. She walked and
walked, a half-hour, an hour, slowly making her way around a route
that took her past one of the last remaining elderly oak groves in the

area. She lingered there, studying the etched bark of the trees and sensing their wisdom. She pushed on, greeting the local cats that one by one met her at certain familiar points and welcomed her feline attention.

Nearing home, she felt invigorated, wide-awake and focused. She looked forward to her work, to finishing the project and starting a new one, perhaps one she had been thinking of for a long time. She anticipated seeing Aidan; she savored her anticipation of whatever the day would bring. Yes, they were on the brink of something, something brilliant and necessary. It was a thing they both wanted and needed, that only the two of them could give to each other. Aunt Emily was right; Aunt Virginia was right. *Be fearless.* The sun made drops on the roses glisten and sparkle. They were like her mind and her resolve to complete herself. It was time. The fullness and liberation of the moment filled her, and she found herself home, at her own door. There was much to do. She let herself in. The vivid drawings on her work table drew her to them. She leaned over, touched them gently with her fingertips and said, "Yes. We're Home now."

THE END

About the Author & the Writing of Emily & Virginia, a Novel

Robert McDowell ran away from home in the San Gabriel Valley when he was 7 in an attempt to reach England. Why? He wanted to meet and stay with Virginia Woolf's sister, the painter Vanessa Bell.

"I didn't get far," says McDowell. "I planned to walk and hitch rides to San Pedro where I'd been taken deep-sea fishing a couple of times. I knew boats would be there and I thought maybe I could sneak aboard a tramp steamer bound for England (I discovered tramp steamers in a movie)."

The runaway's mother picked him up at the entrance to the 605 exchange near Arcadia and took him home where he was grounded for a week, maybe two. Or three. It was a long time, the author reports, until he felt he was no longer under intense surveillance. Then it happened. Vanessa Bell died in England the day before his 8th birthday. There would be no meeting the beautiful painter and closest childhood confidante of her sister, Virginia.

McDowell had already experienced visitations—some might call them hauntings—from Emily Dickinson and Virginia Woolf. The two women, dead 20 and 75 years in 1961, sat on his bed and talked to him and to each other. Because he loved them, the child did not think this strange. He was already a believer in Familiars and soon his two Authors showed up everywhere—in his secret thicket cave on the grounds of the Ramona Convent (where he read some of

Virginia's novels and Emily's poems for the first time), at Marguerita
Elementary School and Alhambra High, at sporting events (Virginia
more than Emily), stores and libraries. Virginia never showed up at
dental appointments because she'd had too many teeth pulled and
Emily avoided eye exams. Both could become irritated when the author's mother took him in tow to shop for clothes, but both loved
recitations, sing-alongs and romps in the woods.

The visits between worlds have gone on throughout the author's
life, but they took on a different focus in 2014. Gradually, McDowell
realized that his Authors were instructing him and encouraging him
to write a novel—this novel—about them teaming up and intervening
in the life of a conflicted young woman. At times, it almost felt as if
the Poet and Novelist, exacting, entertaining editors both, were delivering whole passages and poems through the channel between them
and their younger charge. The process took a bit more than five years
and eleven versions before all were satisfied. The result is this novel.
May you delight in it as much as "They" did in creating it for you.

Robert McDowell is the author, co-author, editor and translator of
numerous collections of poetry, essays and fiction, including *On Foot,
In Flames,* which was a finalist for the Oregon Book Award and *Sweet
Wolf: Selected & New Poems* (2021). A Woolrich Fellow at Columbia
University, he co-founded Story Line Press, serving as director and
editor for 22 years and selecting and guiding into print more than
250 volumes of poetry, fiction, creative non-fiction, criticism and
drama.

With the poet and critic Mark Jarman, he created and edited *The
Reaper,* a literary journal discovering the resurgence of narrative and
formal poetry in the 1980s. He created the Rural Readers Project
and co-created The Poets Prize, an annual award for the best book of
poetry published in the previous year. He served on the panel that

recommended the appointment of Lawson Inada as Poet Laureate of Oregon. His poems, criticism, fiction and translation appear in books from Free Press/Simon & Schuster, Henry Holt and Company, University of Pittsburgh Press, University of Michigan Press, New Directions, Penguin Series of Eastern European Classics and The Salmon Publishing (Ireland).

CPSIA information can be obtained
at www.ICGtesting.com
Printed in the USA
LVHW072255060521
685769LV00010B/11/J